IMAGES
of America

ST. JOHNS

ON THE COVER: The Mormon Church sent 102 Mormon families to St. Johns to help bolster the Mormons' numbers, and this picture shows some of them arriving. Most only stayed a couple of years because the dry land couldn't support such a large number of people and many nearly starved. (Courtesy St. Johns Historical Society and Museum.)

IMAGES
of America

ST. JOHNS

Cameron Udall

Arizona Historical Foundation

ARCADIA
PUBLISHING

ISBN 978-0-7385-5628-4

Published by Arcadia Publishing
Charleston, South Carolina

Printed in the United States of America

Library of Congress Catalog Card Number: 2007941879

For all general information contact Arcadia Publishing at:
Telephone 843-853-2070
Fax 843-853-0044
E-mail sales@arcadiapublishing.com
For customer service and orders:
Toll-Free 1-888-313-2665

Visit us on the Internet at www.arcadiapublishing.com

To my dad, Steve, for providing me with a lifetime of adventures in history.

Contents

ACKNOWLEDGMENTS

There are many people who helped make this book a reality. I owe a huge debt of gratitude to Barbara Jaramillo, who provided her amazing pictures, books, and other information on the Hispanic community of St. Johns. Special thanks go to the volunteers at the St. Johns Family History Center, who kindly opened during their off-hours to help aid my research. Vaughn Wilhelm, Carol McClain, and Kelly Gunnels from the Apache County Historical Society and Museum also need to be thanked, simply for putting up with me.

I truly appreciate the people at the Apache County Sheriff's Office for digging out the 1880s sheriff's docket and for allowing me to scan the picture of Tomas Perez. Ruth Patterson and Michelle Udall both provided great pictures. Albert S. Anderson and his two daughters, Lisa Anderson Whaley and Shayla Anderson Taylor, always came through for me when at the last minute I fired off an e-mail to them for information on their family, and for that I am grateful. I also appreciate Roger Heap, the current principal of St. Johns High, for always taking the time to respond to similar e-mails, which provided important information and statistics on the high school I couldn't find otherwise.

My editor, Jared Jackson, and publisher, Devon Weston, at Arcadia Publishing were both incredibly patient when I needed a little extra time to tell St. Johns's history. Both my parents deserve a big thank-you for buying me the computer and scanner for this project, as well as putting up with my phone calls and questions at all hours.

And lastly, my husband, Joel Larson, deserves my biggest thank you of all, not just for making the off-hand remark that led me to write this book, but for putting up with more during a first year of marriage than any husband should have to.

INTRODUCTION

We cannot understand our history unless we see it whole and tell it true.

—Stewart L. Udall,
former U.S. congressman
and secretary of the interior

There have been a lot of things said about St. Johns. For instance, it is said that the Mormons were passing through the area and said, "We'll just wait here till the wind dies down"—127 years later, their descendants are still waiting. Mo Udall said, "St. Johns may not be the end of the earth—but you sure as hell can see it from there." And then one twilight evening, a resident looked at the sky and said, "For such a small town, St. Johns sure does have pretty sunsets," and *that* is the truth.

Truth is a tricky thing, and sometimes what was once truth gets lost along the way, giving way to a new truth. For instance, the naming of St. Johns has been told for generations and goes something like this: St. Johns was originally called El Vadito ("little crossing") after a toll bridge was built in the early 1870s. Sometime around 1874, Sol Barth changed the name to San Juan in honor of the first female resident, Maria San Juan de Baca, but when the citizens applied for a post office in 1880, the postmaster changed the name to St. Johns.

The actual application for the post office, written in June 1880 by district attorney C. A. Franklin (known as A. F. Banta), tells this story:

> Sir—your petitioners, residents of St. Johns, do most respectfully represent that from present information, we believe your department has been willfully deceived by a certain class of citizens of Arizona calling themselves "Latter Day Saints." By false and atrocious misrepresentations they have so far imposed upon your department as to have a post office established at their *wagon camp*, and by naming such post office St. Johns. For better information of yourself and department, and that if any errors have been committed they may be corrected, we herewith present the following facts, to-wit:
>
> During the year A.D., 1874, the town of Saint Johns was located—at which time not a single "Latter Day Saint" was residing within the limits of this Territory—and now contains a resident (gentile) population amounting to 600 souls. The school census, taken in 1879, gives 148 school children. About three or four months ago, the aforesaid "Latter Day Saints," most of whom are foreign paupers (as Secretary Evarts very sensibly and truthfully puts it) and nipped to the United States at the expense of the Mormon Church, have located and are now living in wagons, tents and jacotas on the Little Colorado, one mile and a half below St. Johns; and for the express purpose of misrepresenting matters abroad, and more particularly to your department, they have had the "cheek," or imprudence to usurp the name of this town, and have called their wagon train camp by the name of Saint Johns. Saint Johns has the legal right to the name, and had the latter days sufficient understanding,

> by consulting the session laws of the Tenth Legislative Assembly, they there would have found that this place has the legal right, as therein recognized, to the name of Saint Johns. The undersigned, citizens and civil officers of the county of Apache, do earnestly request that your department make a note of the foregoing facts, and if you have been led into an error in this respect, to do us the favor to correct such error. And furthermore, we respectfully request that a post office be established at SAINT JOHNS, with S. E. Stover as Postmaster. Our Delegate to Congress, the Hon. John G. Campbell, can inform you of the facts as above stated, and that at the last general election, November 5th, 1878, there were polled at St. Johns 231 votes. The town of St. Johns is now the county seat of Apache County and from this fact alone is entitled to U.S. mail service. We have recently been informed that the Department has seen fit to order mail service between Fort Wingate, N.M. and Fort Apache, A.T., such route being designated as "route No. 39, 124," passing through Zuni villages, Saint Johns and Shomlain, if such is the case then by all means give us a post office, and your petitioners will ever pray. We severally under our solemn affirmation do affirm the foregoing to be true to the best of our information.

On June 8, 1880, the Mormons' post office was discontinued, and on July 26, 1880, another post office was opened in St. Johns with S. E. Stover as the postmaster. The battle of the post office may have been the first between the Mormons and original settlers, but it certainly would not be the last.

St. Johns has gone through a number of changes since those early days, and it is doubtful that if an early settler were to see the town now they would even recognize it. The behemoth structure known as the Salt River Project power plant can be seen perched at the outskirts of town and, at night, looks bigger than the town itself. But in many aspects, St. Johns hasn't changed at all. The wind still blows incessantly, asparagus can still be picked at the ditch, hollyhocks still grow wild, and people still flood irrigate from water in the Little Reservoir.

It is a remarkable little town with an even more remarkable story.

One

THE MAKING OF A TOWN

Spanish pioneers were the first to arrive and settle in the area known as St. Johns. Mormon scouts had been sent by the Mormon Church as early as the 1860s to find land to colonize. Reports on the area were generally dismal, referring to it as "an inhospitable and forbidding waste" or "fearfully barren." As the Mormons had been forced to flee three states previously, the issue wasn't the quality of the land, but its remoteness. Thus, when Mormon scout Ammon Tenney recommended the area to church authorities, he was told to buy.

On November 19, 1879, Ammon Tenney entered into an agreement with the Barth brothers, Solomon and Morris, to purchase all the land and all the water for 750 head of American cattle. On October 6, 1880, David King Udall arrived to serve as the first bishop. Fearing the vagueness of the original bill of sale, David King drew up a quitclaim deed that defined the boundaries the Mormons were to purchase, which was now 1,200 acres for 770 head of cattle. It is unknown whether or not the land was actually the Barths to sell, but the Mormons bought it believing that they were buying a good title to the land and water.

Unlike the Hispanic settlers, the Mormons didn't choose to settle in St. Johns—they were told to do so by church authorities. It is highly unlikely that any of the Mormons would have chosen to leave their friends, families, and homes in Utah to settle there otherwise. But when the church authorities told the members to "hold St. Johns at all costs," the two factions, the "Mexicans and the Mormons," squared off—one faction to fight for land they believed was rightfully theirs, the other to fight for land they didn't even want—and in the midst, a town was born.

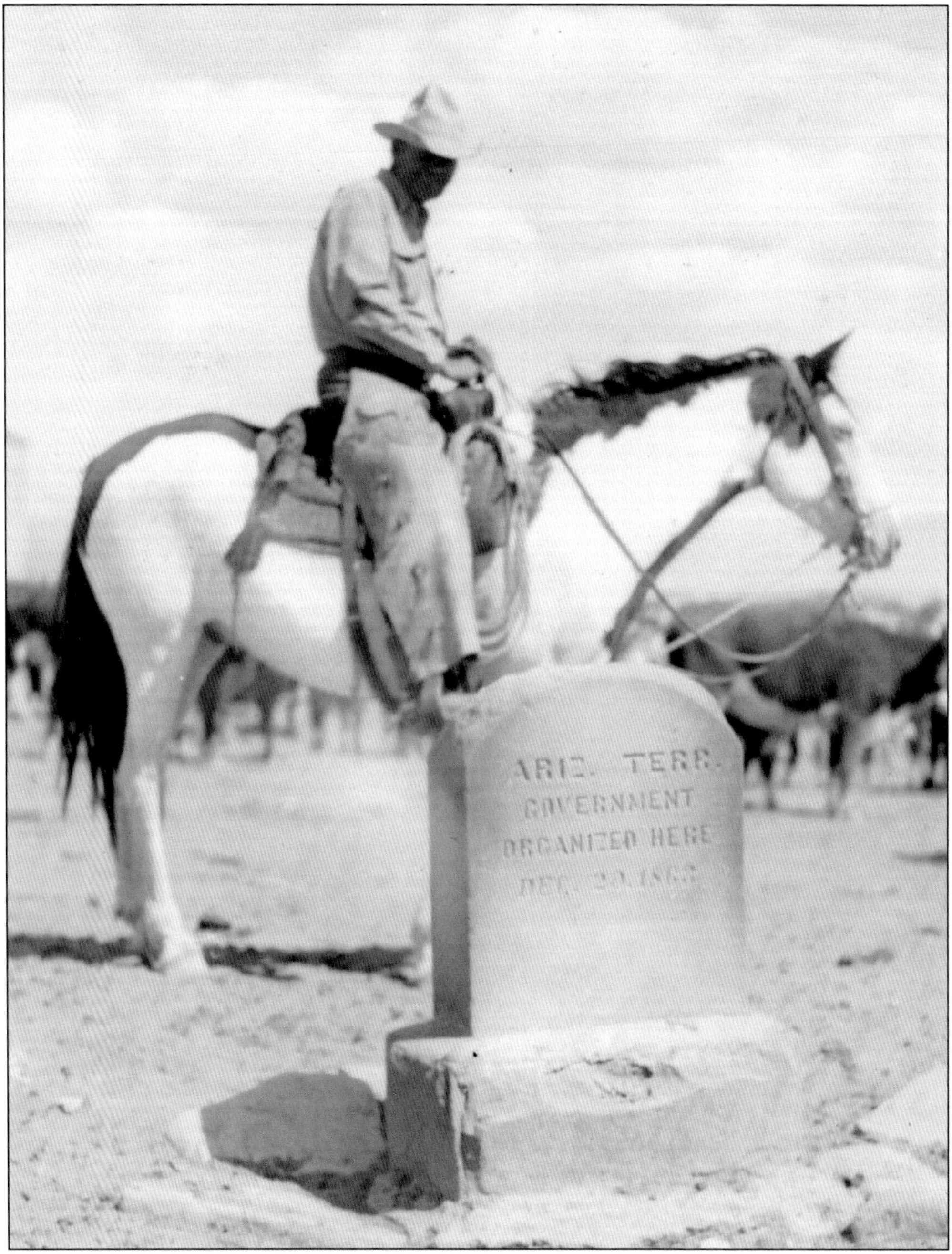

After the first efforts to create an Arizona Territory from what was then the New Mexico Territory failed, the Civil War and concern for control of potential railroad routes to the riches of California brought approval for an Arizona Territory in 1863. President Lincoln appointed the civil officers who left Washington, D.C., in August and entered the territory on December 27. Unsure if they were actually within the territory's borders, the officers traveled two more days to Navajo Springs, where the national colors were raised and the territorial government formally inaugurated. This marker, north of St. Johns, commemorates that place. (Courtesy St. Johns Historical Society and Museum.)

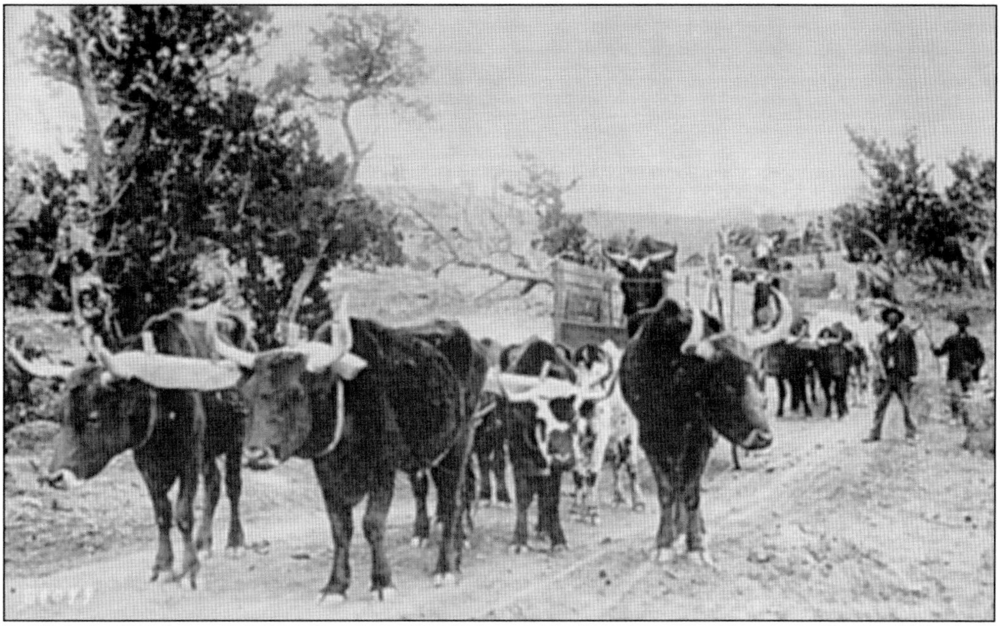

Ox-drawn freight trains, like the one pictured here, were used to haul grain and hay to military outposts such as Fort Wingate and Fort Apache. Freighters between these two particular forts crossed the Little Colorado River at a rock crossing known as El Vadito. (Courtesy National Archives.)

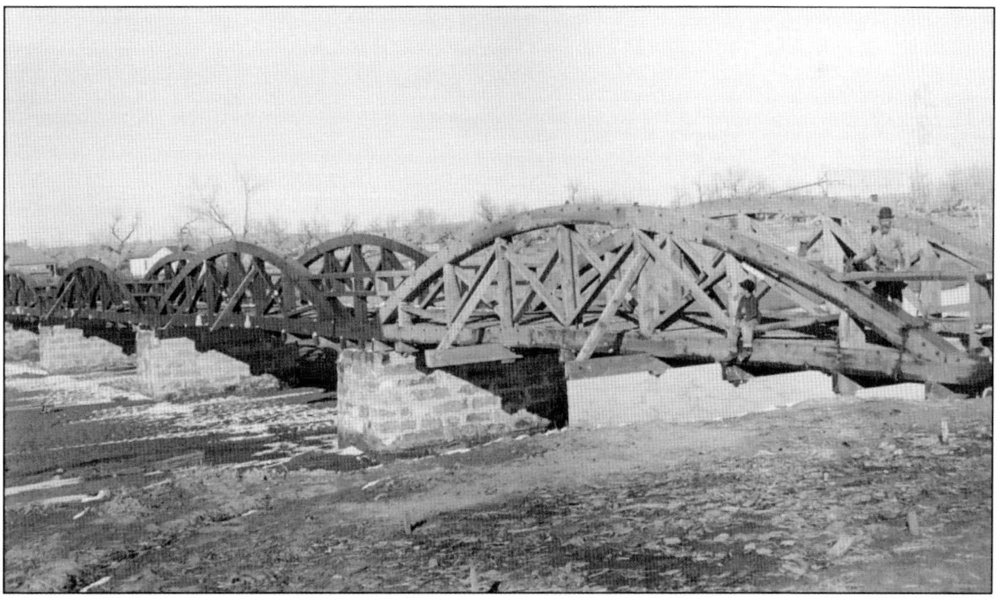

This toll bridge was built in 1879 after the 10th Legislative Assembly granted the exclusive right to build it to Solomon Barth. The toll to cross was 25¢ for a wagon with one or two animals and 10¢ for every additional two animals. There was no charge for a beast of burden, a horse or mule with a rider, or a person on foot. The next day, the same legislature created Apache County. (Courtesy St. Johns Historical Society and Museum.)

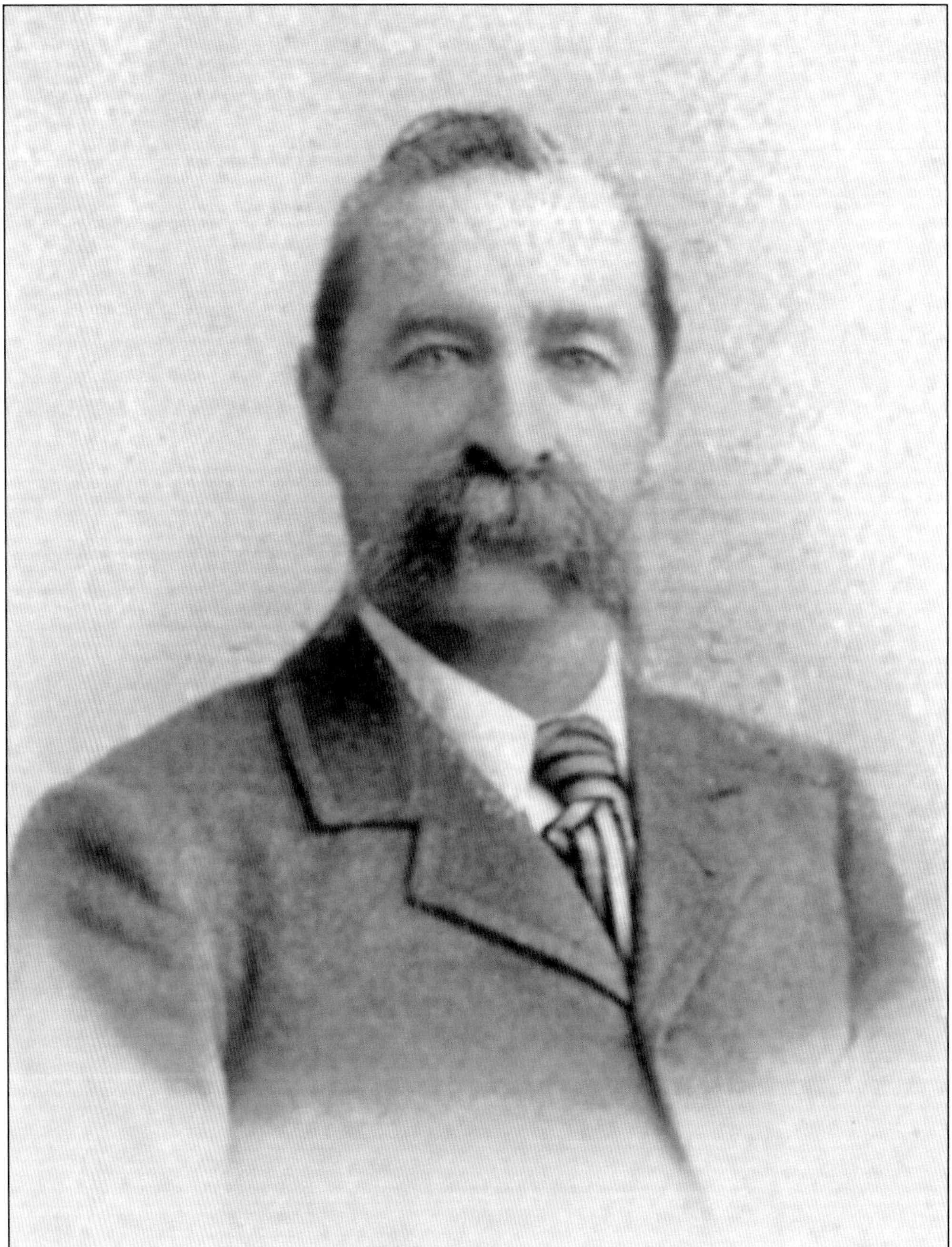

Solomon "Sol" Barth came to the United States from Prussia in 1856 and was an early freighter to Fort Apache. He moved to St. Johns around 1874, and in 1879, he and his brother Morris sold 1,200 acres of the town to the Mormons. This picture was taken in 1896 when he was a member of the council (now called the House of Representatives) for the 19th Territorial Legislature. (Courtesy Arizona State Library, Archives and Public Records, Archives Division, No. 98-1531.)

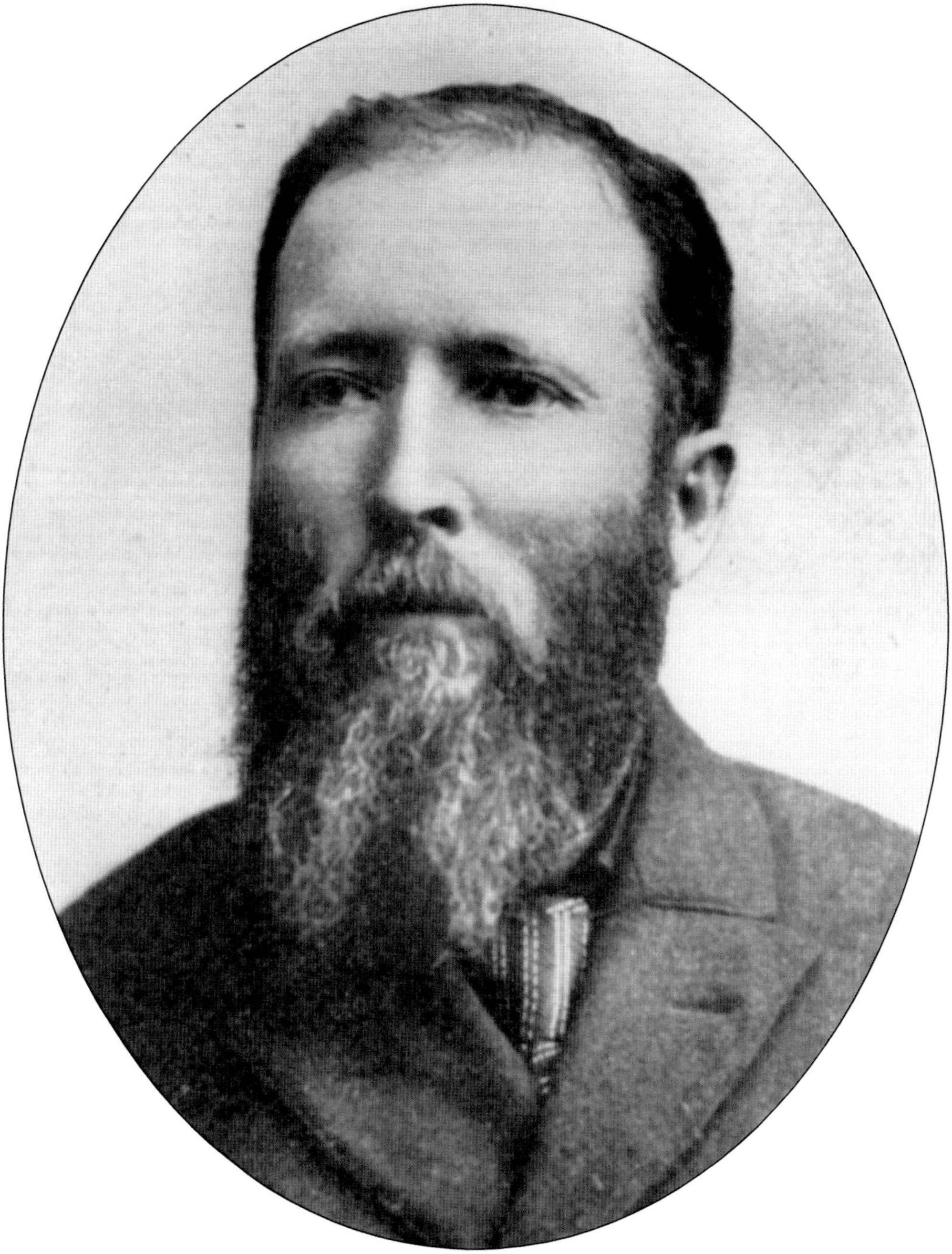

David King Udall was called by the Mormon Church to serve as the first bishop of St. Johns. Leaving his family and new home, he left Kanab, Utah, with his wife, Luella "Ella," in September 1880 and arrived in St. Johns on October 6. Pursuant to church policy he took a plural wife, Ida Hunt, two years later. Udall later served in the territorial legislature, where he helped pass the bill giving women the right to vote in Arizona. He is also the patriarch of the Udall political dynasty. His heirs include state legislators, U.S. congressmen, a U.S. senator, superior court judges, Arizona Supreme Court chief justices, a U.S. Circuit Court judge, county attorneys, an attorney general, and a secretary of the interior. (Courtesy Arizona Historical Foundation.)

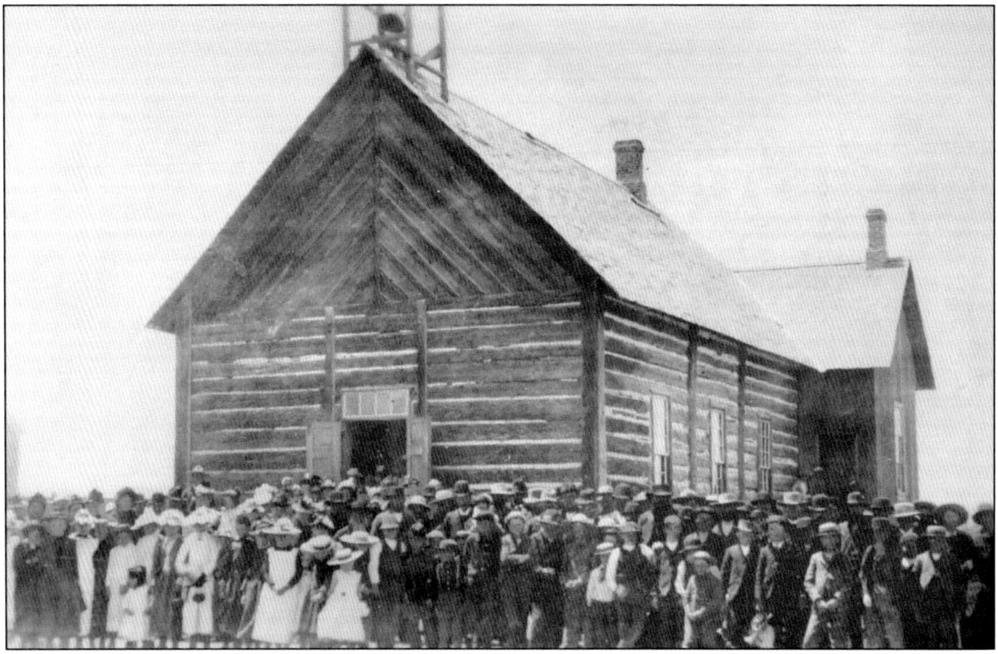

The Assembly Hall, built in 1881, served as the Mormons' church and principal gathering place. This picture was taken in 1887 after the hall was made larger by increasing the stage, giving the building the shape of a "T," the original design. (Courtesy St. Johns Family History Center.)

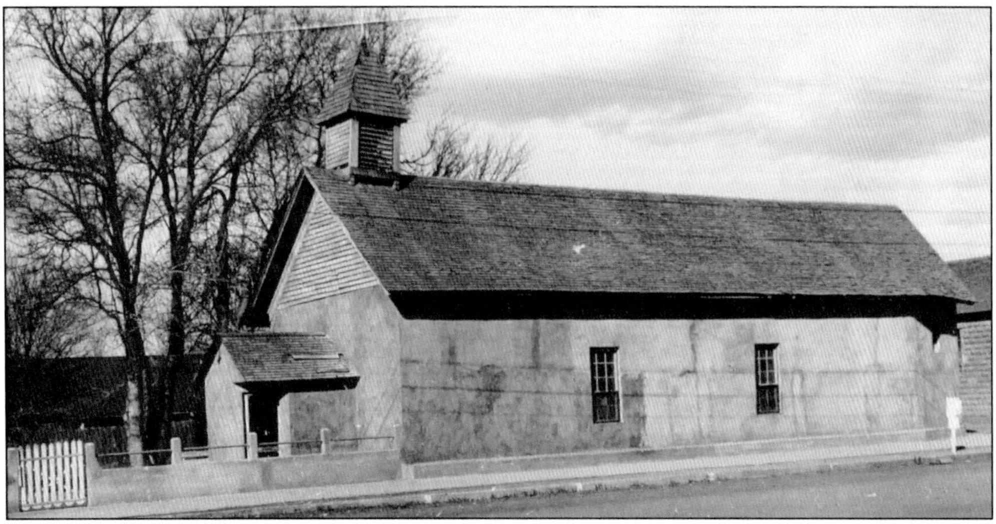

When he arrived in St. Johns, Fr. Pedro Maria Badilla discovered that the community had begun building a Catholic church several years earlier but had to stop because of a lack of funds. Father Badilla worked side by side with his parishioners to build this church, dedicated as the San Juan de Baptista Catholic Church in 1881, which was the first Catholic church in Apache County. (Courtesy Barbara Jaramillo.)

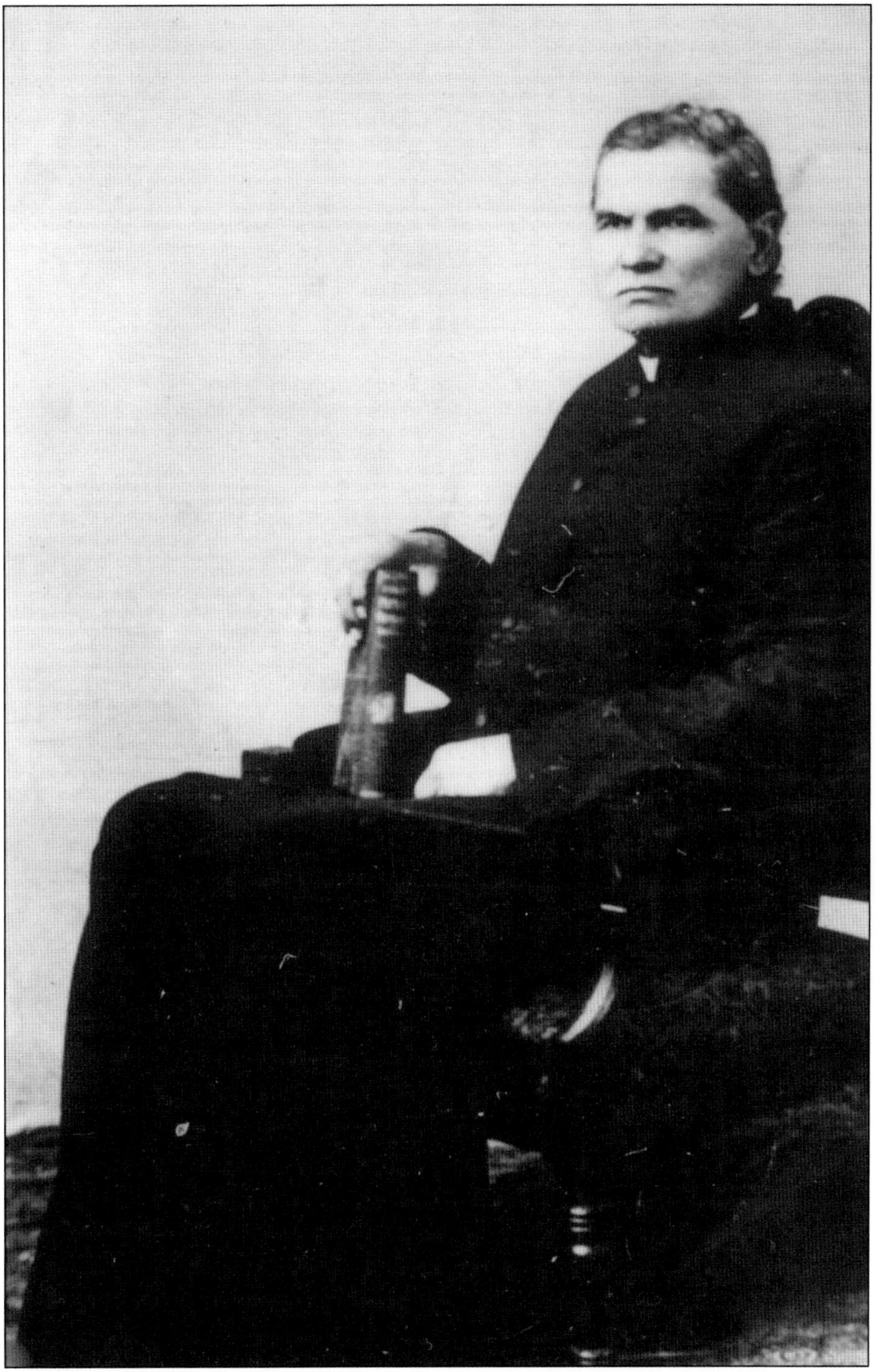

Fr. Pedro Maria Badilla arrived in St. Johns on August 2, 1880, to serve as the town's first priest. He walked from Tucson to Holbrook, where Señor Sarafin Apodaca met him and took him to St. Johns. The entire Catholic community was so happy with his coming that they walked to the outskirts of town to meet him. (Courtesy Barbara Jaramillo.)

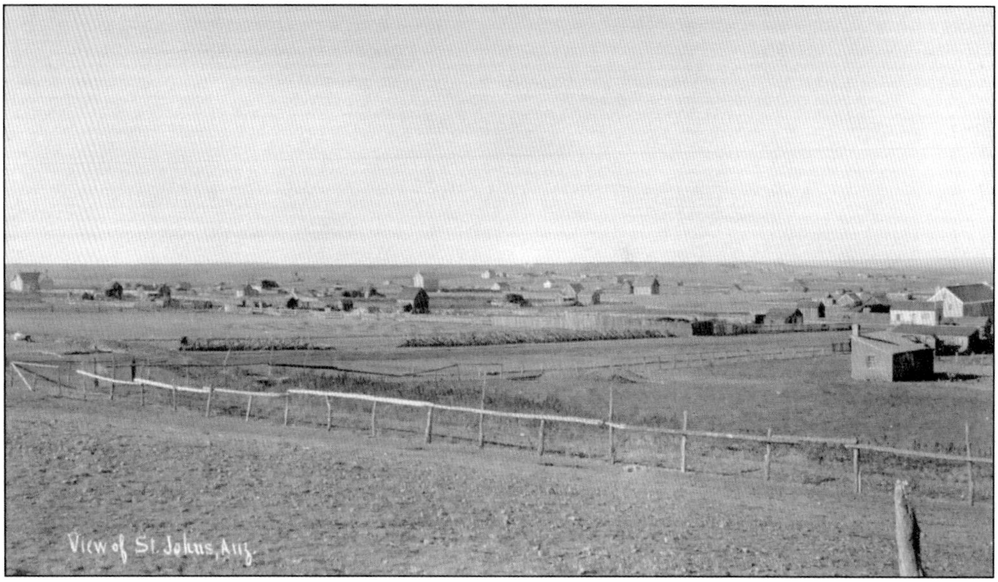

St. Johns (above, around 1885, looking northwest) was laid out by David King Udall and Christopher Kempe using a cactus and the North Star to block off town lots, which were all 24 rods each way. The business district (below) was initially blocked off the same way, but the board of supervisors decided to run Commercial Street directly through two of the blocks. (Both courtesy St. Johns Family History Center.)

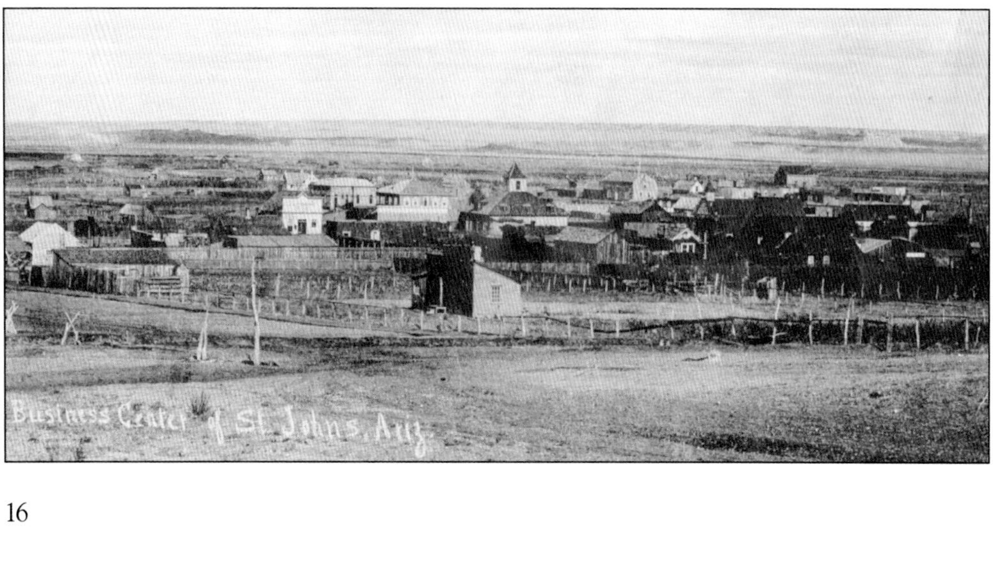

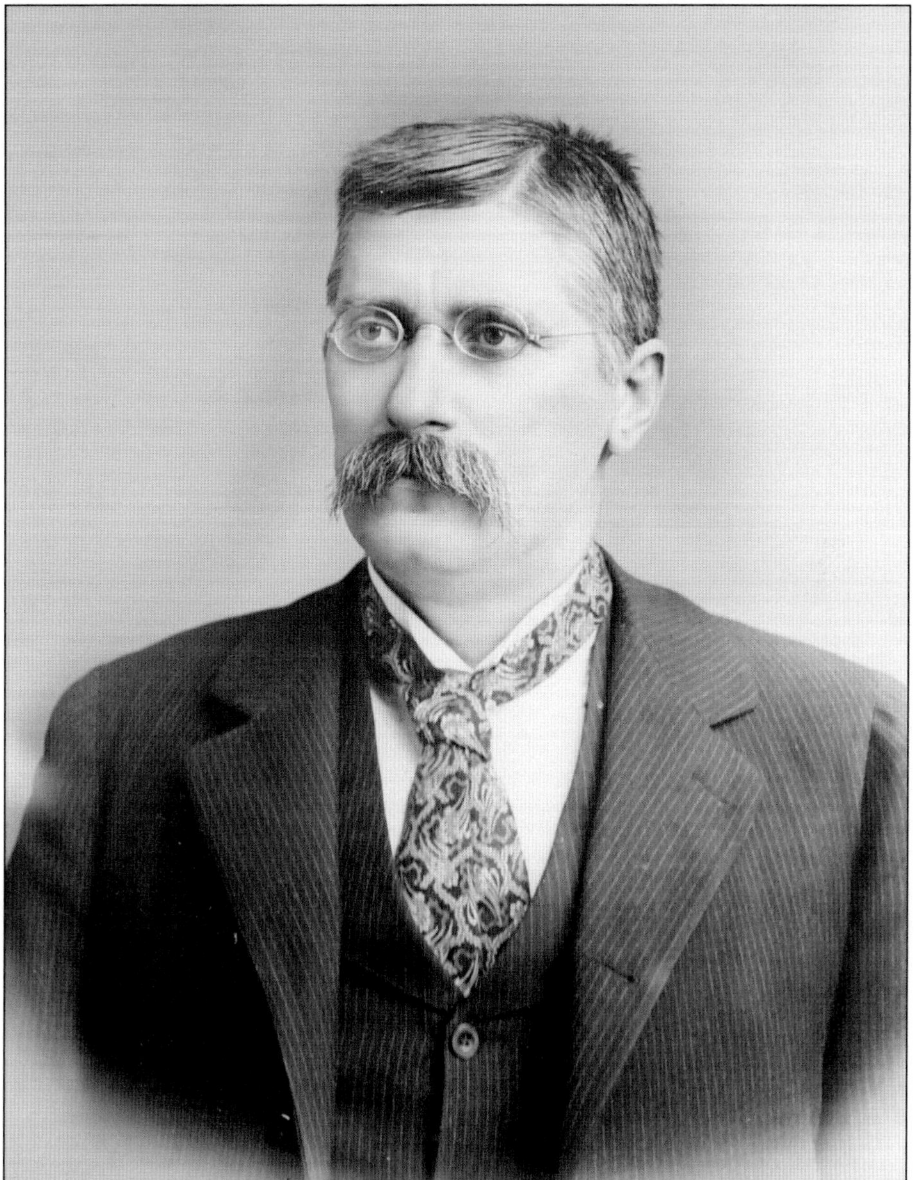

Don Lorenzo Hubbell, pictured here, came to St. Johns in 1878 and opened a store. After the Mormons began to survey the town, Hubbell handed D. K. Udall a letter written by justice of the peace Marcos Baca and signed by 30 townspeople (Hubbell's was the second signature), which stated in part, "We have seen members of the Mormon sect, surveying, driving stakes, and living under their wagon covers, making preparations [to transfer] themselves to the surroundings of our town. This we believe to be entirely your work. The object of this is to notify you that you had better give it more thoughtful deliberation and desist desiring to establish the members of the Mormon Church in said place. We see in your determination only the intention of surrounding and oppressing us. We will not feel it inconvenient to show that we will place all the means in our power and within our reach to impede the establishment of the Mormons in the surroundings of this town. This you shall take for a town protest. We hope you will desist in your purpose." (Courtesy Arizona State Library, Archives and Public Records, Archives Division, No. 02-9367.)

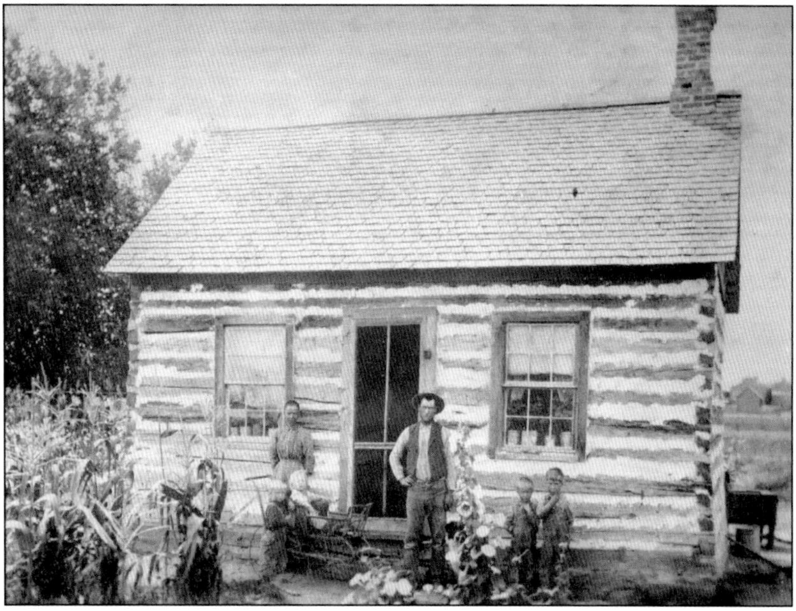

The Mormons' homes were initially built of logs like the Davis home, shown here, and the Holgate home, below. (Courtesy St. Johns Family History Center.)

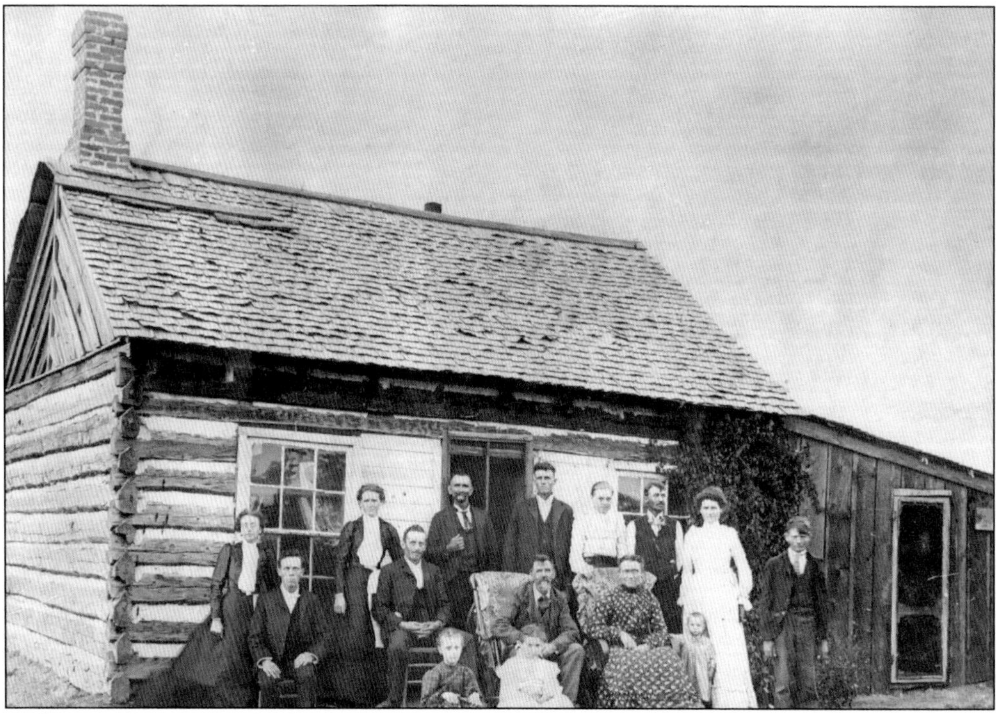

William Holgate and wife Eliza were among the first Mormons to arrive and are shown here with their family in front of their home. From left to right are (first row) Ruth Holgate, Ruth's friend (unidentified), William, Eliza Holgate, and an unidentified grandchild; (second row) Miriam Holgate and husband Fred Rothlisberger (seated), Mattie Holgate, Jake Rothlisberger, unidentified, William Holgate, Hannah Sorenson Holgate, Elijah Holgate, Mary Holgate, and Lester Holgate. (Courtesy St. Johns Family History Center.)

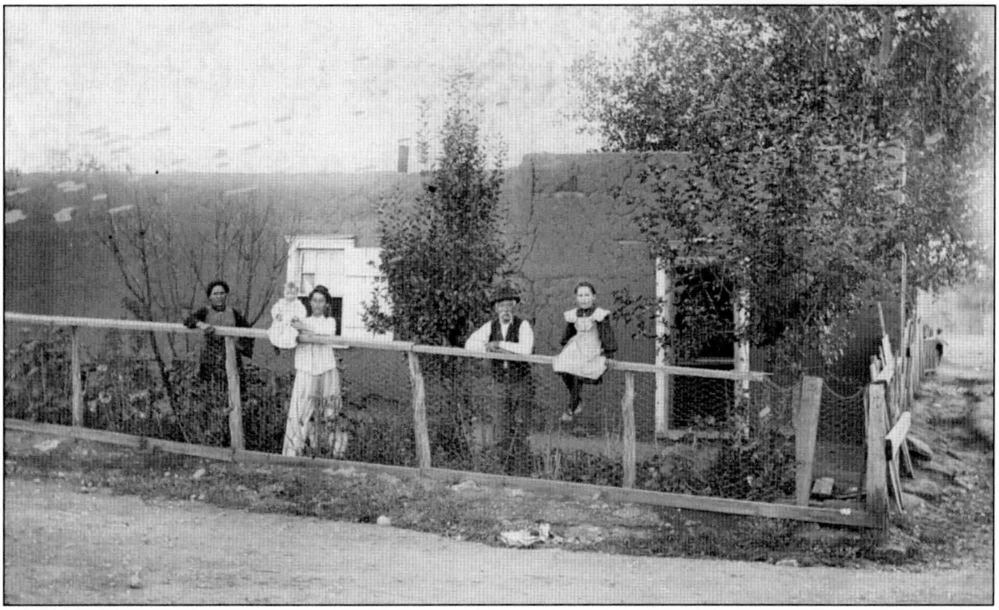

The Hispanic residents made much sturdier homes of adobe (above) and cooked in adobe bread ovens, similar to the Zuni people (below). (Both courtesy Barbara Jaramillo.)

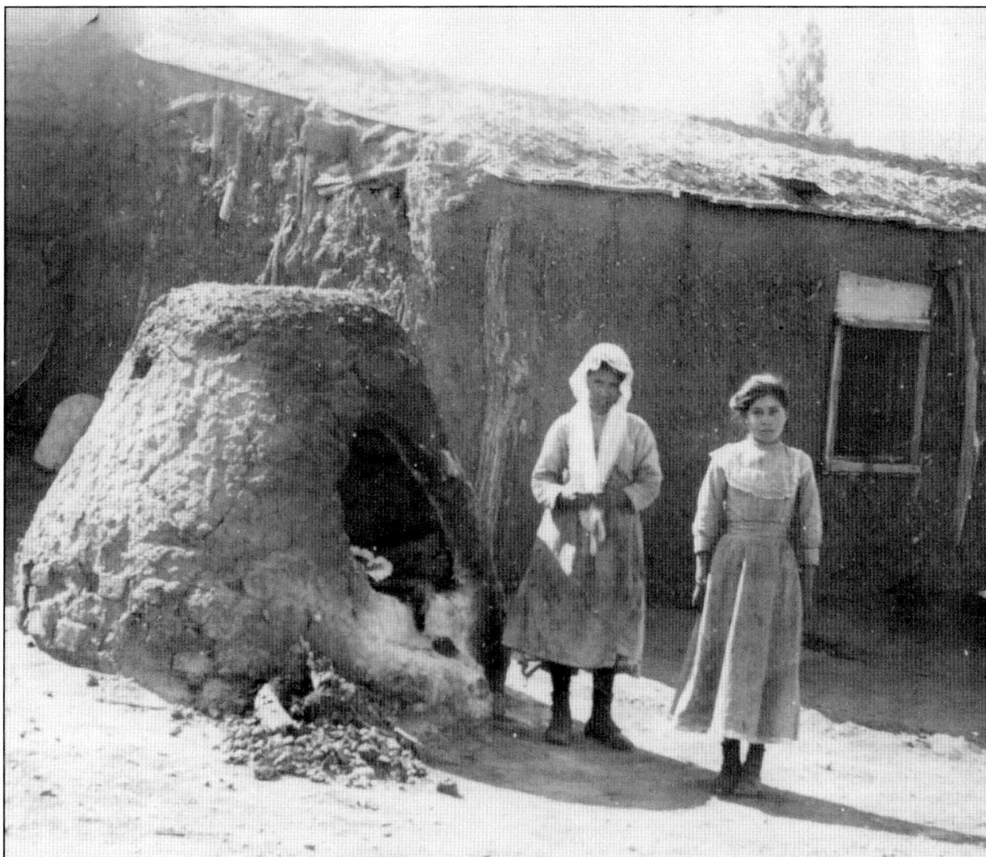

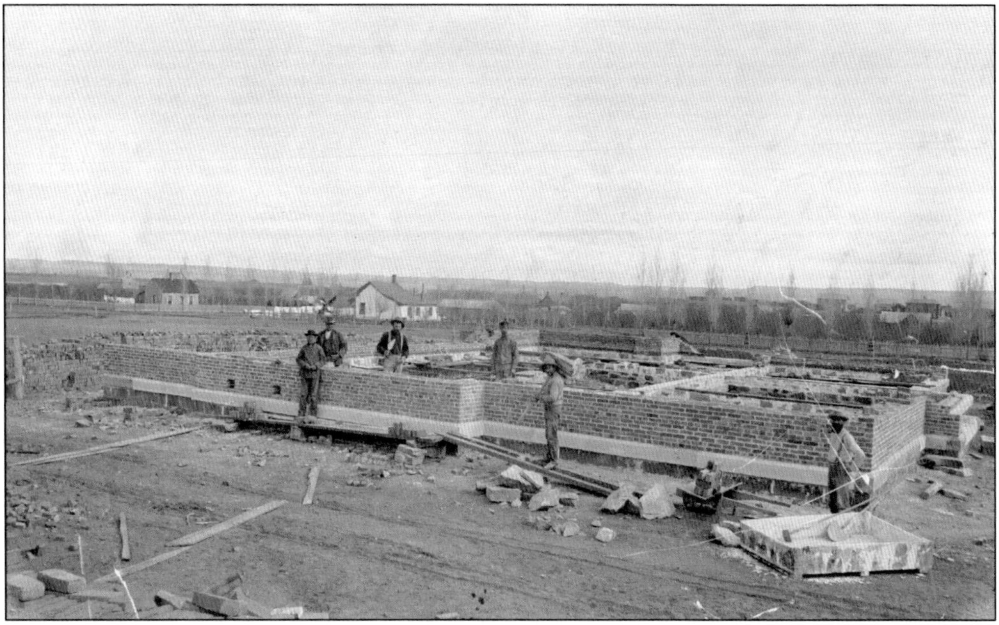

William Holgate and Jens Sorenson opened a brickyard and turned out thousands of "Mormon bricks," which were used to construct houses and buildings. The tithing office, shown above being built, was finished in 1885 and was one of the first buildings to be constructed by the Mormons with Mormon bricks. As a substantial brick building, the tithing office served a number of functions. It is shown below in the late 1890s when students for the St. Johns Stake Academy still met on the top floor. (Both courtesy St. Johns Historical Society and Museum.)

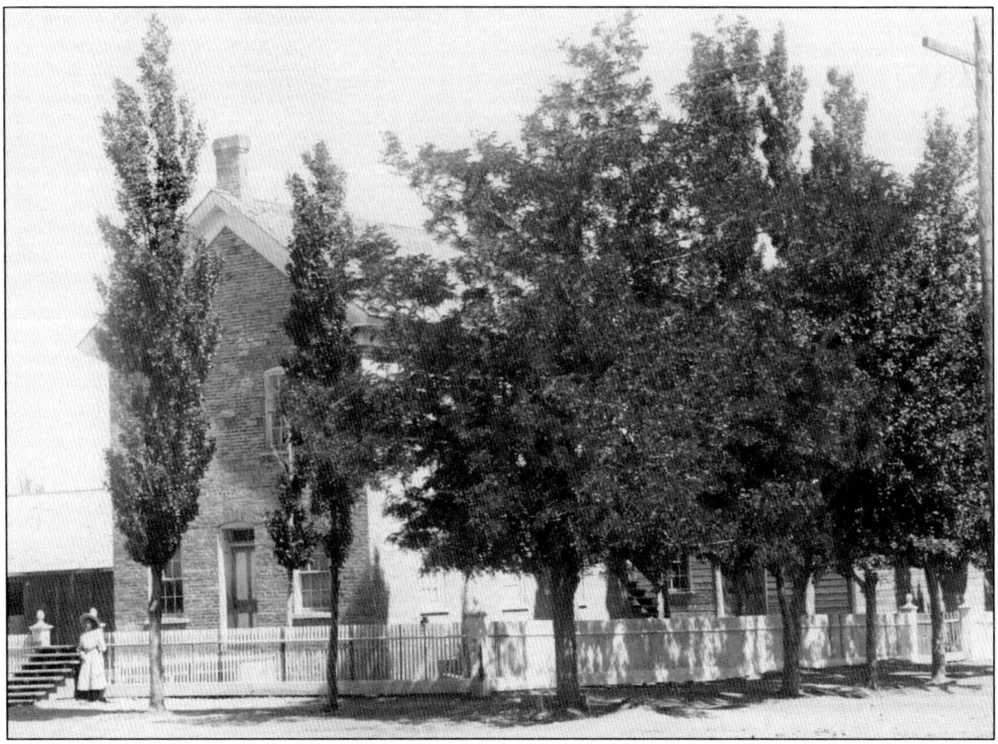

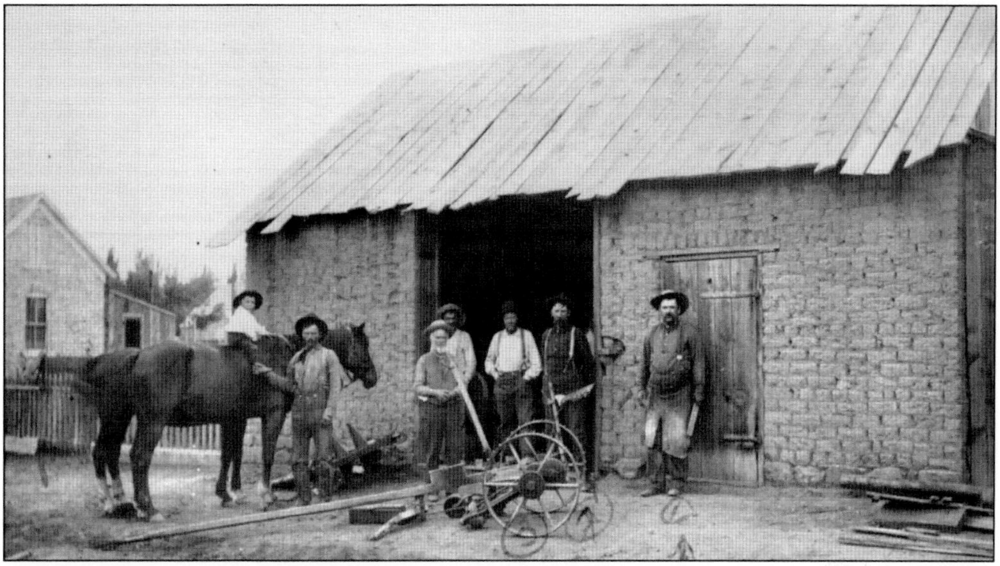

Marinus Christensen's blacksmith shop was built of adobe and less likely to burn down than the more common buildings constructed during that time of wood. Christensen was the town blacksmith for nearly 30 years, having learned the trade from his adopted father, Ove Overson. This picture, taken in 1898, depicts a typical scene for those days. From left to right are David Overson on the horse with his father, David, at the horse's head; Seth Russell; Henry Platt; Andrew Jensen; William Gibbons; and Marinus Christensen. (Courtesy Northern Arizona University, Cline Library, Special Collections and Archives, General Collections.)

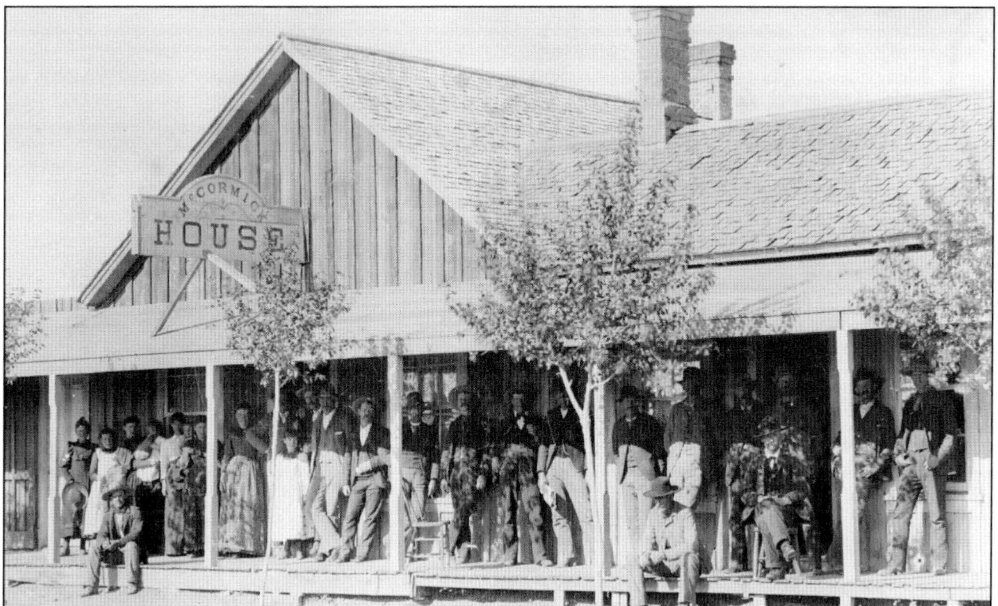

The McCormick House, shown here with boarders on the front porch, was one of the earliest boardinghouses in St. Johns and boasted containing everything to make a person's stay comfortable, like new furniture, neatly fitted-up rooms, and gambling from early morning until late at night without intermission. They also offered a stable and corral with the best in hay and grain, so parties who wished to could feed their own horses. (Courtesy Barbara Jaramillo.)

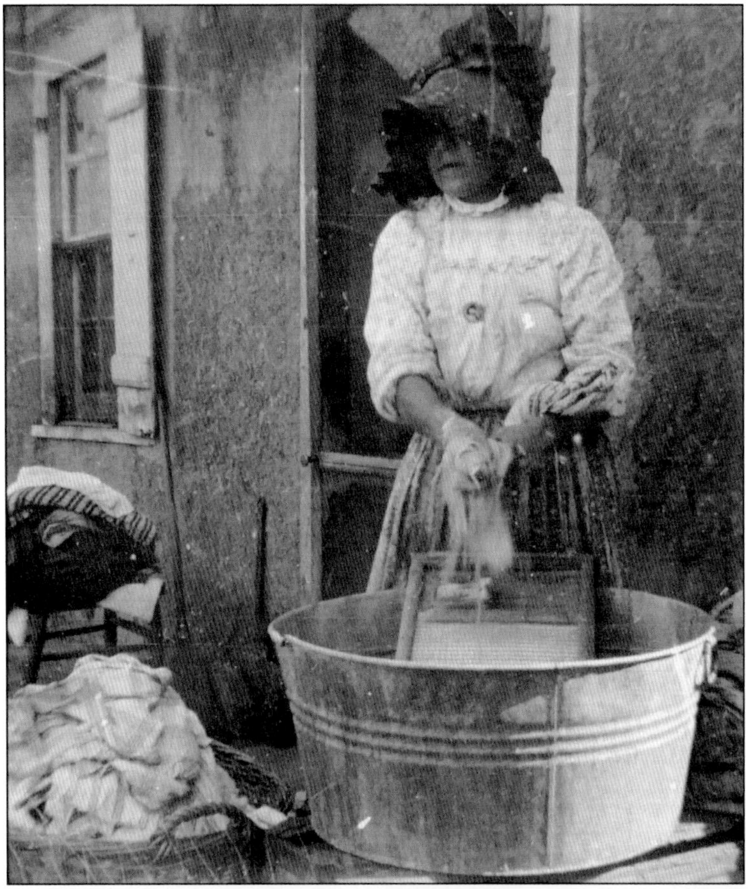

Women in St. Johns lived in almost primitive conditions and frequently in the shadow of disaster, as is evidenced in the left photograph where a shotgun is in easy reach of an unidentified woman doing her washing. Monotony punctuated with crisis and a void of social amenities characterized their daily lives and can be seen in the face of an unidentified woman, below, milking a cow. (Both courtesy St. Johns of the Historical Society and Museum.)

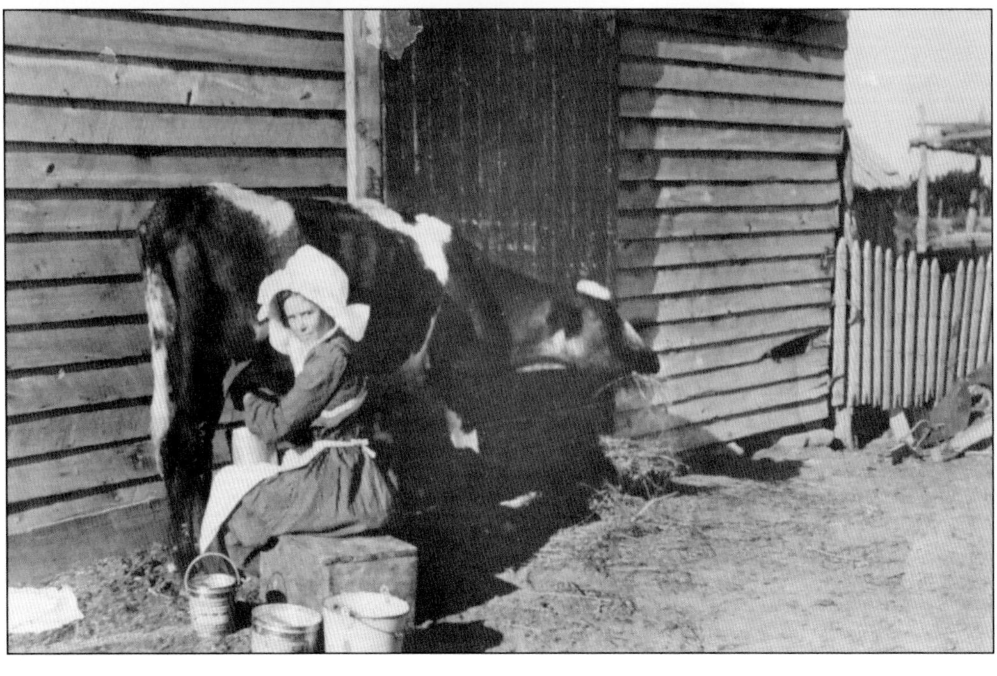

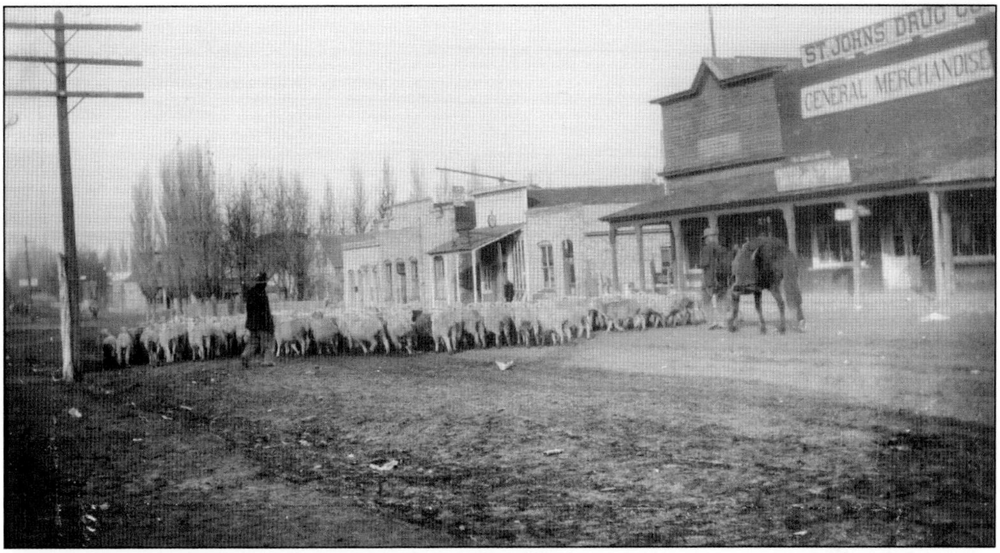

Because Commercial Street ran directly to the bridge, cattle and sheep were driven down the center of town, shown here, which not only kicked up rocks of every size but left quite a mess. (Courtesy St. Johns Historical Society and Museum.)

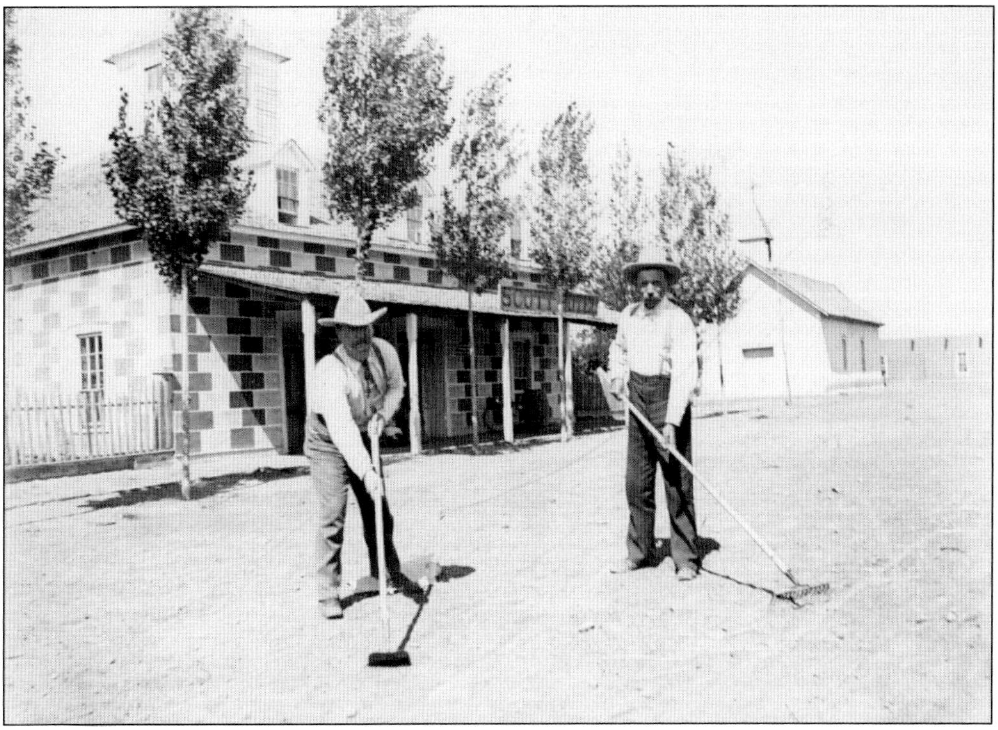

Merchants along the street were responsible for clearing this mess. Here Isaac Barth (left) and Reamer Ling take a moment to pose for a photograph while raking in front of the Barth Mercantile (not shown) and the Scott Hotel, which would later be known as the Barth Hotel. (Courtesy St. Johns Historical Society and Museum.)

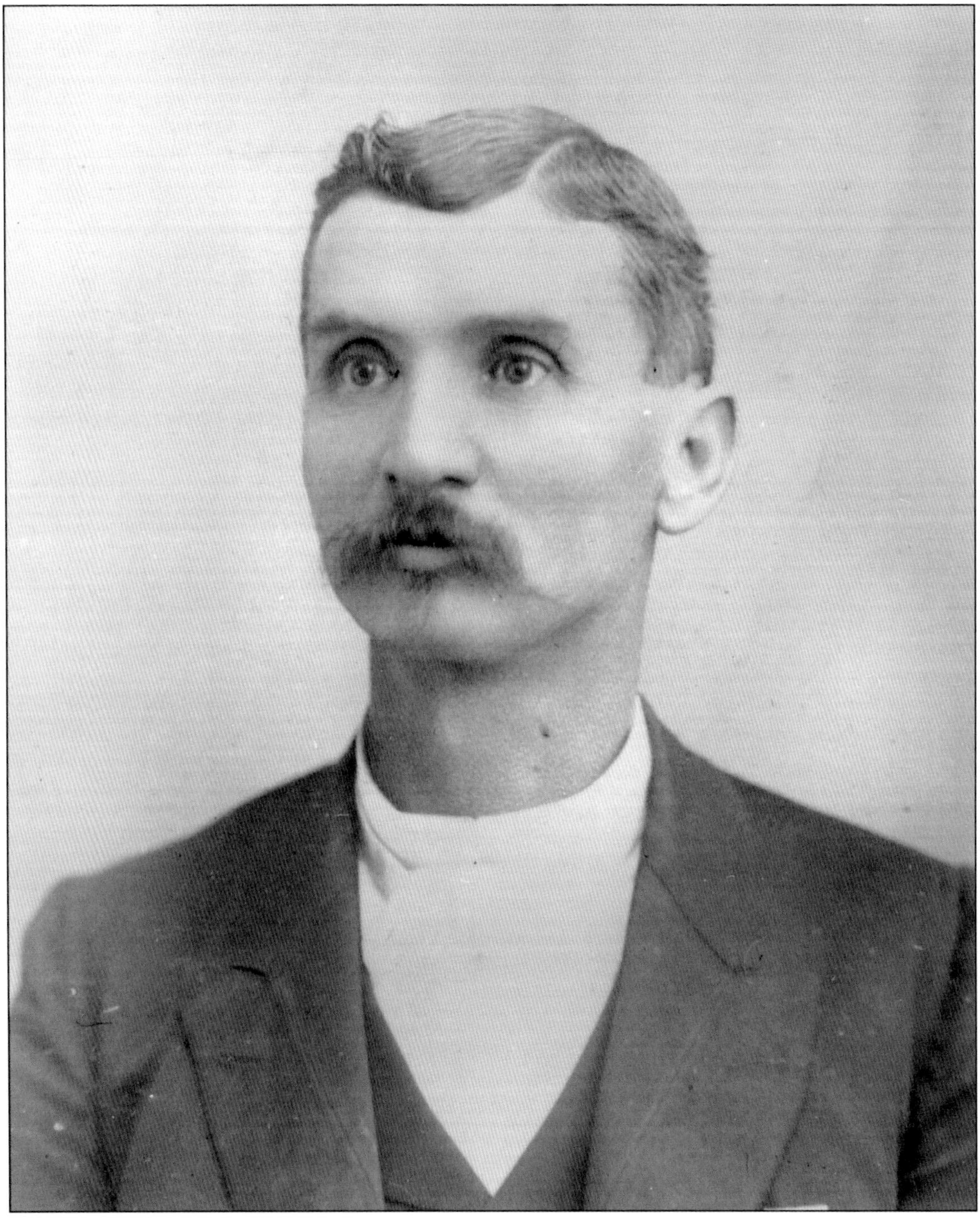

Albert Franklin "A. F." Banta is one of Arizona's most colorful early settlers. Born in Indiana in 1843, his formal education would total only 12 months, which ended when he was 11. Early in the Civil War, he joined the Missouri Militia. After being unfortunately misidentified as a spy and threatened with death, he took the alias Charles Albert Franklin and fled to Arizona, arriving in 1863. As a member of the 10th Territorial Legislature, he introduced and passed a bill organizing Apache County. During his life, he organized nine newspapers in Arizona, including the *Arizona Pioneer* in St. Johns in 1882, which he later sold to the Mormons, who changed the name to the *Orion Era.* (Courtesy St. Johns Historical Society and Museum.)

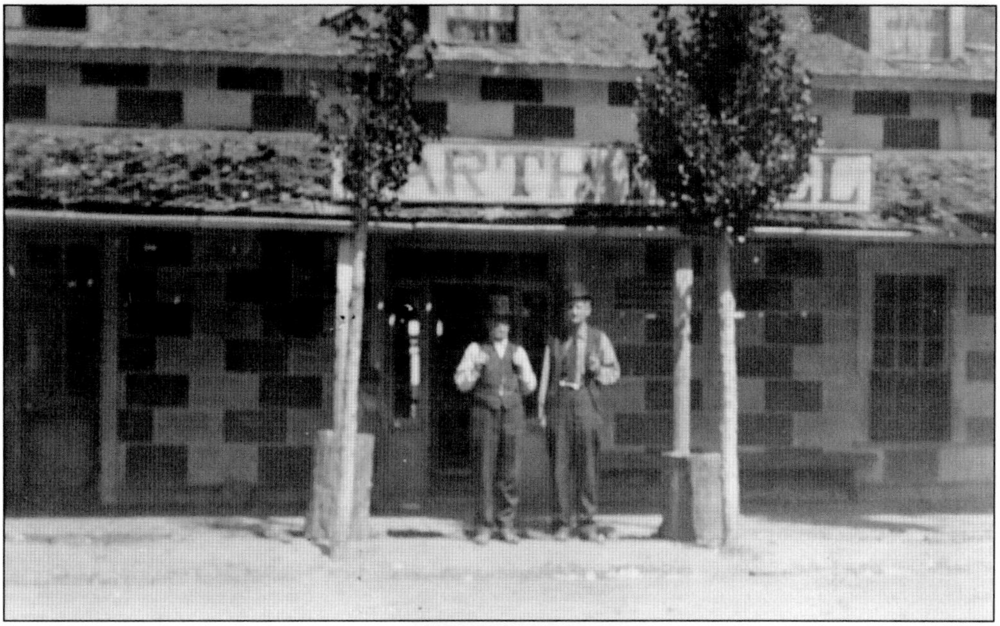

A. F. Banta (right) and Sol Barth (left), shown here in front of Barth's hotel, had a dispute that led to Barth trying to choke Banta, who in turn began to carve upon Barth's head with a penknife. Upon hearing the skirmish, Barth's brother Nathan fired a .44 bullet straight through Banta's neck. Banta survived and Sol's thumb was a digit shorter. (Courtesy Arizona State Library, Archives and Public Records, Archives Division, No. 97-6507.)

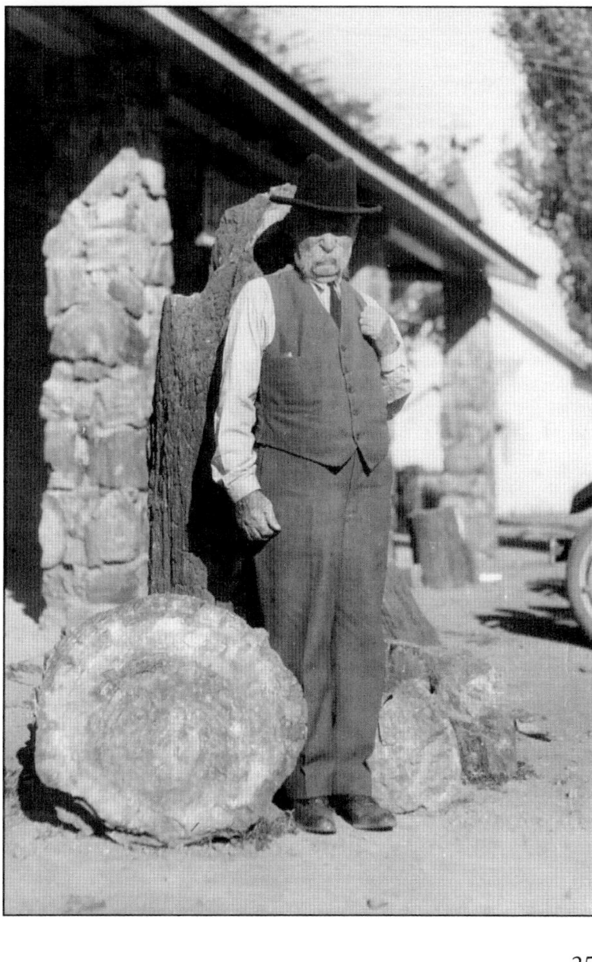

Sol Barth, shown here, stands in front of his hotel. (Courtesy St. Johns Historical Society and Museum.)

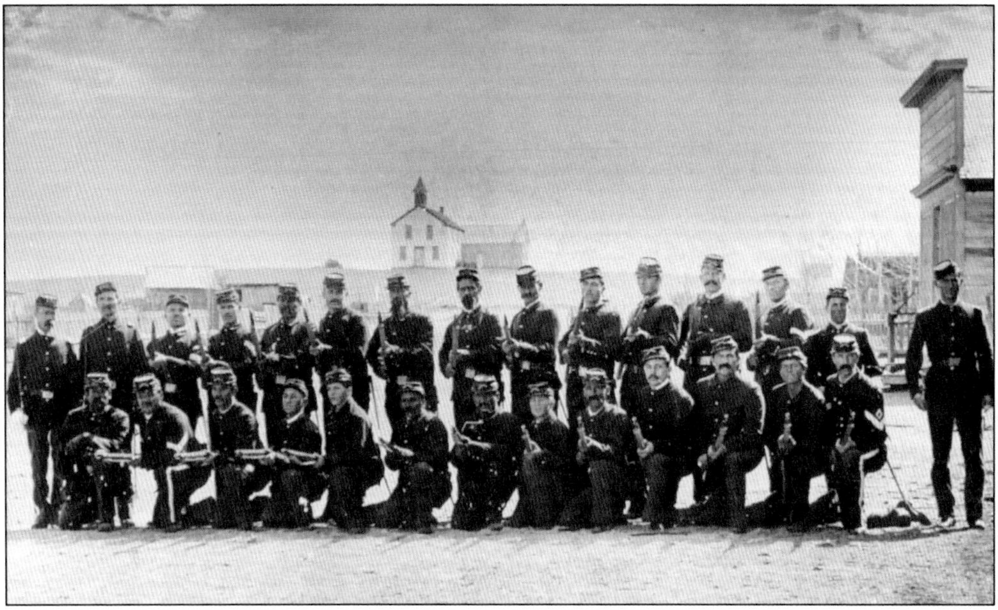

In 1891, A. F. Banta helped to organize Company K, National Guard of Arizona, which was stationed in St. Johns until 1905. This photograph was taken in 1892 down the street from the White School House. Those identified are (kneeling) Walter Scott second from left, Jerry Gonzales third from left, Martin Jensen fifth from left, Luis Chavez sixth from left, and Sydney Morgan Craig fourth from right; (standing) Charles Jarvis at far left, Ben Schuster third from the left, and Capt. Charles Estes at far right. (Courtesy St. Johns Historical Society and Museum.)

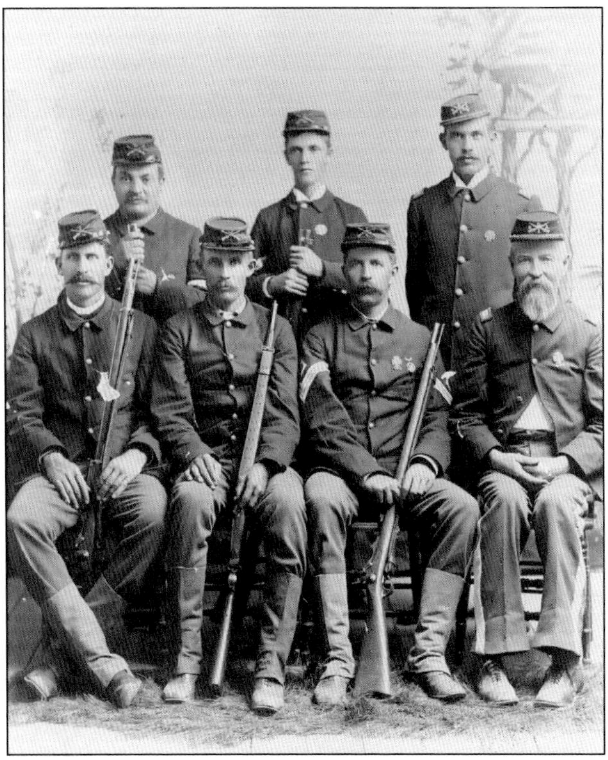

Members of Company K pose for a formal portrait. They are, from left to right, (first row) Jim Claybrook, Ed Bergman, Fred Nelson, and Art ?; (second row) Walter G. Scott, Martin Jensen, and Sydney M. Craig. (Courtesy Barbara Jaramillo.)

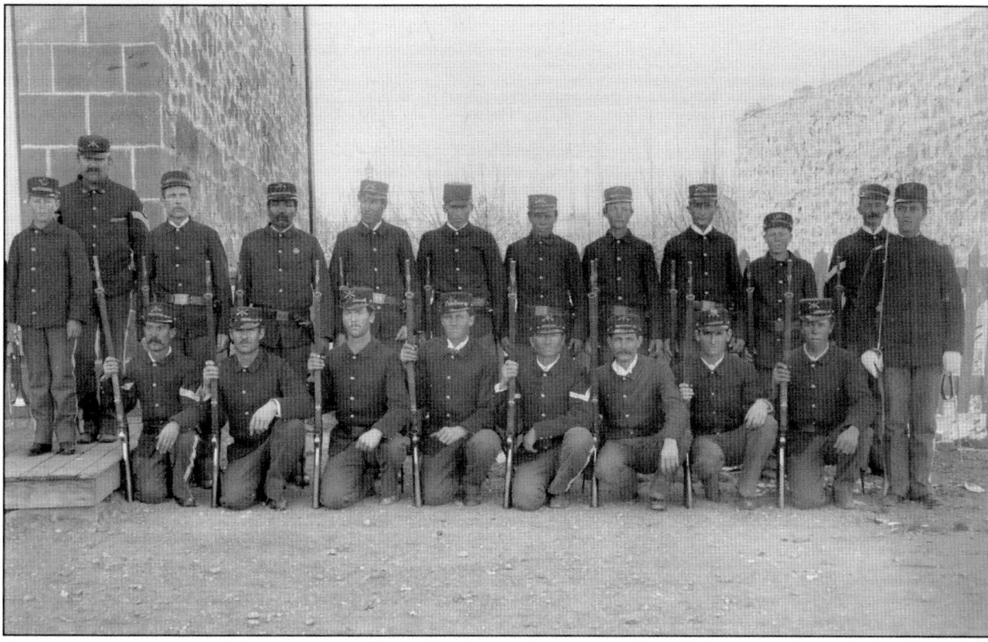

Company K, pictured here in 1896 beside the armory, are, from left to right, (kneeling) Jerry Gonzales, Fred Davis, George Waite, Willard Holgate, Fred Nelson, Frank Thomas, Frank Nicoll, and Will Jones; (standing) Arthur Jarvis, Marinus Christensen, John T. Patterson, unidentified, Andrew Gibbons, John Brown, Henry Jones, unidentified, Emer Plumb, Reuel Jarvis, Elijah Holgate, and Martin Jensen. (Courtesy St. Johns Family History Center.)

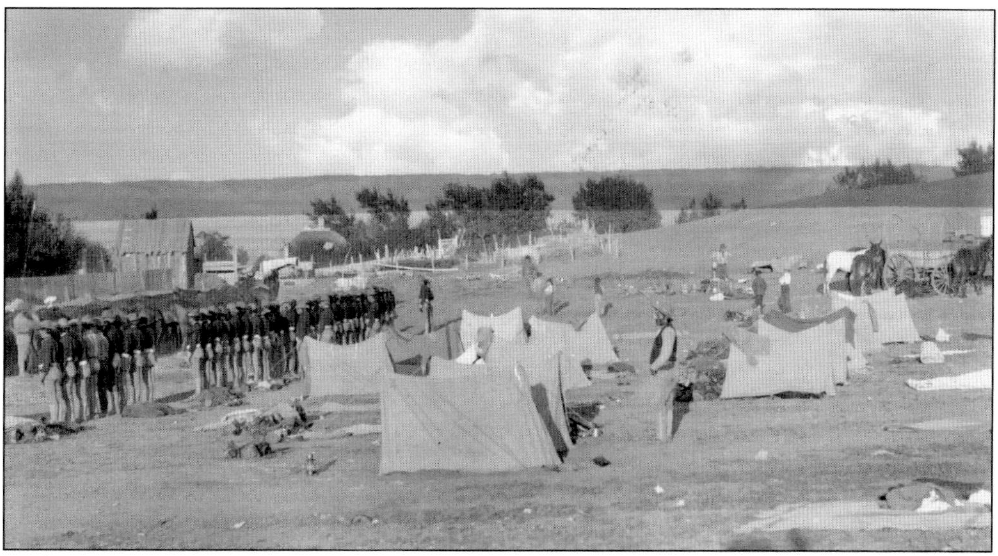

In this picture, Company K gets into formation for drills just outside St. Johns. (Courtesy St. Johns Family History Center.)

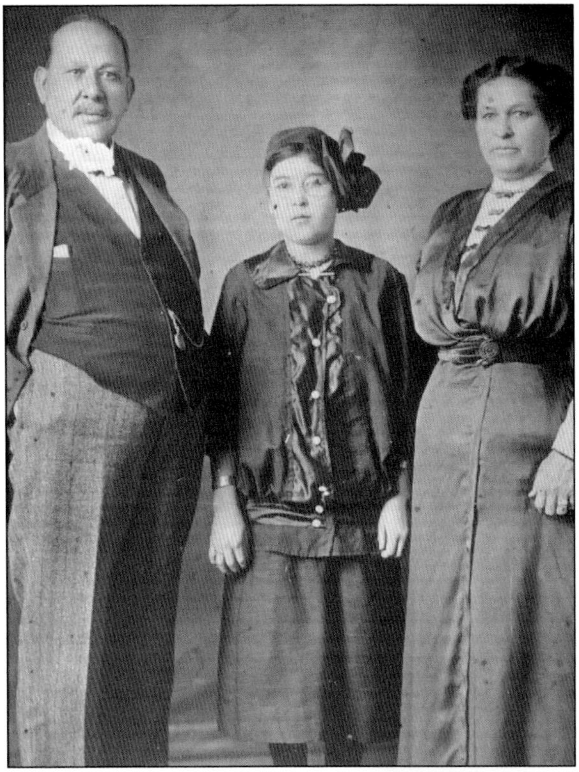

Alfred Ruiz was a St. Johns lawyer, district attorney, clerk for the district court, Apache County recorder, U.S. commissioner, superintendent of schools, and highly respected man noted for his immaculate dress and pride in his appearance. He did the 1880 census for St. Johns and served as both the clerk and recorder for Apache County as well as the superintendent of schools. This picture, taken in 1905, shows him with his niece and wife, Rufina Trujillo de Ruiz. (Courtesy Barbara Jaramillo.)

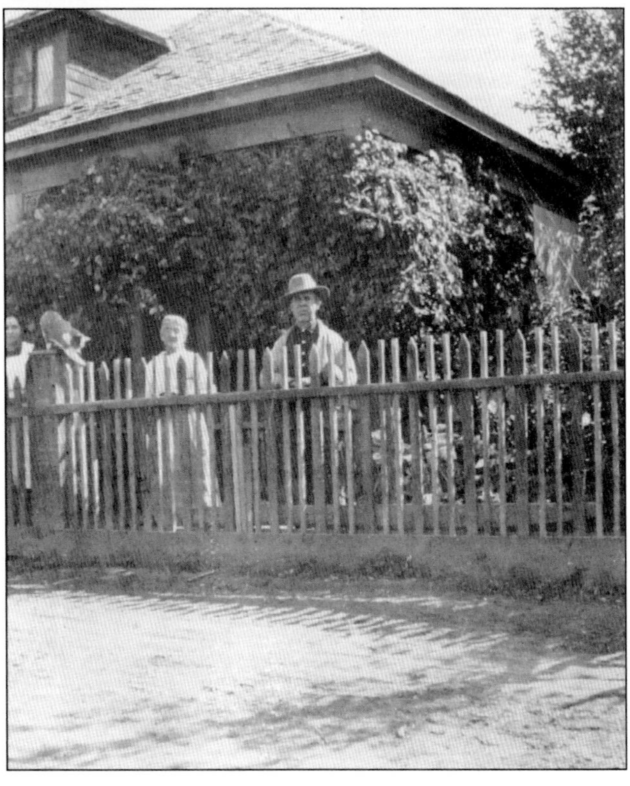

This picture shows the house of Santa Cruz Carrillo, a local musician. In the yard are, from left to right, Beatrice Gallegos, Mrs. Brown, and Carrillo. Father Badilla held the first mass at this house. (Courtesy Barbara Jaramillo.)

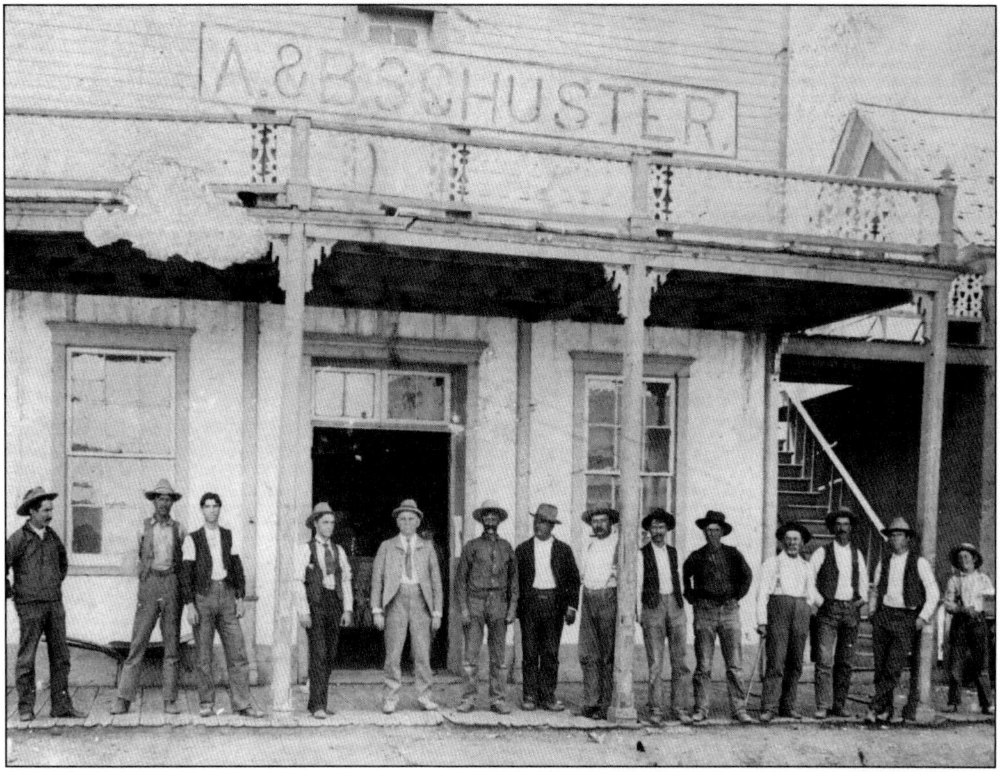

Twin bothers Adolf and Ben Schuster opened their first store in Holbrook in 1884; their motto was "The friendly store, since 1884." This store, built in St. Johns in 1891, was destroyed by fire in 1915. In this picture, Ben Schuster (in front of the door wearing a tie) stands with a row of unidentified townspeople and customers. (Courtesy Northern Arizona University, Cline Library, Special Collections and Archives, General Collections.)

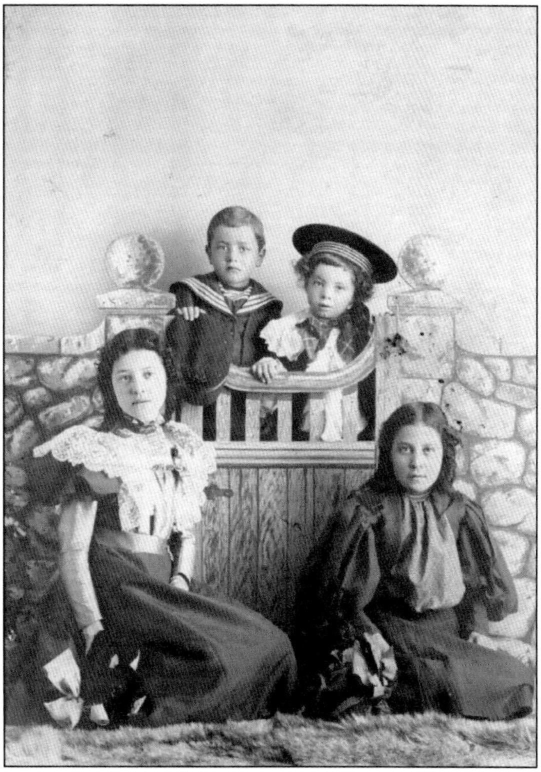

Ben Schuster's sisters-in-law Barbarita (first row, left) and Mamie Baca (first row, right), nephew Sydney M. Craig Jr. (second row, left), and eldest son Arthur Schuster (second row, right) pose for a photograph. (Courtesy St. Johns Historical Society and Museum.)

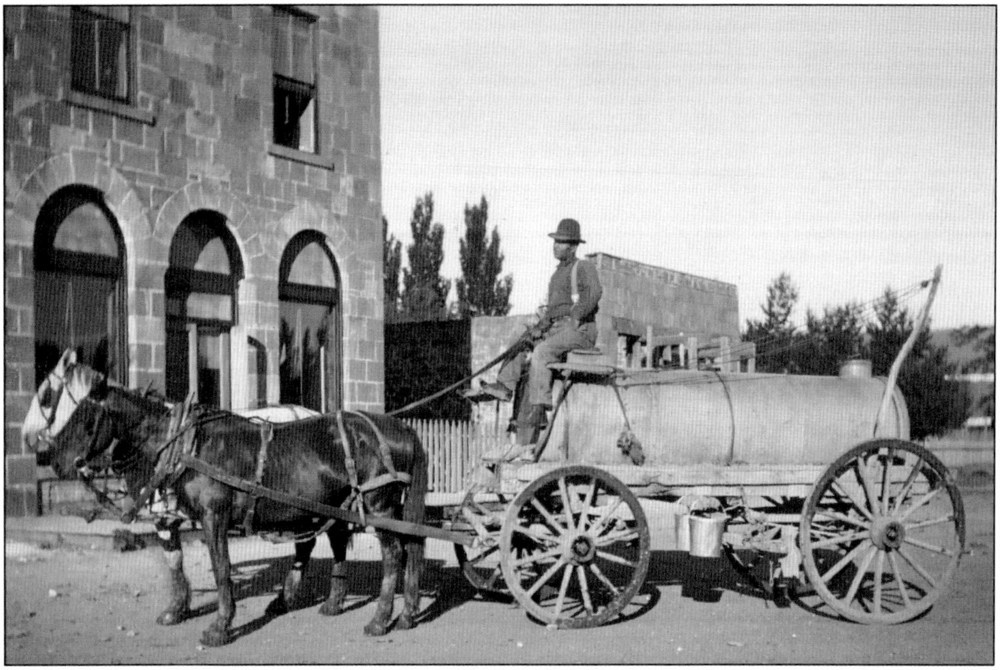

The only source of running water was the river or ditches, which the people drank from until Alexander McIntosh discovered a freshwater spring outside town. McIntosh sold the spring to the Richeys, who put a water tank on the back and sold water to businesses and door-to-door for 5¢ a bucket. In these photographs, Benjamin Richey delivers water to the armory (above) and the Monarch Saloon (below). From left to right in front of the saloon are (in front) Teofilo Duran (far left), Nathan Barth (on horse), Dr. Louis Barth (standing right beside Nathan), and Sol Barth (standing in front of wagon with arms folded); (on wagon) Monico Garcia, Jacob Armijo, and Benjamin Richey; (behind horse) five unidentified men; (beginning at horse's nose) Moroni Richey, Marcor H. Peterson, Martin Jensen, and Marinus Christenses. (Both courtesy St. Johns Family History Center.)

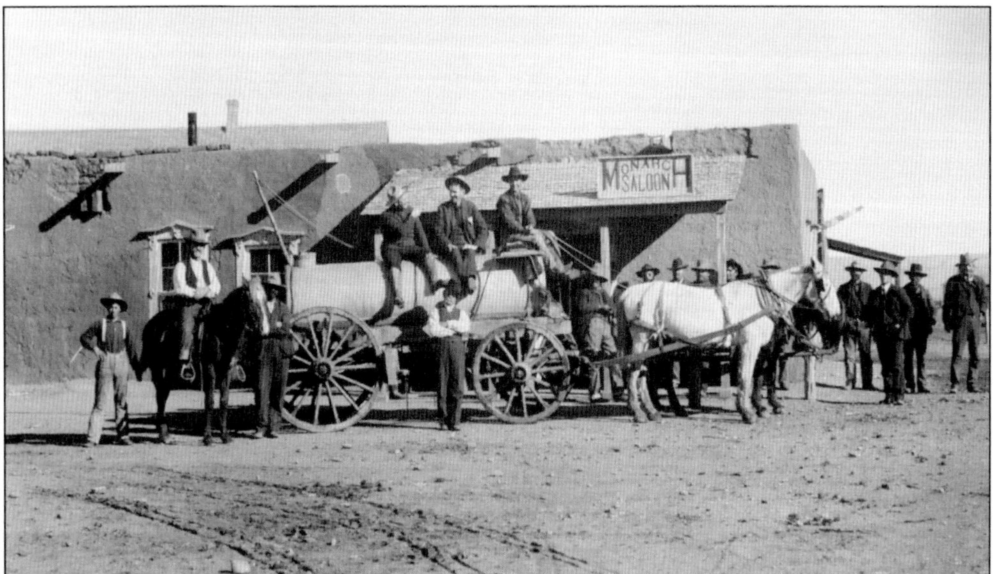

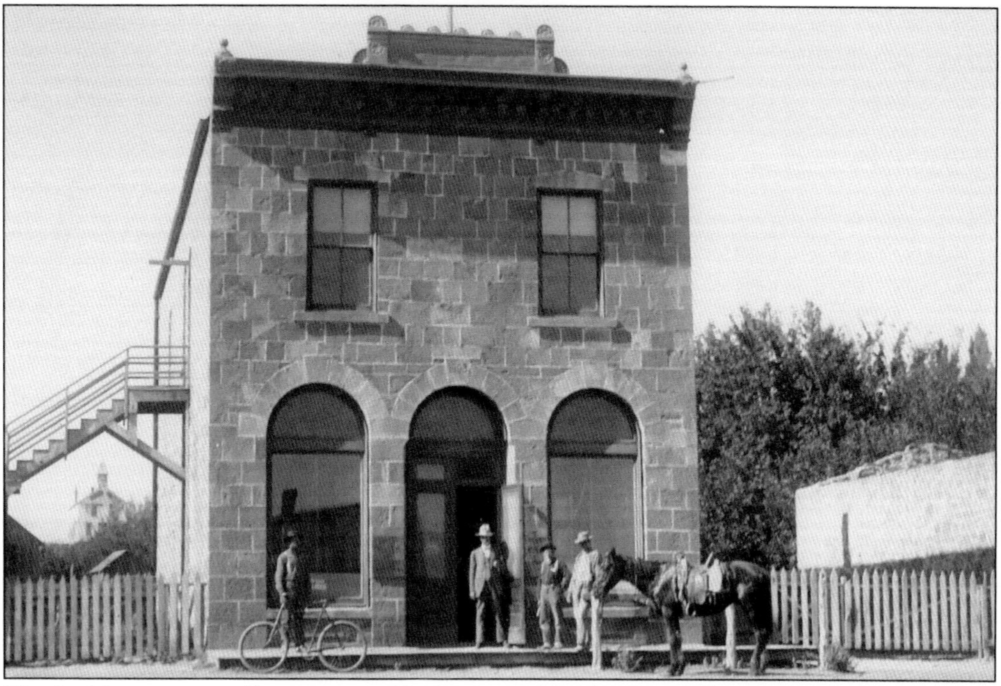

This building was initially constructed by Company K as Armory Hall in 1892. It later became the Merchant's and Stockman's Bank on the bottom floor, and various town newspapers were printed on the second floor. Standing in front from left to right are Henry Overson with his bicycle, Fred Nelson in the door, Ove Overson, and Jacob Hamblin. (Courtesy St. Johns Family History Center.)

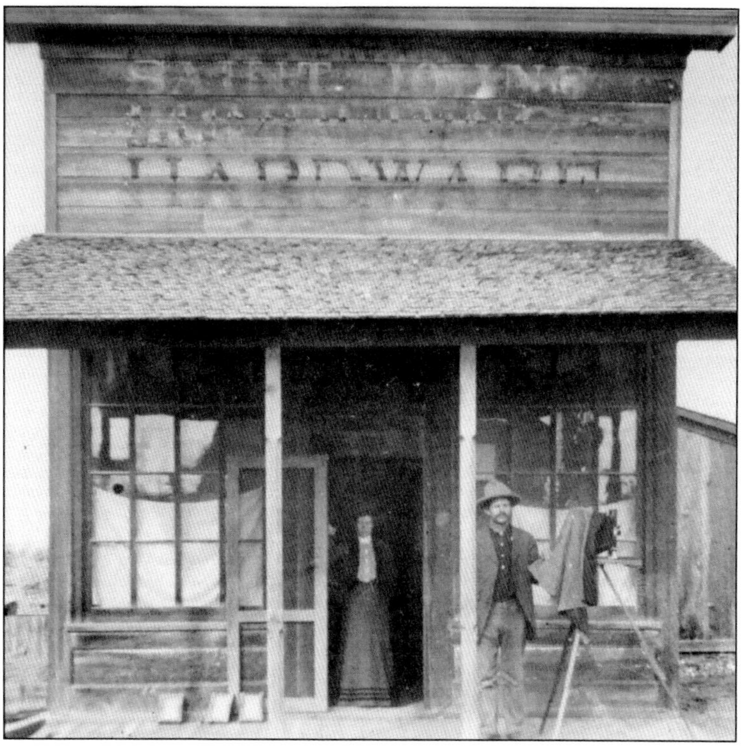

This building was a hardware store before becoming a photography studio and gallery run by Henry Overson and his wife, Margaret. Margaret learned the photography trade from her father, Charles Jarvis, and took over the business when Charles died, working as the town photographer for over 50 years. Pictured are Stella Jarvis Peterson standing in the doorway and Henry Overson standing out front with a camera. (Courtesy St. Johns Family History Center.)

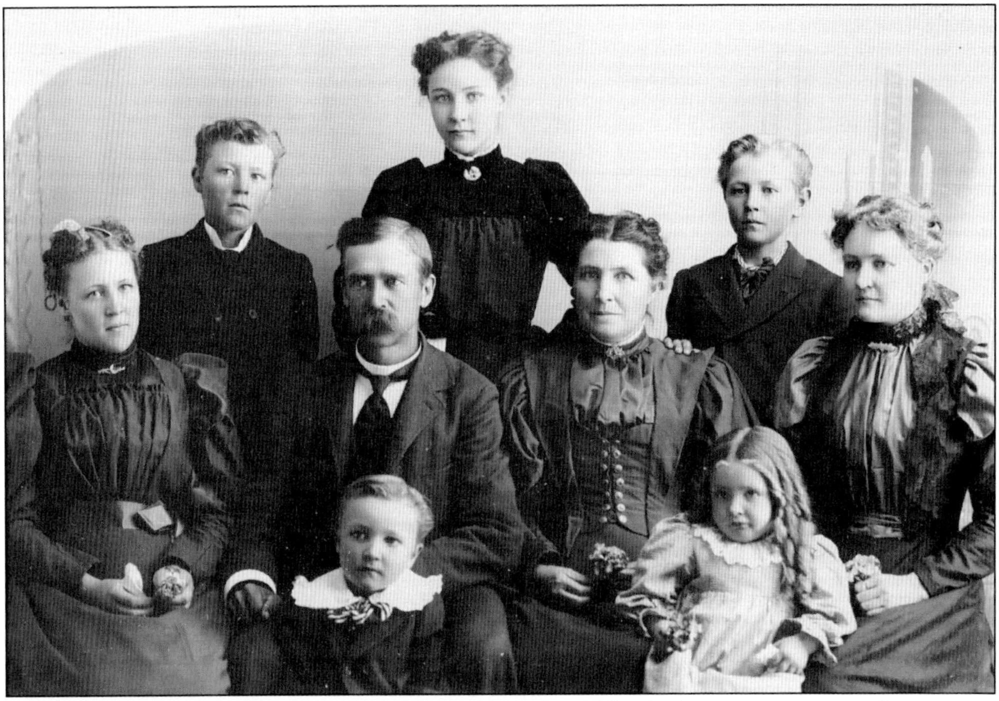

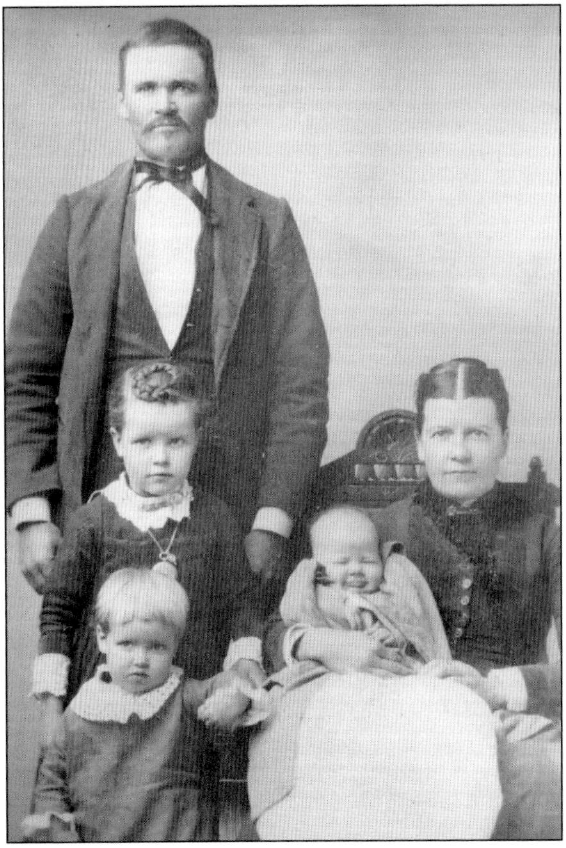

Charles Jarvis was a man of many talents and at one time or another was a postmaster, teacher, photographer, bandleader, and practical dentist, pulling all the loose teeth and some that weren't so loose. He is pictured here with his family, and from left to right they are (first row) Albert and Lois; (second row) Annie, Charles, Margaret, and Maggie; (third row) Reuel, Stella, and Arthur. (Courtesy St. Johns Historical Society and Museum.)

John Henry Heap and his wife, Mary, arrived in St. Johns in 1881 with $5 in cash, two sacks of grain, and a wagon with a team—which was stolen from them shortly after their arrival. He supervised the building of two reservoirs. Pictured here are John Henry, Mary, and their three oldest children, Elva (in front of John Henry), Mary Ellen (in front of Elva), and Ward (on Mary's lap). (Courtesy St. Johns Family History Center.)

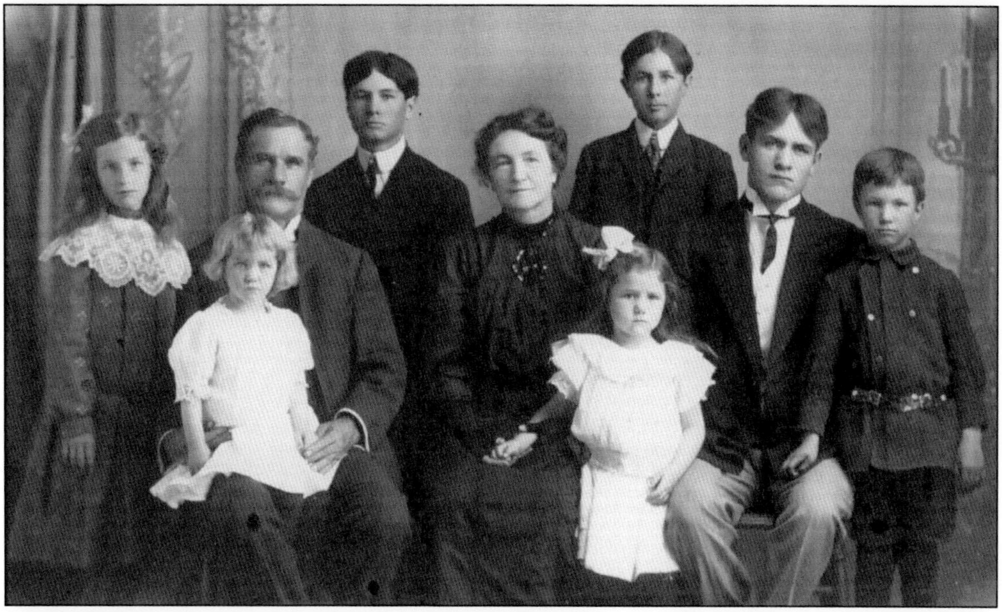

Joseph Bowman Patterson first met his wife, Emily, while working for her father in Nevada in 1879. After hearing that Emily's family had been called to settle in St. Johns, he followed to claim Emily as his bride. Arriving in 1880, his and Emily's wedding was the first in the new Mormon settlement. The family, shown here from left to right, includes (first row, girls in white) Amy and Emily (or Tem as she was called); (second row) Mona, Joseph, Emily, Joy, and Don; (third row) Gay and Earl. (Courtesy St. Johns Historical Society and Museum.)

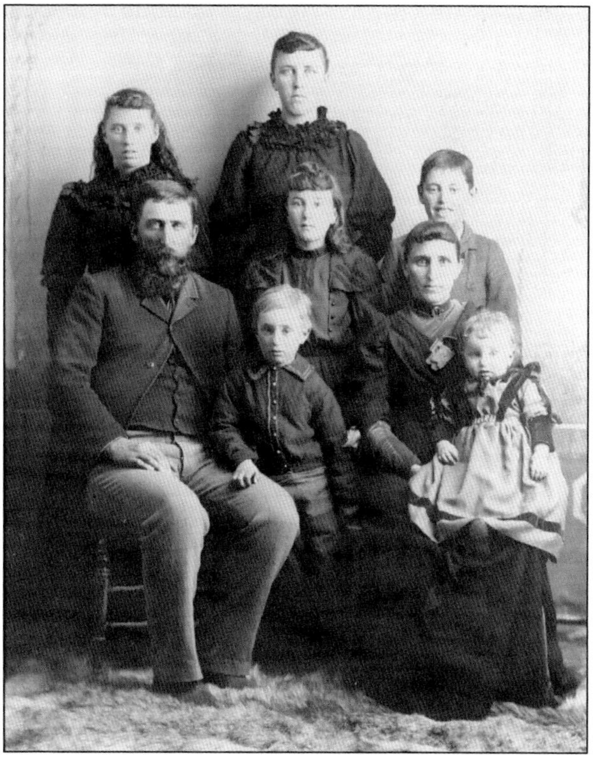

The Berry family, shown here from left to right, includes (first row) William Wiley ("W. W."), Gerald, Jennie (behind Gerald), Rachel, and Eulalia (on Rachel's lap); (second row) Alice, Levenia, and Wiley. They were a family that experienced both great achievements and great sorrows. Wiley was murdered (see chapter two), and all of Jennie's children (the Palmer children) drowned when the Lyman Dam broke. Rachel became the first female in the United States to be elected to a state legislature; W. W. served as the Apache County sheriff and was later killed in a car crash, which crippled Rachel. (Courtesy St. Johns Historical Society and Museum.)

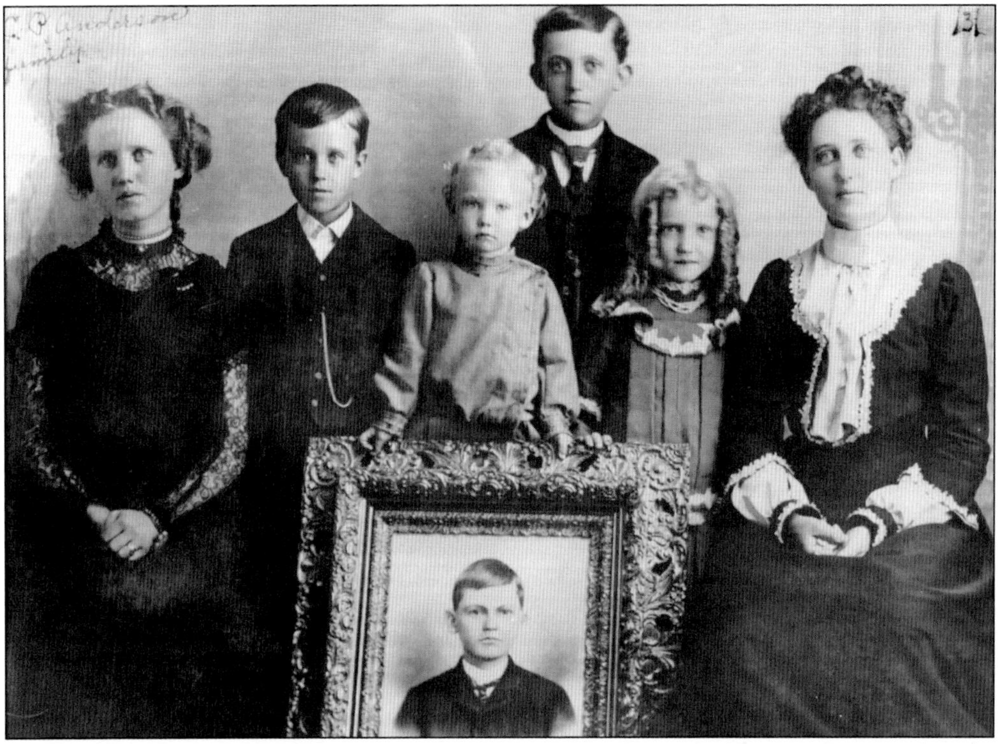

Charles Pehr Anderson and his wife, Anna Louise, arrived in St. Johns in 1884. C. P. bought stock in the then community-held St. Johns Drug Company in 1890. He purchased all the stock in 1904 after establishing the Anderson Mercantile. The Anderson children, pictured here, were all highly accomplished musicians, druggists, and merchants. From left to right they are Josephine, Alfred, Carl (standing behind a picture of the eldest son, Charlie), Albert, Annie, and Letty. (Courtesy St. Johns Family History Center.)

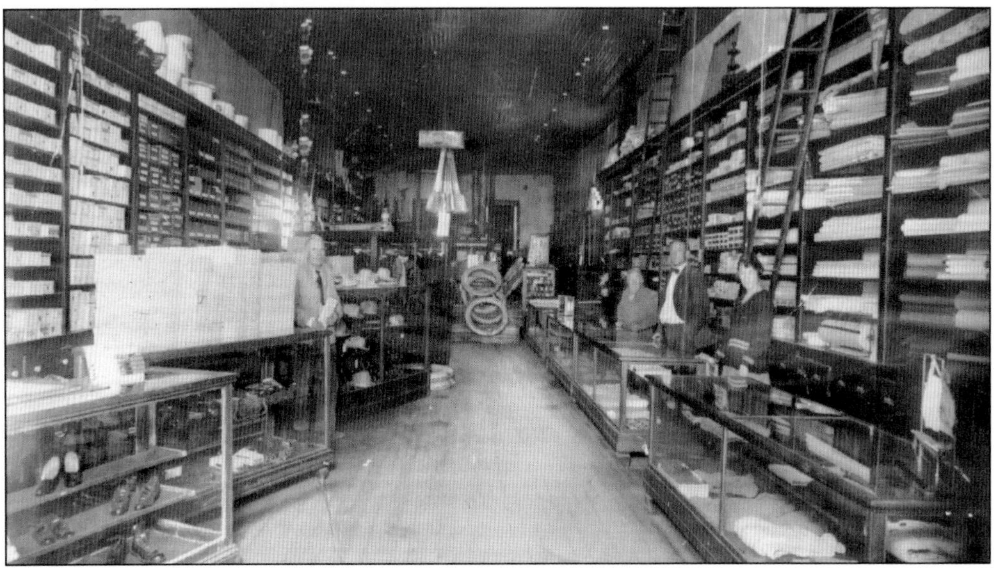

This picture shows the inside of the Anderson Mercantile, or "A Merc" as it appeared around the turn of the century. (Courtesy Michelle Udall.)

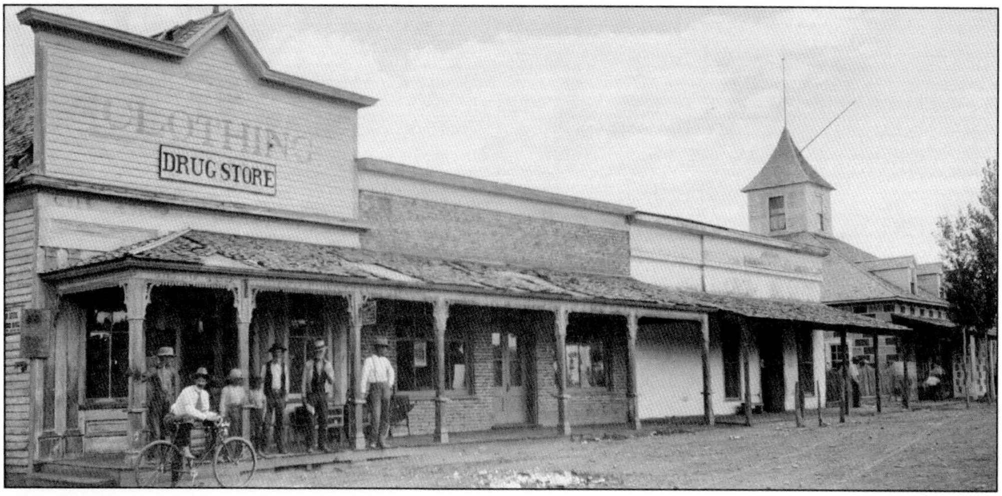

The Andersons, wanting to build a bigger drugstore but not wanting to waste the building they already had, decided to have the old wooden drugstore, shown here on the north side of Commercial Street, moved across the street. Frances Day was hired for the job. Unfortunately, Day's equipment broke down in the middle—literally. For two weeks, the old drugstore sat in the middle of the street, where Charles P. Anderson and his son Albert continued to do business. (Courtesy Barbara Jaramillo.)

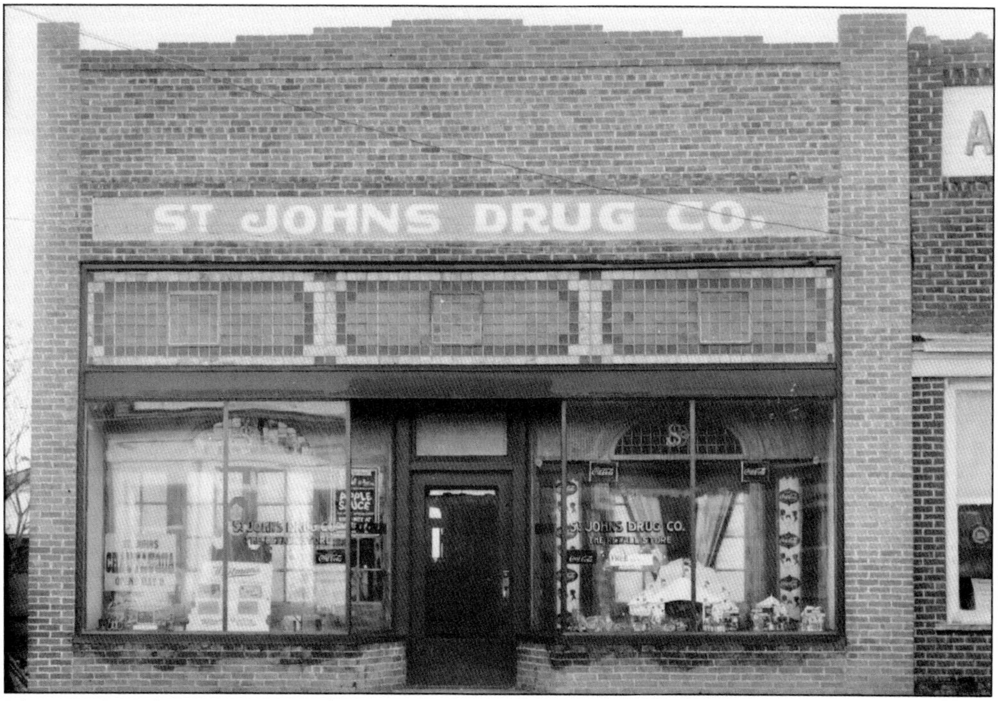

The new St. Johns Drug Store, shown here, was built on the north side of Commercial Street after the old one was moved across the street. The Andersons chose to move the old wooden drugstore across the street, rather than building the new one on the south side, because it was next to Anderson Mercantile. A metal door was installed connecting the two businesses so Albert F. Anderson (who ran the mercantile store) could assist his brother Carl (who ran the drugstore) as needed since both were licensed pharmacists. (Courtesy St. Johns Historical Society and Museum.)

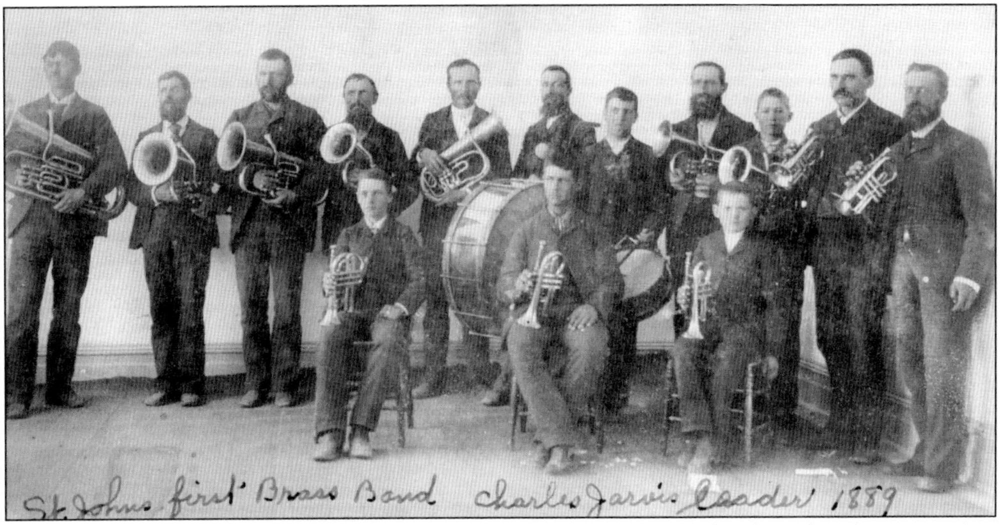

Although life was difficult, there was always time for music. Here the first brass band, organized in St. Johns in 1889, holds still for a photograph. From left to right they are (first row, seated) Martin Jensen, Daniel Wright, and Charlie Anderson; (second row, standing) Charles Davis, Willard Holgate, Marinus Christensen, Orson Arnold, Alma Doxey, W. C. Davis, John Rothlisberger, Fred Davis, unidentified, Charles P. Anderson, and bandleader Charles Jarvis. (Courtesy St. Johns Family History Center.)

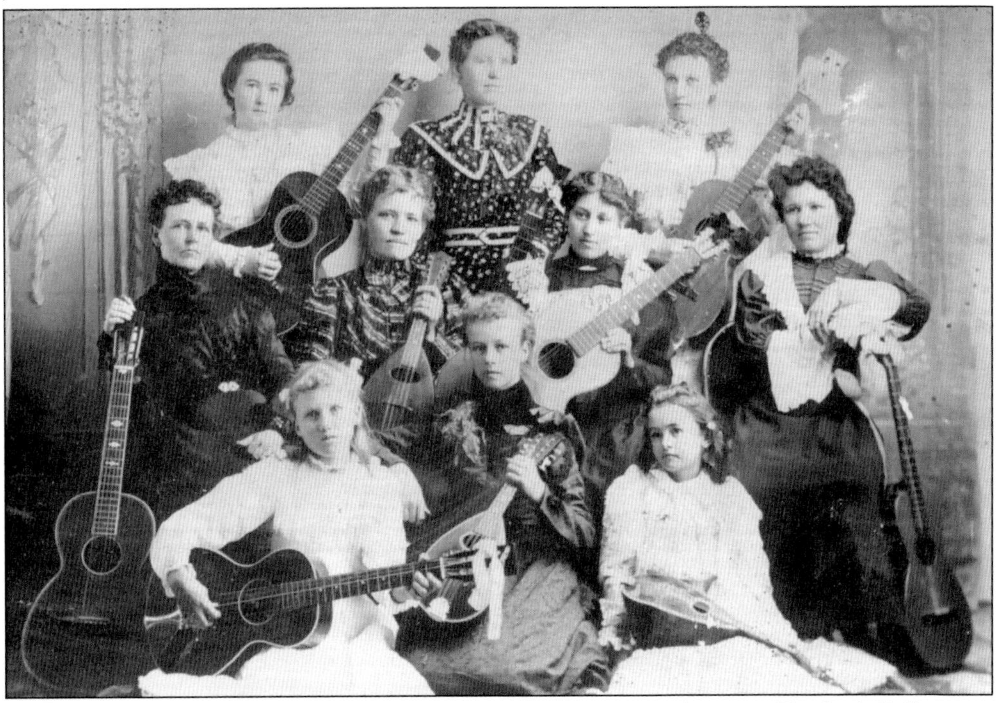

The St. Johns Mandolin and Guitar Club was organized in 1886 by Mary Elizabeth Ballentyne Farr and continued for over a century. The first members, shown here from left to right, are (first row) Josie Anderson, Ethel Farr, and Nell LeSueur; (second row) Mary Elizabeth B. Farr, Olena Kempe, Pearl Peterson, and Mary Jones; (third row) Alice LeSueur, Amanda Kempe, and Louise Freeman. (Author collection.)

Two

Taking Leave of Arizona by the Winchester Route

There were many ways to leave Arizona, but the most common in that day was either "Arizona kickers style" (hanging) or by the "Winchester route" (shooting). Because of the lack of tall trees and the jail's low-hanging door, hangings were difficult, so most outlaws and other unfortunate people left St. Johns by the Winchester route. Although there were probably many before, the first to make the news was the killing of Pete Clanton (or Blanton) in 1877. Pete and friend Joe Spencer, both members of a gang of horse thieves, were in St. Johns on "business" when they were recognized by some locals, who tried to arrest both. Instead, Pete and Joe holed up in Maurice Barth's house. The house was immediately surrounded and both were ordered to surrender; only Spencer obeyed. Three men went into the house to arrest Pete—two were shot dead and the other was seriously wounded. Instead of sending more men in through the door to be shot, the men surrounding the house made as if to leave but instead quietly climbed on the roof. While Pete looked out the window believing he had won, the roof was suddenly stripped off as one man quickly fired a shot into Pete's breast, killing him instantly. Spencer, after being told he would be taken out of St. Johns to some sort of safety, was found later strung up on a tree not even a mile away. Outlaws and other ne'er-do-wells met similar fates.

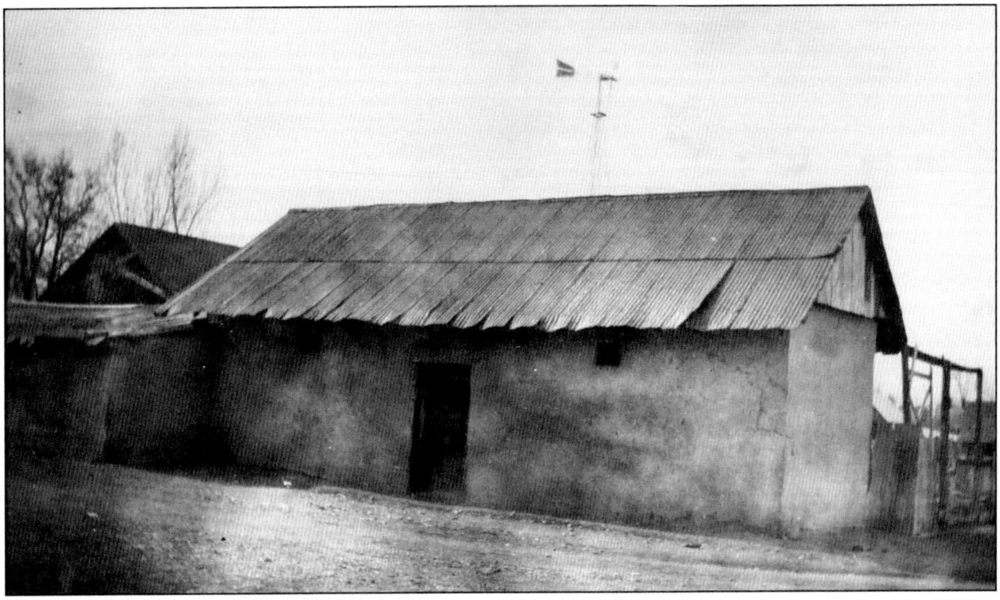

The first Apache County Jail, shown here, was a one-room adobe structure built in the early 1880s. In 1881, William "Wild Bill" Campbell and "Thick-Lipped" Joe Waters were in this jail for the murder of William Blanchard and Joe Barrett. After the jailor left on a "convenient" errand, at least 100 men descended on the jail and hanged both men in the doorway of the jail. Because the doorway was too low, somebody had to bring a little extra rope to tie a prisoner's legs up behind his back before he could be hanged. (Courtesy St. Johns Family History Center.)

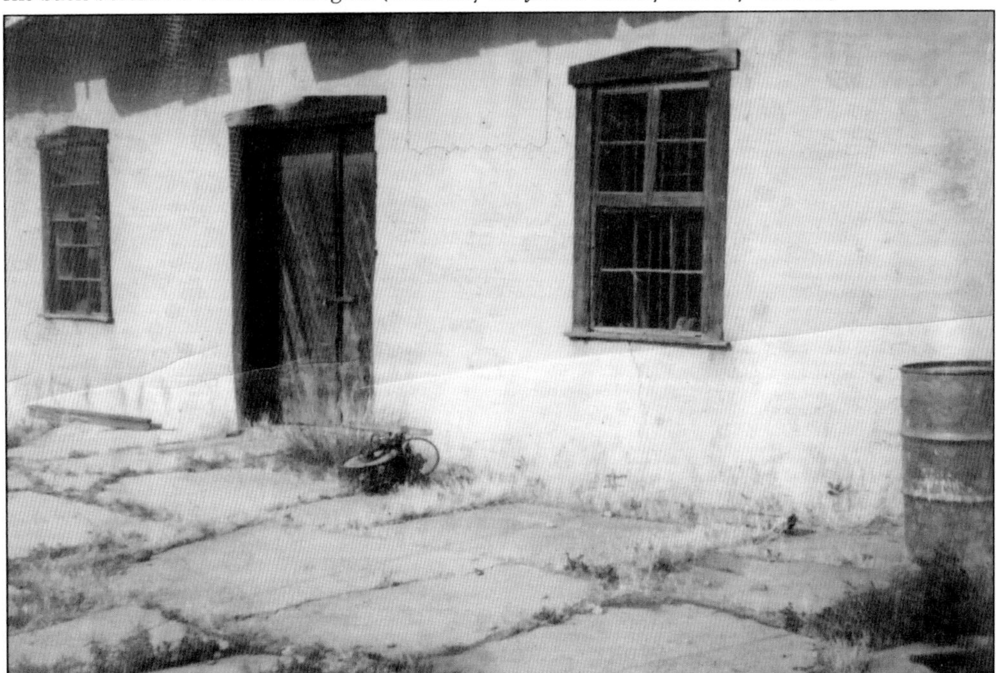

Because of the old jail's inhumane conditions, a new jail was built across the street in 1885, and the old adobe jail was remodeled in 1886 as an office for the board of supervisors, as shown in this picture. (Courtesy St. Johns Historical Society and Museum.)

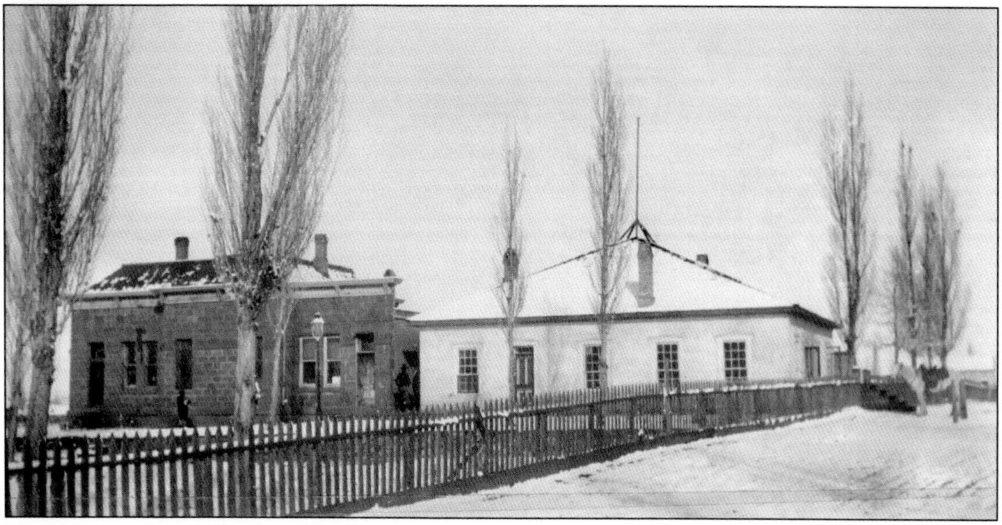

This picture shows the first Apache County Courthouse (right, built in 1880) and the new jail. When a new courthouse was built, these buildings were remodeled and turned into Coronado Elementary School. (Courtesy St. Johns Historical Society and Museum.)

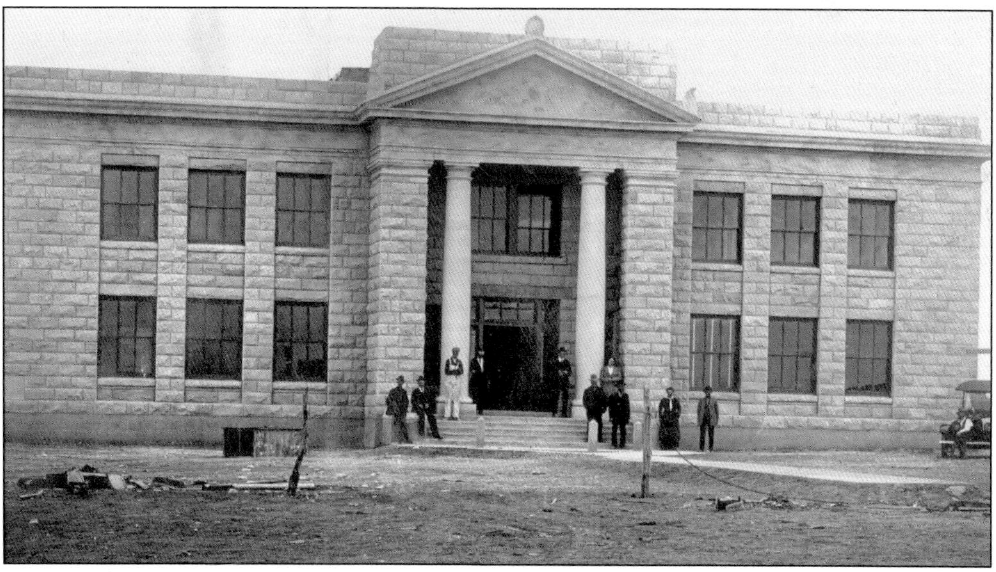

By 1915, the growing county was in dire need of a bigger courthouse, which, shown here being built, finally happened in 1918. (Courtesy St. Johns Family History Center.)

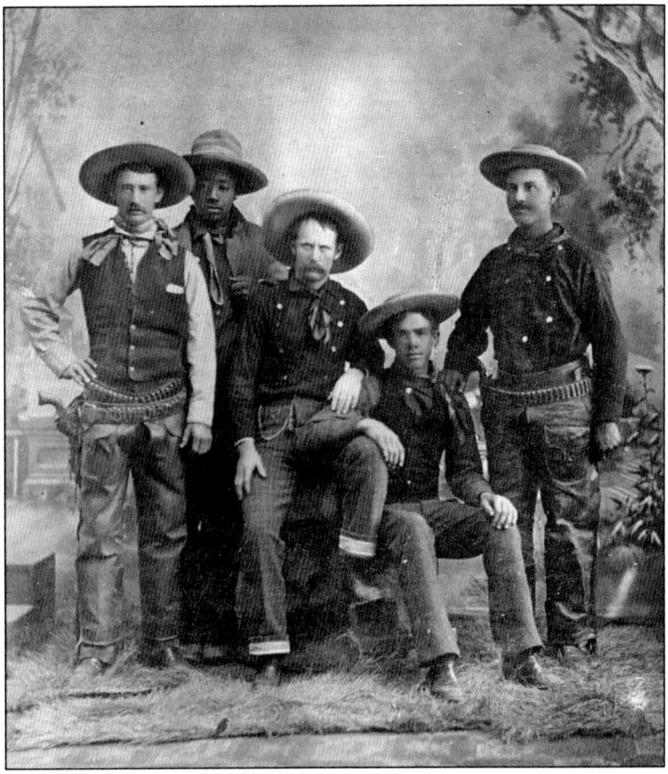

In the 1860s, the land was used for grazing sheep. That all changed when the Greers arrived in 1878 with a large herd of cattle and some cowboys. Soon a sort of battle ensued between the cowboys and sheepherders to the degree that there was bound to be a showdown. That showdown came on June 24, 1882. The Greer gang, shown here from left to right, includes Joseph Woods, Jeff Tribbet, Nat Greer, Hiram "Hi" Hatch, and Albert Porter. (Courtesy Arizona State Library, Archives and Public Records, Archives Division, No. 97-9493.)

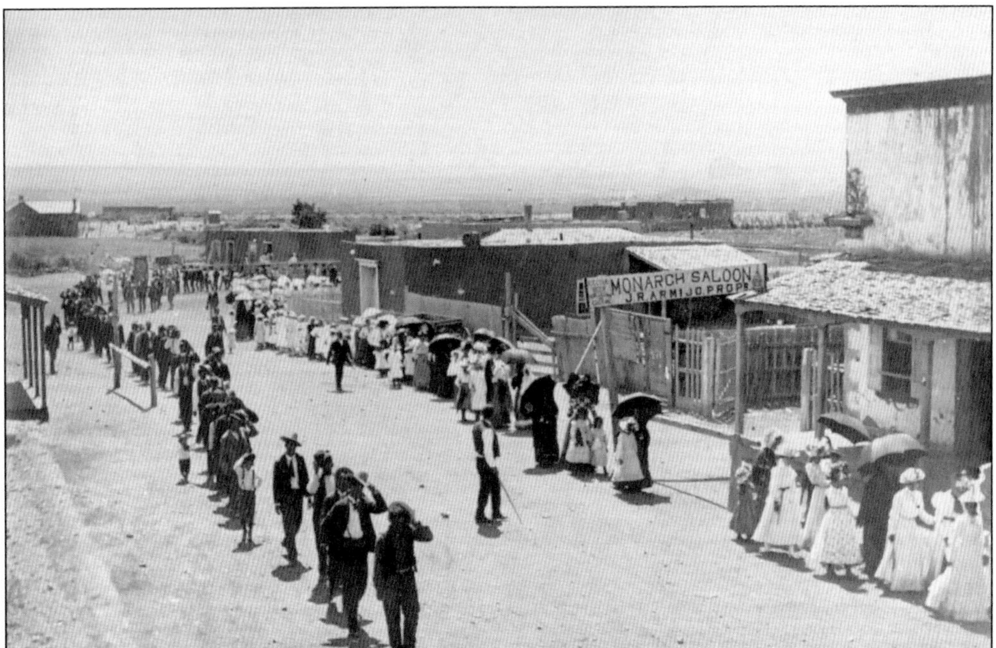

Since the beginning of the settlement, the Hispanic people of St. Johns have celebrated the Feast of St. John the Baptist, or San Juan Day, on June 24. In 1882, musicians, acrobats, and a bullfight were on the ticket and the Greers were told not to come. (Courtesy Barbara Jaramillo.)

This made the Greers more determined to attend the festivities, and they let the Hispanics know that they intended on coming and coming armed. Sheriff Tomas Perez (right) heard of the Greers' plan and told them not to come to town armed, but they disregarded the sheriff and arrived in town well armed. (Courtesy Apache County Sheriff's Office.)

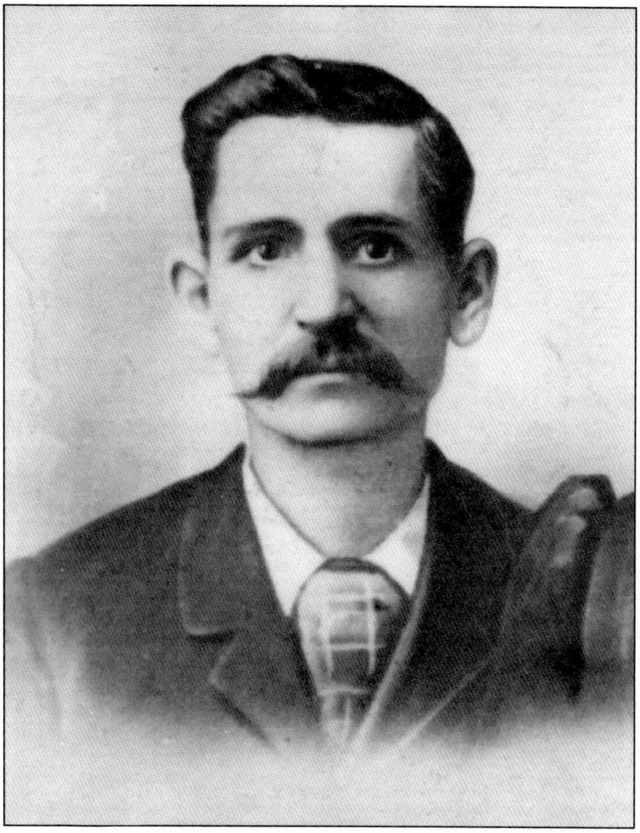

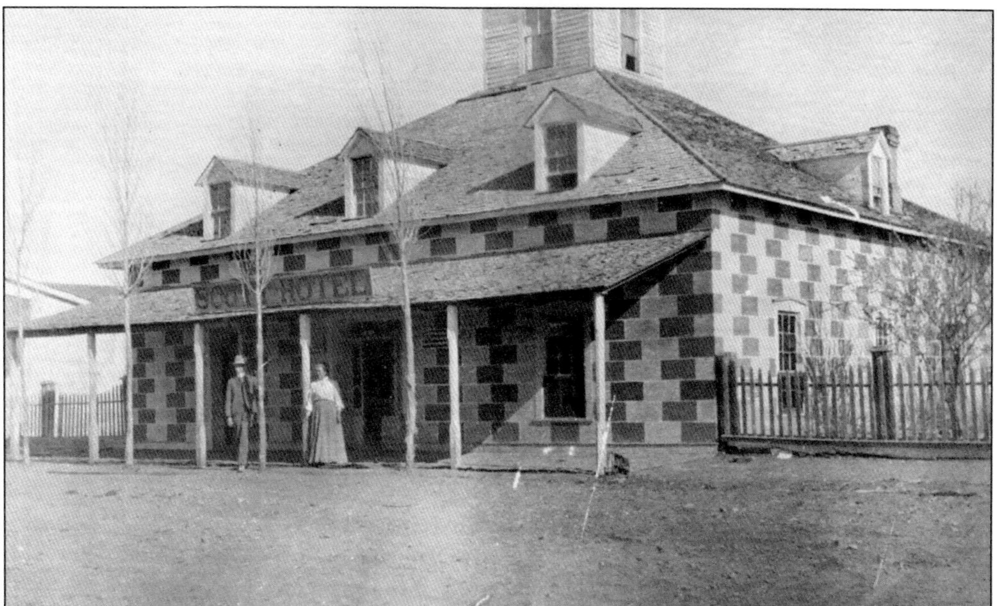

Soon rifle bullets and pistol balls ripped through the air, and a running battle was in progress. The Hispanic shooters took shelter in the Barth Hotel. (Courtesy St. Johns Historical Society and Museum.)

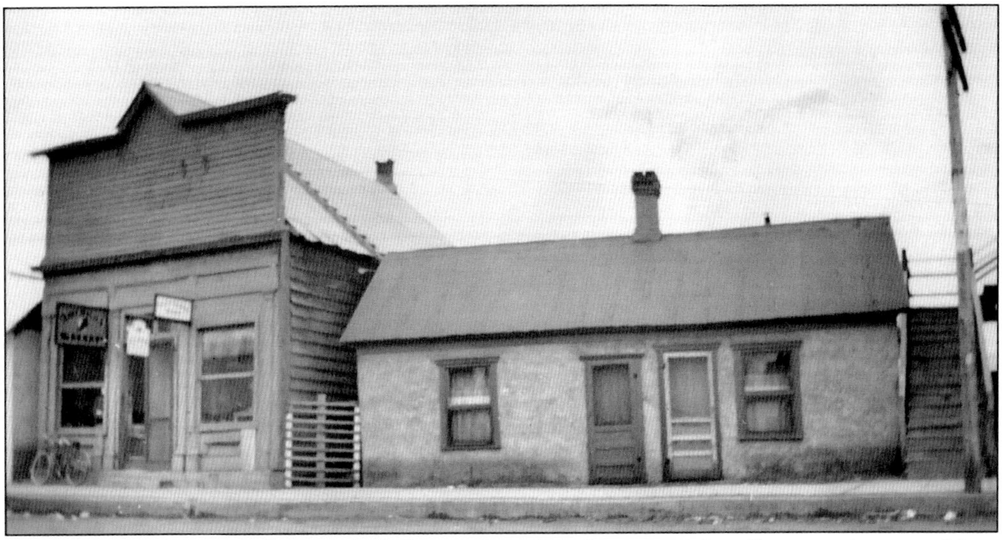

The Greers and their cowboys took shelter in this adobe house on Main Street and returned fire. Hi Hatch was shot in the shoulder and Harris Greer in the hand. When Jim Vaughn went to the window, he was shot in the neck below the chin, the bullet exiting the back of the head, and he bled to death. (Courtesy St. Johns Family History Center.)

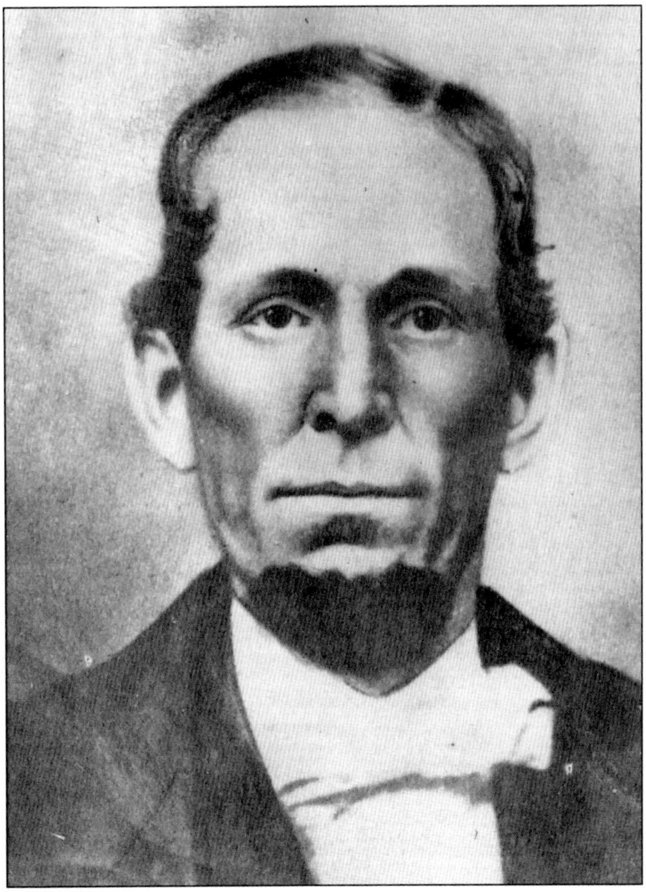

After 15 to 20 minutes of shooting, Nathan Tenney, 70 years old and a friend to all, walked up the street with a white flag. The shooting stopped, and Tenney entered the house with the Greers and told them to surrender. They agreed. When Tenney opened the door and stepped out, he was shot in the head and died immediately. It is unknown to this day who shot him. (Courtesy St. Johns Family History Center.)

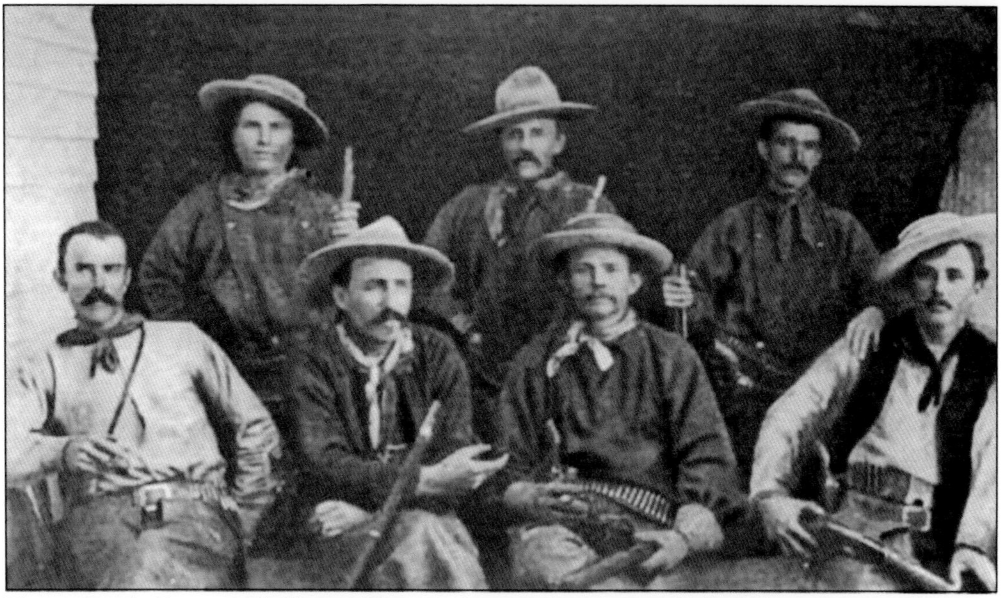

Henry Smith (first row, left) and Thomas Carson (beside Smith) had the largest cattle ranch south of St. Johns, running nearly 10,000 head of cattle, which they branded "24." Ike and Phin Clanton had a "Z4" brand and, with the skillful use of a running iron, rustled thousands of cattle from Smith, Carson, and Ernest Tee. (Author collection.)

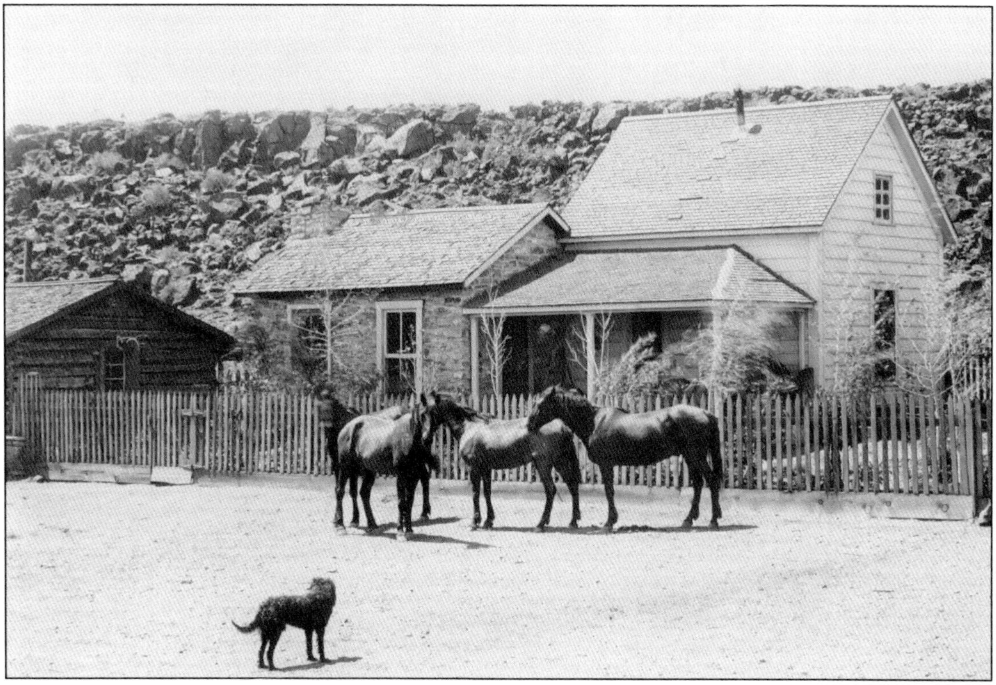

The headquarters for the Smith, Carson, and Tee ranch is shown here, located outside St. Johns. (Courtesy St. Johns Historical Society and Museum.)

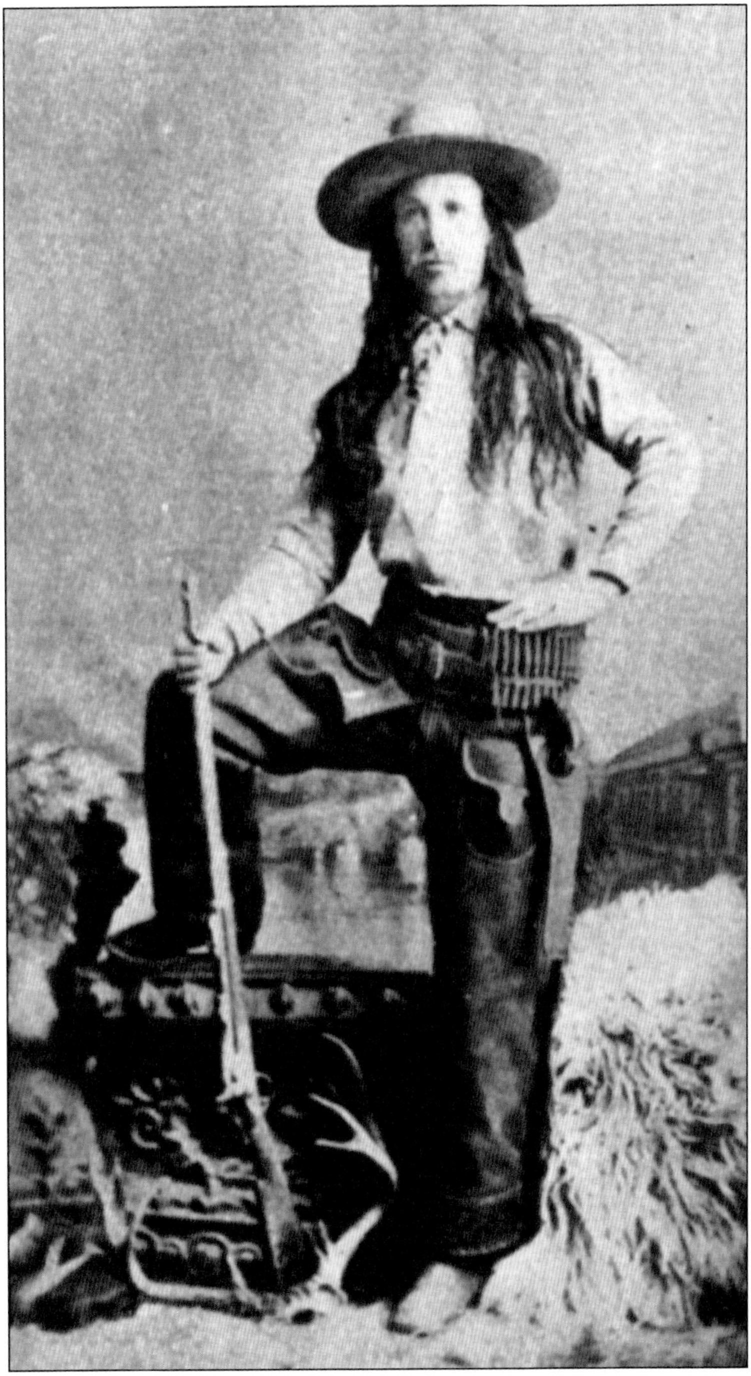

Commodore Perry Owens, Apache County's sixth sheriff, took office in January 1887. By March 25, indictments and warrants had been issued, mostly against cattle rustlers like Ebin Stanley and Ike and Phin Clanton. When he left office only two years later, the outlaws were either dead (like Ike Clanton) or in prison (like Phin Clanton). A true western frontier sheriff, Owens left Apache County a safer place. (Courtesy Arizona State Library, Archives and Public Records, Archives Division, No. 97-7750.)

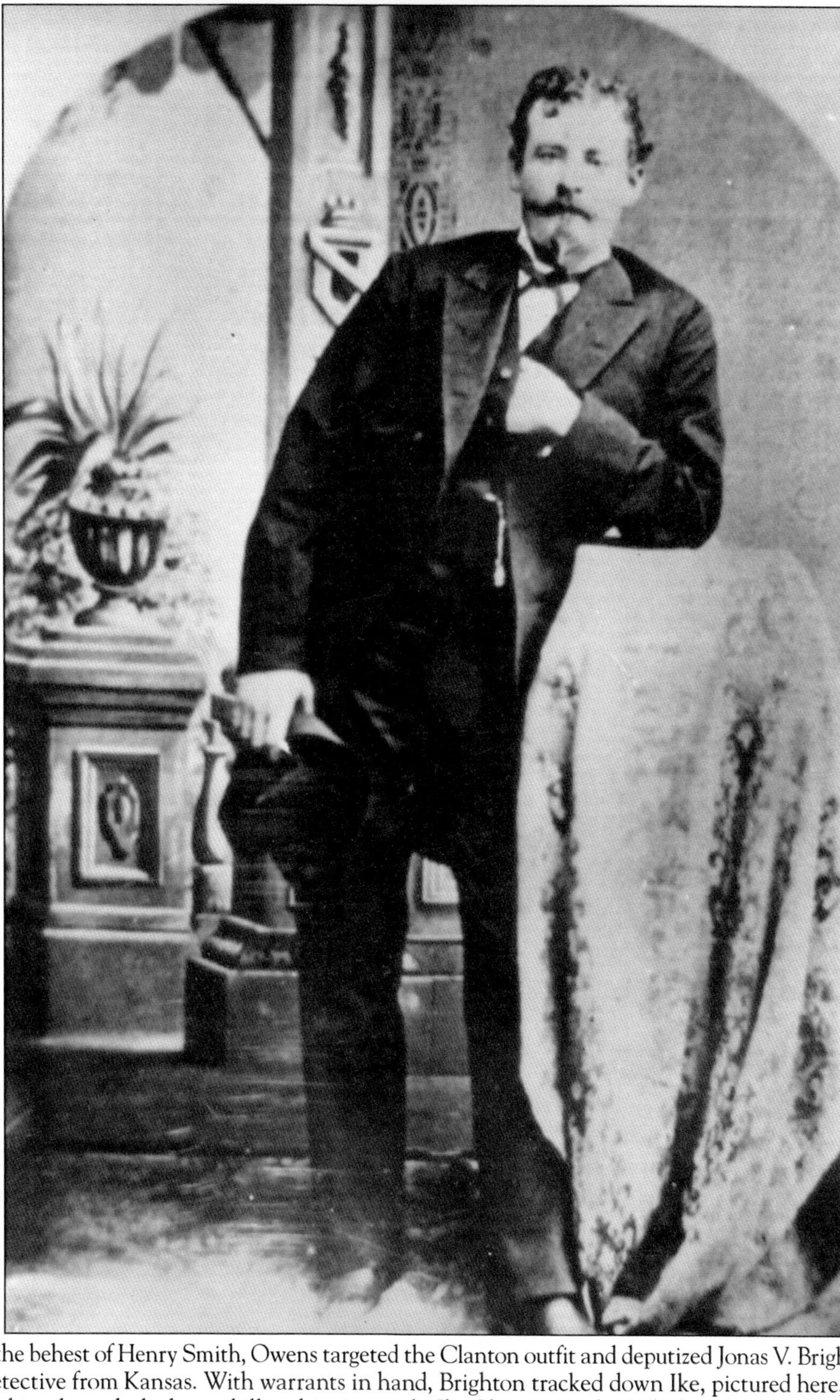

At the behest of Henry Smith, Owens targeted the Clanton outfit and deputized Jonas V. Brighton, a detective from Kansas. With warrants in hand, Brighton tracked down Ike, pictured here, and shot him through the heart, killing him instantly. Ike Clanton was buried where he fell. (Courtesy Arizona State Library, Archives and Public Records, Archives Division, No. 97-7485.)

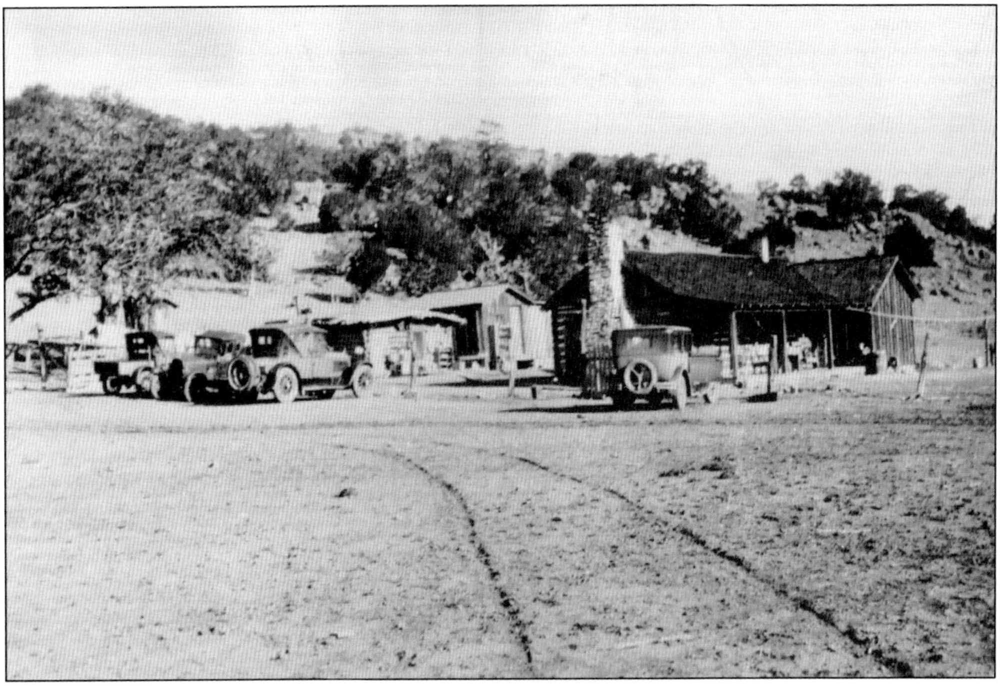

The Clantons, Isaac "Ike" and Phineas "Phin," moved to this homestead outside of St. Johns in the summer of 1882. It was here that the Clanton outfit, which included Ebin Stanley and Lee Renfro, rendezvoused with stolen cattle and horses and where Lee Renfro shot and killed Isaac Ellenger for no apparent reason. (Courtesy Arizona State Library, Archives and Public Records, Archives Division, No. 97-7488.)

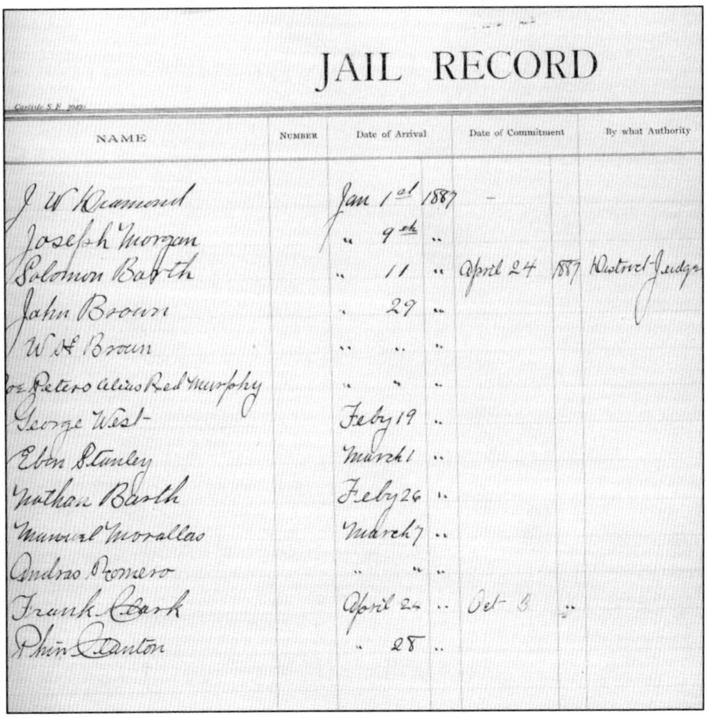

JAIL RECORD

NAME	NUMBER	Date of Arrival	Date of Commitment	By what Authority
J W Diamond		Jan 1st 1887	–	
Joseph Morgan		" 9th "		
Solomon Barth		" 11 "	April 24 1887	District Judge
John Brown		" 29 "		
W H Brown		" " "		
Joe Peters alias Red Murphy		" " "		
George West		Feby 19 "		
Ebin Stanley		March 1 "		
Nathan Barth		Feby 26 "		
Manuel Morallas		March 7 "		
Andrao Romero		" " "		
Frank Clark		April 24 "	Oct 3 "	
Phin Clanton		" 28 "		

The year 1887 was a busy one for Sheriff Owens, as shown by this jail record. Sol Barth was arrested and convicted for forging county warrants, and his brother Nathan was arrested for trying to bribe the jury in Sol's case. John Brown, William Brown, Red Murphy, and George West were all arrested for rustling, and all broke out. Ebin Stanley and Phin Clanton were both arrested for cattle rustling, and Frank Clark was arrested for killing Patrick Mullen in the Monarch Saloon. (Courtesy Apache County Sheriff's Office.)

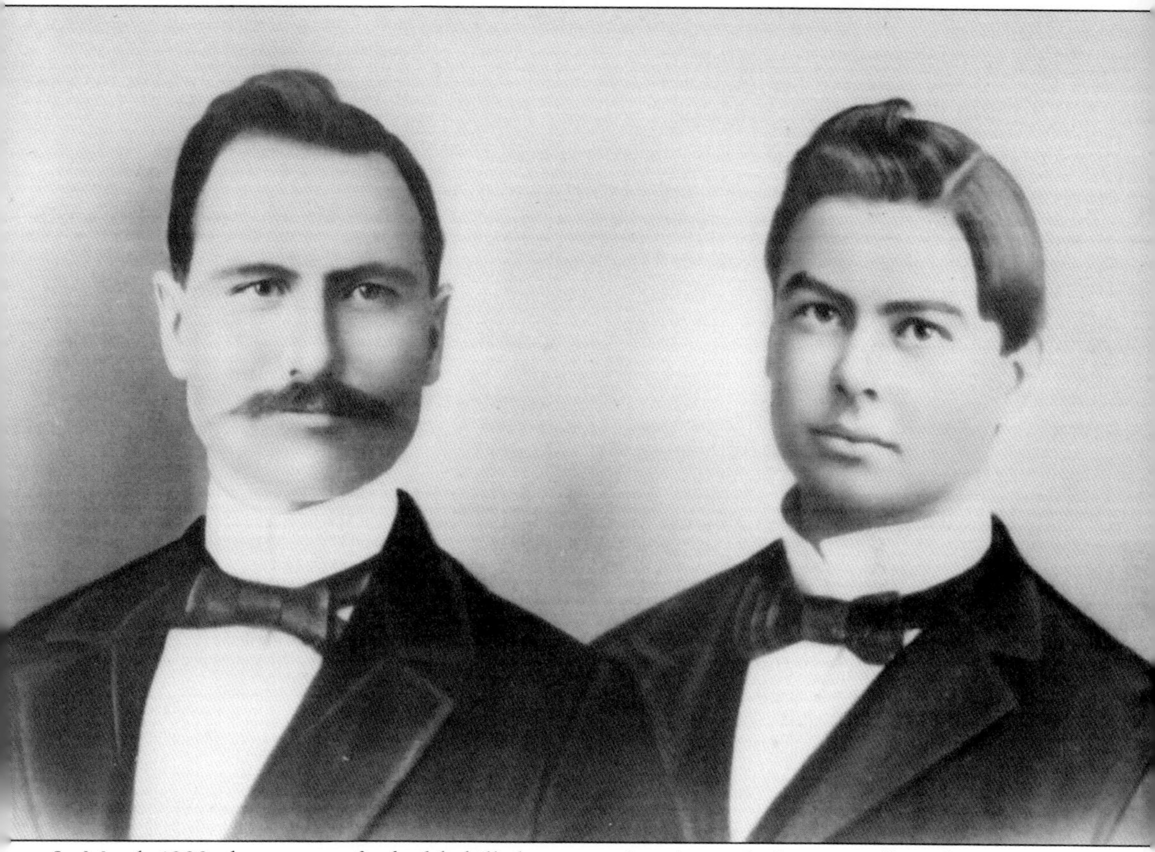

In March 1900, the carcass of a freshly killed cow was found outside Springerville and reported to Sheriff Ed Beeler, who formed a posse and began pursuit. Later that day, a group of outlaws was later spotted at the bridge outside St. Johns, and a new posse consisting of Gus Gibbons (right) and Frank LeSueur (left) went in pursuit. The next day, when the two young men hadn't come home, another group went out looking for them. The men were found outside St. Johns. The killers had lain in wait for the two as they led their horses up the rocky and steep terrain. Frank was shot in the neck and between the eyes, killing him instantly. Gus initially suffered only a body wound and ran. Chasing him down, the outlaws shot him three times in the head. (Courtesy St. Johns Family History Center.)

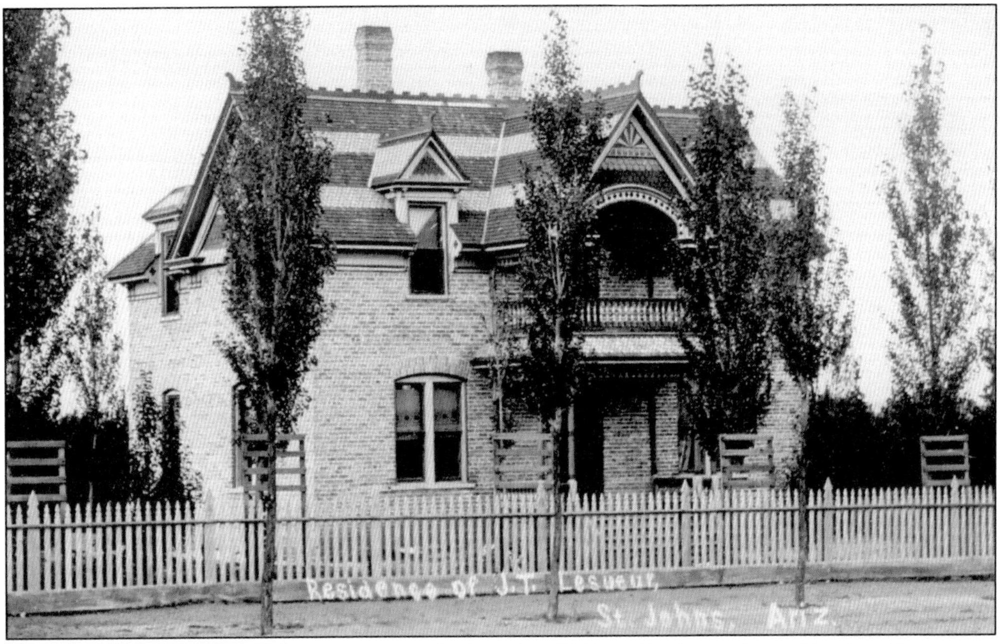

The John T. LeSueur home, shown here, was built in the 1880s and is the residence Frank LeSueur grew up in. It was designed by Ralph Ramsey, the architect and maker of the Eagle Gate in Salt Lake City. (Courtesy Arizona State Library, Archives and Public Records, Archives Division, No. 96-2106.)

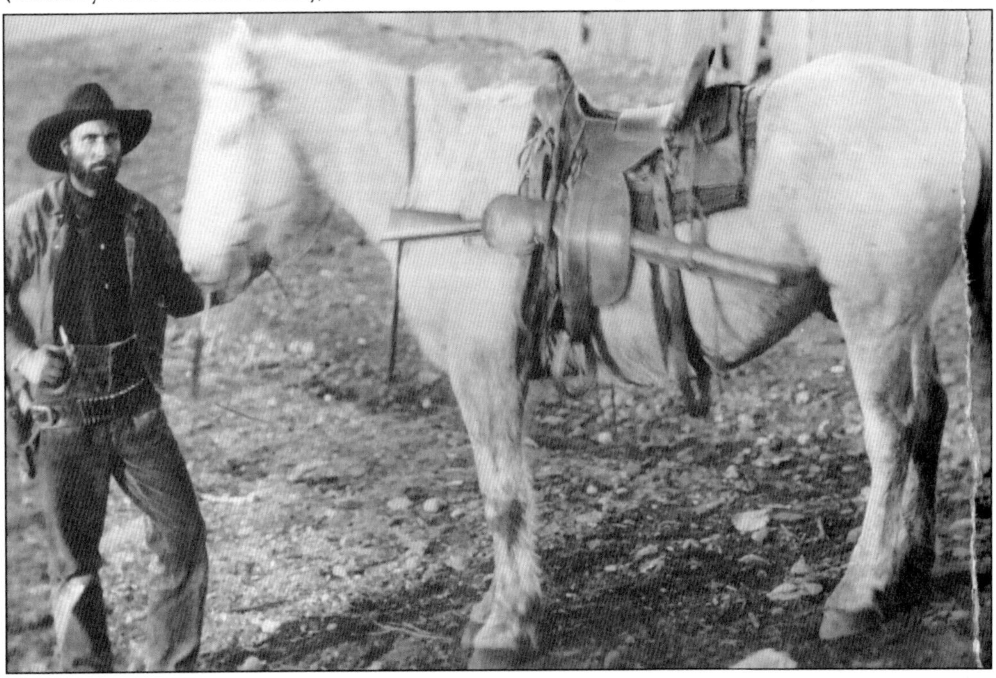

Gus's brother William, pictured here, was with his uncle Dick Gibbons when the bodies were found. He and Dick stayed with them all night while someone went to town for a wagon. Because the terrain was too rocky and steep for the wagon to make it all the way to the bodies, William put them both on this horse and walked out 2 miles to where the wagon could reach them. (Courtesy St. Johns Family History Center.)

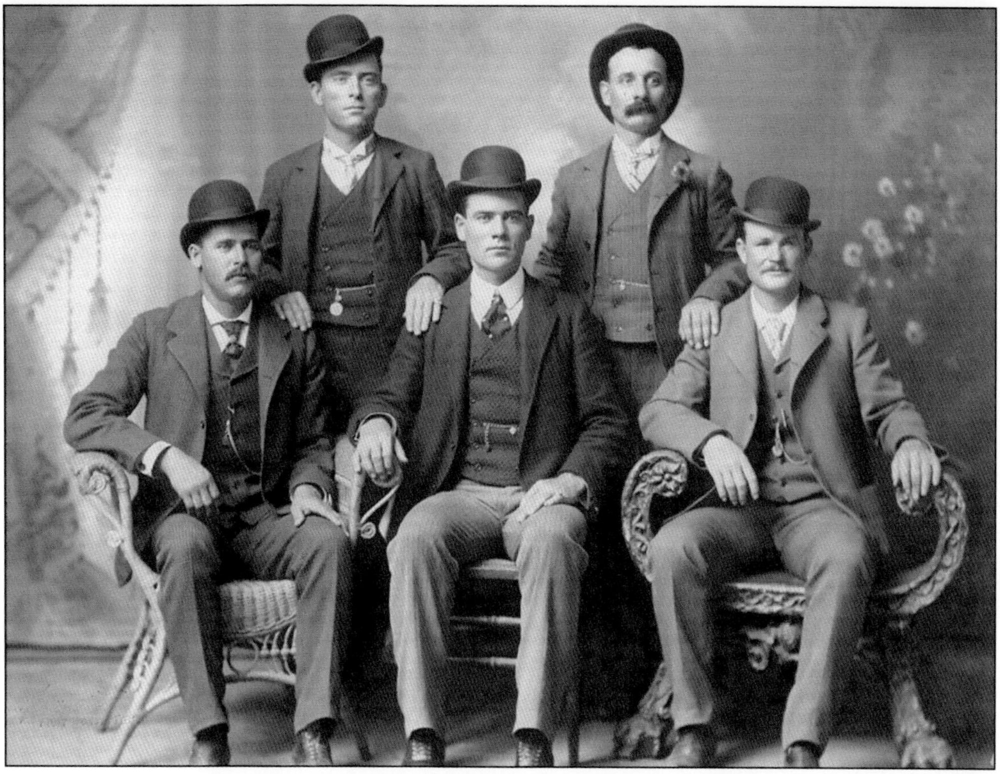

Known as the "Fort Worth Five," the notorious Wild Bunch posed for the John Swartz Photography Studio in Fort Worth, Texas, in 1900. They are, from left to right, (first row) Harry Longabaugh ("The Sundance Kid"), Ben Kilpatrick ("Tall Texan"), and Robert Leroy Parker ("Butch Cassidy"); (second row) William "Will" Carver and Harvey Logan ("Kid Curry"). Parker, using the name James Lowe, was jailed in St. Johns with "Red" Murphy (not pictured Wild Bunch member), using the name Bruce Weaver. (Author collection.)

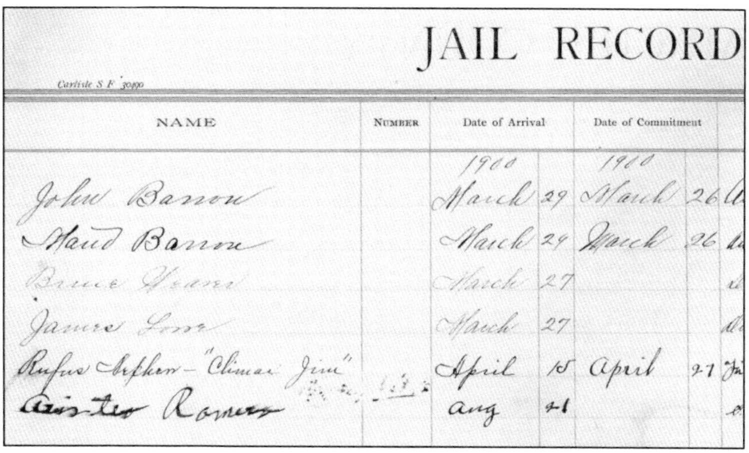

JAIL RECORD

Carlisle S F 30490

NAME	NUMBER	Date of Arrival		Date of Commitment	
		1900		1900	
John Barron		March	29	March	26
Maud Barron		March	29	March	26
Bruce Weaver		March	27		
James Lowe		March	27		
Rufus Upham – "Climax Jim"		April	15	April	27
Aristeo Romero		Aug	21		

This copy of the Apache County Jail record shows that Bruce Weaver (Red Murphy) and James Lowe (Butch Cassidy) were inmates. (Courtesy Apache County Sheriff's Office.)

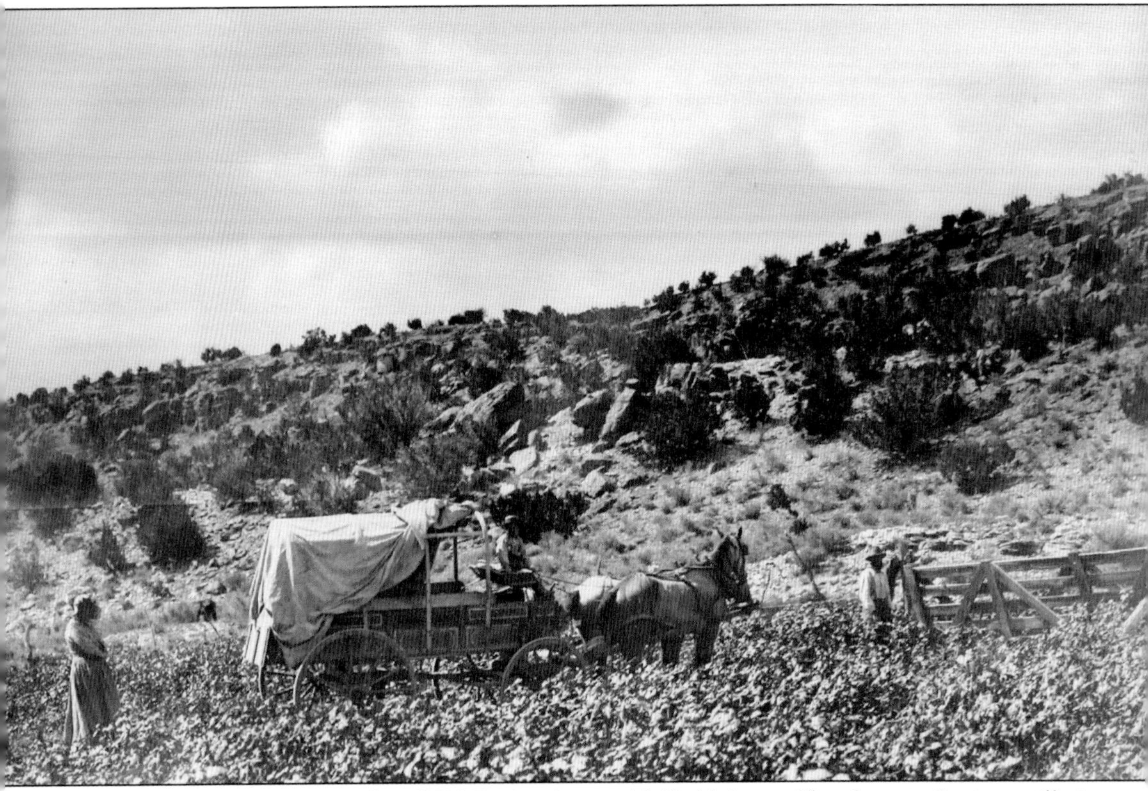

In January 1901, former sheriff Ed Beeler shot and killed Montie Slaughter in Springerville in Sam Saffell's saloon. Three months later, while delivering some barbed wire, Beeler was shot numerous times as he was opening a gate. Here an unidentified man is standing at the gate where Beeler was shot, and Margaret Jarvis is standing where Beeler's body was discovered. (Courtesy St. Johns Historical Society and Museum.)

Although one of many saloons in St. Johns, the Monarch Saloon, pictured here when it was owned by Walter Darling, had more deaths inside its walls than any of the others. Bartender Frank Clark shot and killed patron Patrick Mullen; owner Walter Darling shot and killed *St. Johns Herald* editor Barry Mathews; and Sam Saffell was shot numerous times over a disagreement during a poker game. (Courtesy Barbara Jaramillo.)

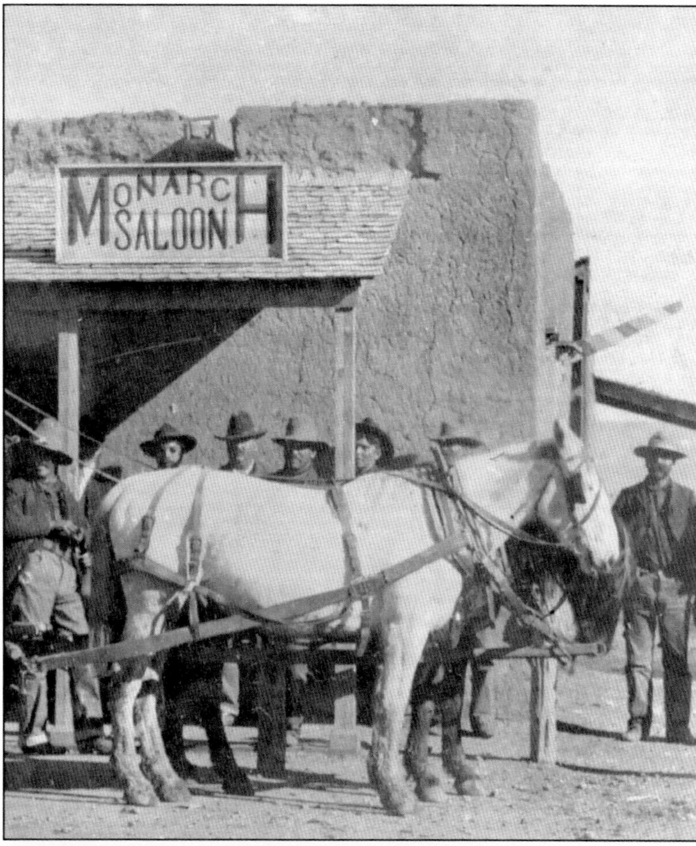

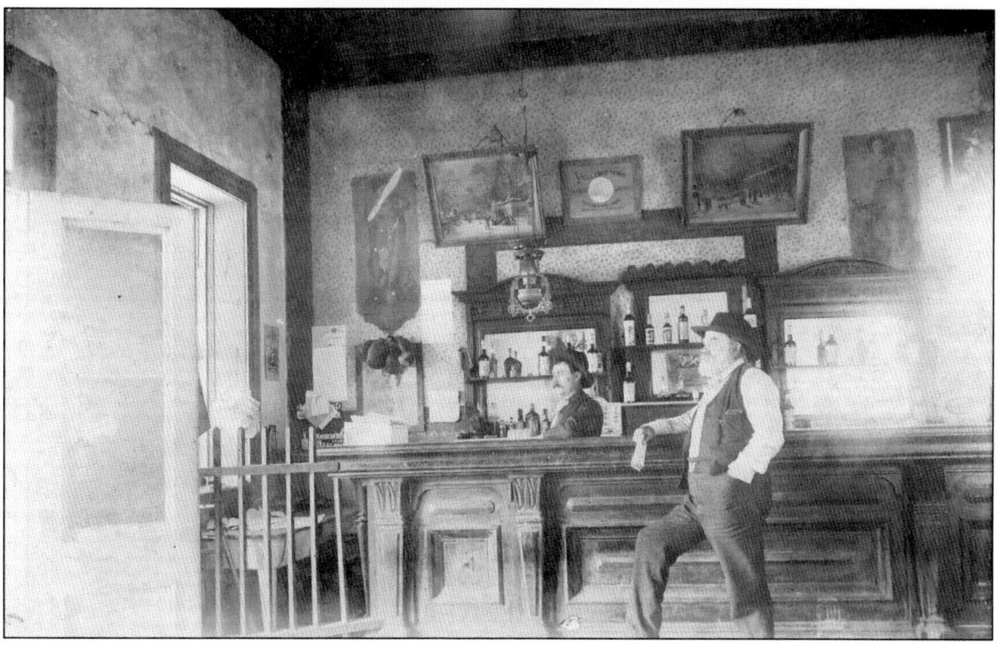

This photograph was taken in the 1890s after Jake Armijo bought the Monarch from Darling. Jake is behind the bar and Capt. John T. Hogue looks out the window. (Courtesy Barbara Jaramillo.)

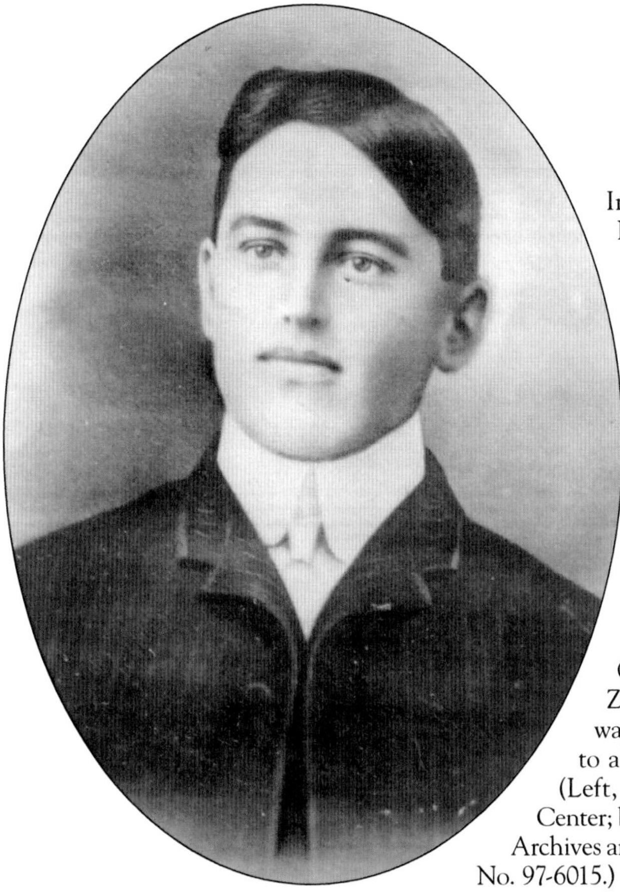

In the winter of 1903, William W. Berry hired Santiago Vigil and his son Juan to help Berry's son Wiley (left) move his sheep from St. Johns, where grass was sparse, to some land in the Salt River Valley. They made camp outside Gisela, which cattlemen had decided was cattle country and were determined to keep sheep out of. On the morning of December 22, Zack and John Booth rode into the camp where they found Wiley and Juan and killed them both. Only Zack was convicted for the crime and was sentenced to death by hanging. On September 15, 1905, in Globe, Zack was led to the gallows, where he waved his hat, stating, "Remember me to all the people up around St. Johns." (Left, courtesy St. Johns Family History Center; below, courtesy Arizona State Library, Archives and Public Records, Archives Division, No. 97-6015.)

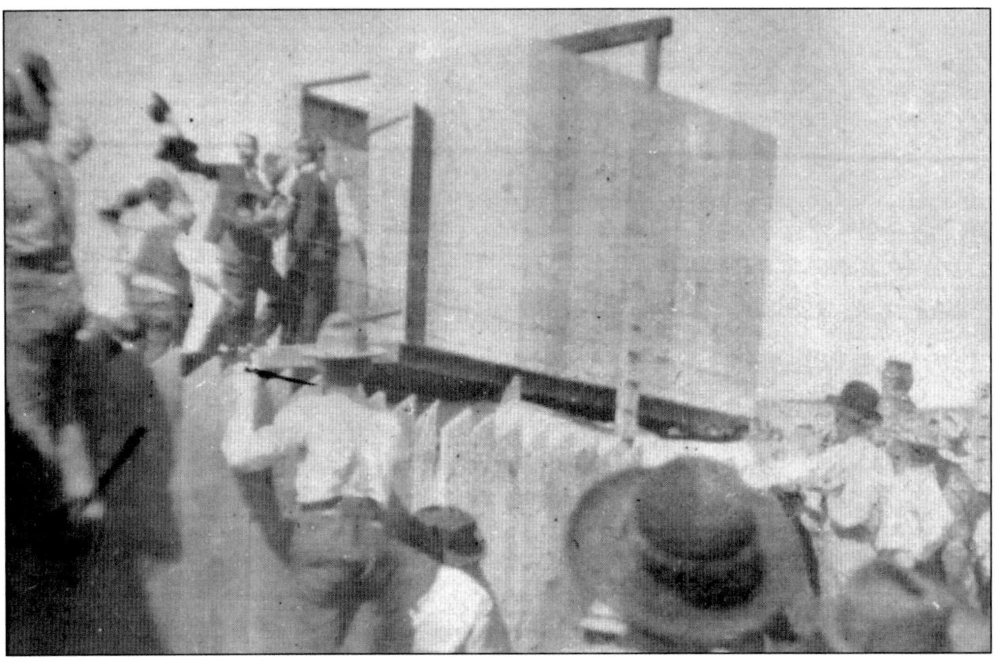

Three

Dam That River

The ability to grow one's own food was critical to survival in the western frontier, and in order or that to happen, water was crucial. The problem with the Little Colorado River was its sporadic nature—during a month of good rain, the runoff could approach 80,000 acre feet, while at other times, at any given place, it could be bone dry. The people began to realize that their survival would depend on their ability to conquer the Little Colorado.

After the sixth dam broke, the leaders of the Mormon Church did something they had never done before—they gathered all the Mormons in the area and released them from their calling as colonizers of St. Johns. Many left, but many decided that the little town they had fought so hard for might actually be worth the fight—and the fight with the river had just begun.

The Mormons who stayed decided they would build a bigger and better dam this time and thought they had done just that with the Lyman Dam. The Ray family—mother Violet, 17-year-old Dewey, nine-year-old Hazel, seven-year-old Ethel, and four-year-old Lily—left Mancos, Colorado, for Tucson in March 1915. Arriving in St. Johns around April 12, they found temporary work at the Lyman spillway, so they camped beneath the dam in the small town of El Tule. April 14, 1915, was the night of the junior prom, and Violet offered to watch the three Palmer children so their parents, Ellis and Jennie, could go to the dance in exchange for sleeping in the house instead of outside in the wagon. Close to midnight, there was a roar of rushing water as the base of the dam gave out. The top of the dam held for an instant, causing a spectacular arch to form over the rushing water. Those who drowned that night were Violet, Dewey, and Hazel Ray; Carrol, Gerald, and Louise Palmer; and Mrs. Savaadra and her infant daughter. Only the bodies of Violet and Dewey were ever found.

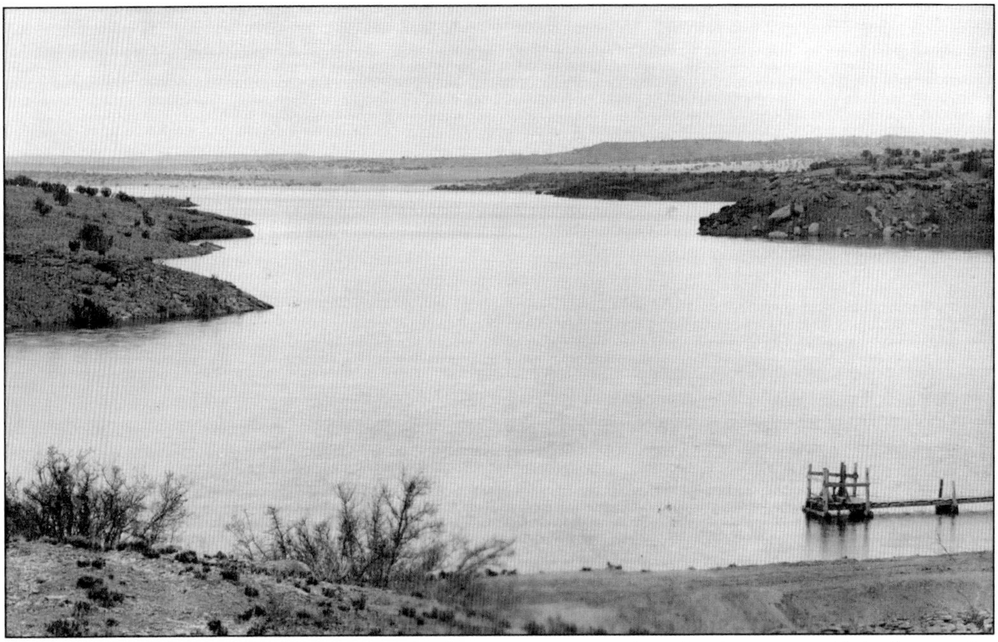

Initially all attempts to use the river water for irrigation was done by digging small ditches at the river and diverting the water onto the land where it was needed. However, the sporadic flow of the river made it nearly impossible to yield successful crops, so the people began to look at other ways to tame the river. The first dam was built sometime in 1885 and created a small storage lake known as the Little Reservoir (or "Little Rezi" as it has been called ever since), shown above. Its capacity could irrigate the small town, but the system required a diversion dam to be built in the middle of the main river, pictured below, to fill the reservoir, and this dam broke every time there was substantial runoff in the river. (Both author collection.)

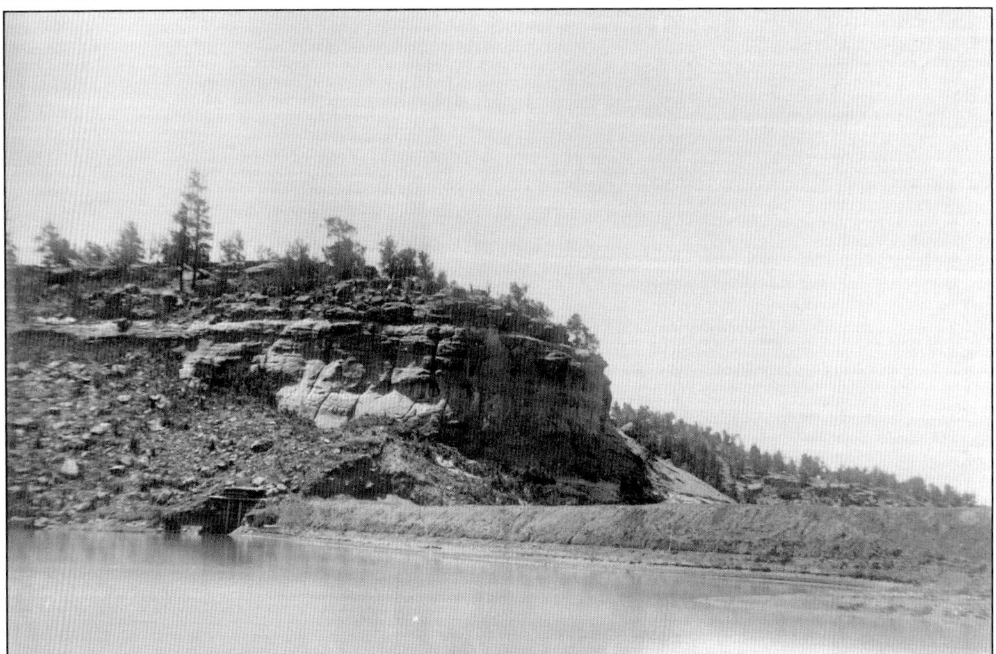

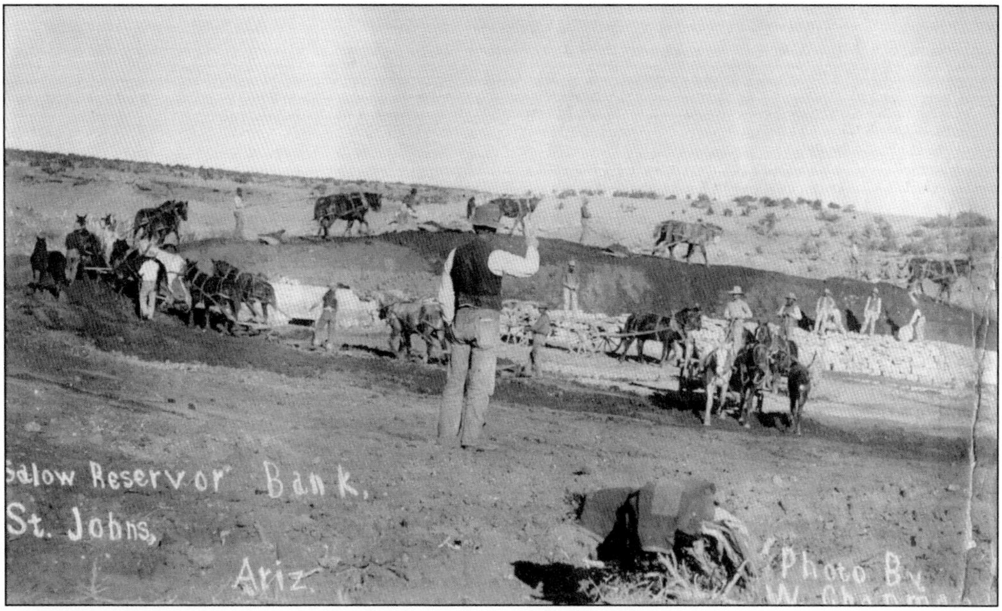

Five more dams were built and washed out before the Salado Dam was built 6 miles outside of St. Johns, the first really big dam to be built on the Little Colorado. In an effort to prevent the dam washing out, the local blacksmith built a special sluice gate, which when opened could augment the capacity of the spillway in case of an emergency. Here John Henry Heap supervises the building of the Salado Dam. (Courtesy St. Johns Family History Center.)

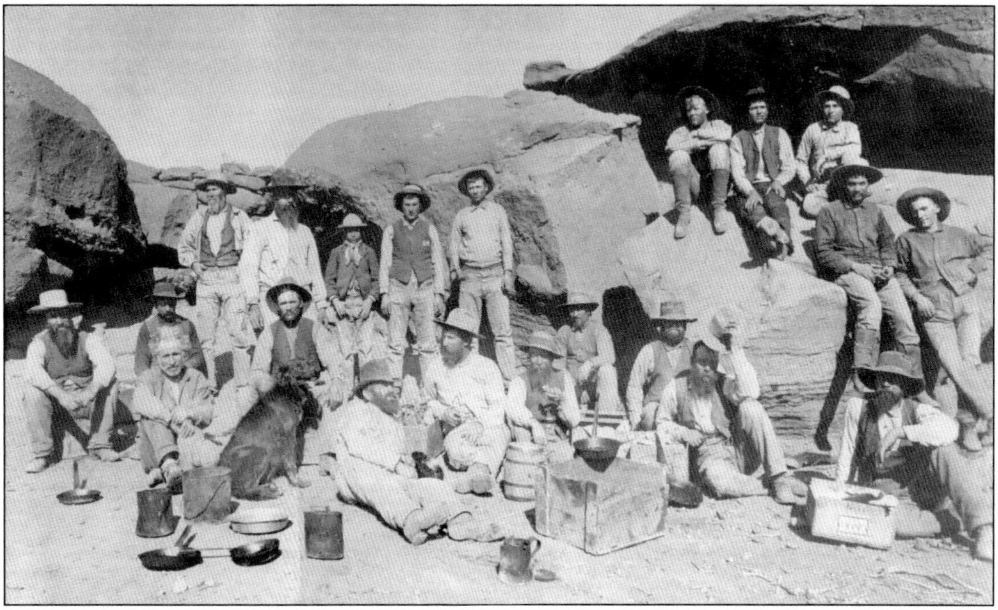

In this picture, the workers on the Salado Dam are taking a lunch break. From left to right are (first row) Andrew V. Gibbons, J. E. White, Dutch George (in front of White), John Henry Heap, E. W. A. Moore, W. W. Berry, Henry Butler, M. H. Peterson, Isaac Thomas, Elijah Freeman, and William Black; (second row) Hyrum Chapman, Thomas Berry, Ramon Gonzales, Julias Cropas, Fred Nielson, (sitting on rock) Bob Overson, Frank Thomas, Welcome Chapman, Seth Russell (in front of Welcome), and Eugene Chapman. (Courtesy St. Johns Family History Center.)

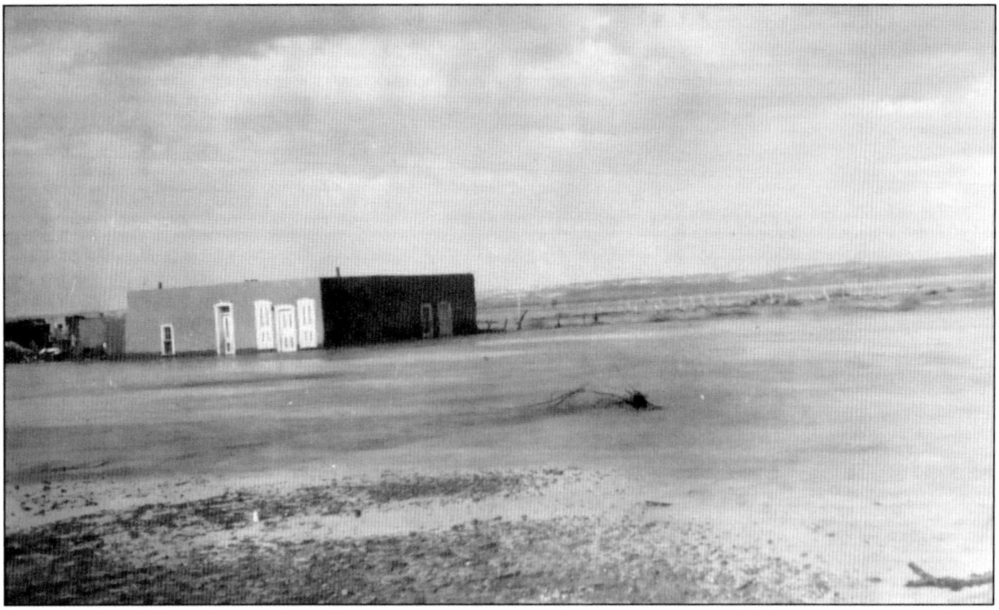

All was well until 1905, when after years of drought it finally began to rain. The reservoir was soon at capacity, but before the sluice gate could be pulled, it broke. All the water went rushing down the river and into the town as seen in this photograph. (Courtesy St. Johns Family History Center.)

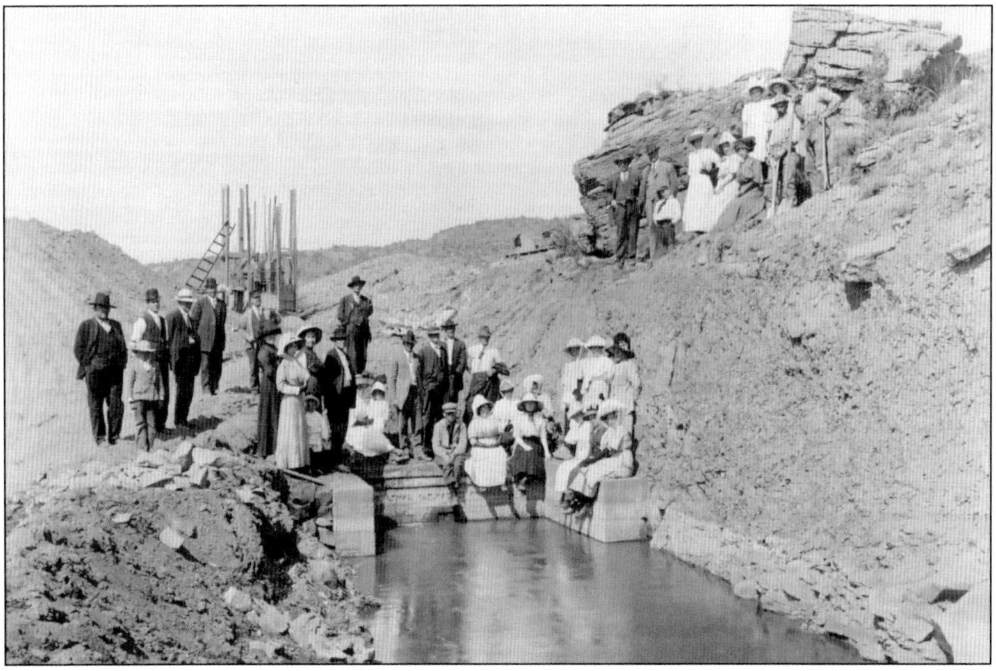

With the help of a group of capitalists from Denver, the people began to build the Lyman Dam in 1910. Three years and $250,000 later, the Lyman Dam, which would hold nearly double the capacity of the Salado Dam, was finally finished. As shown in this photograph taken at the Lyman intake, the people were jubilant and proud, believing they had finally succeeded in conquering the Little Colorado. (Author collection.)

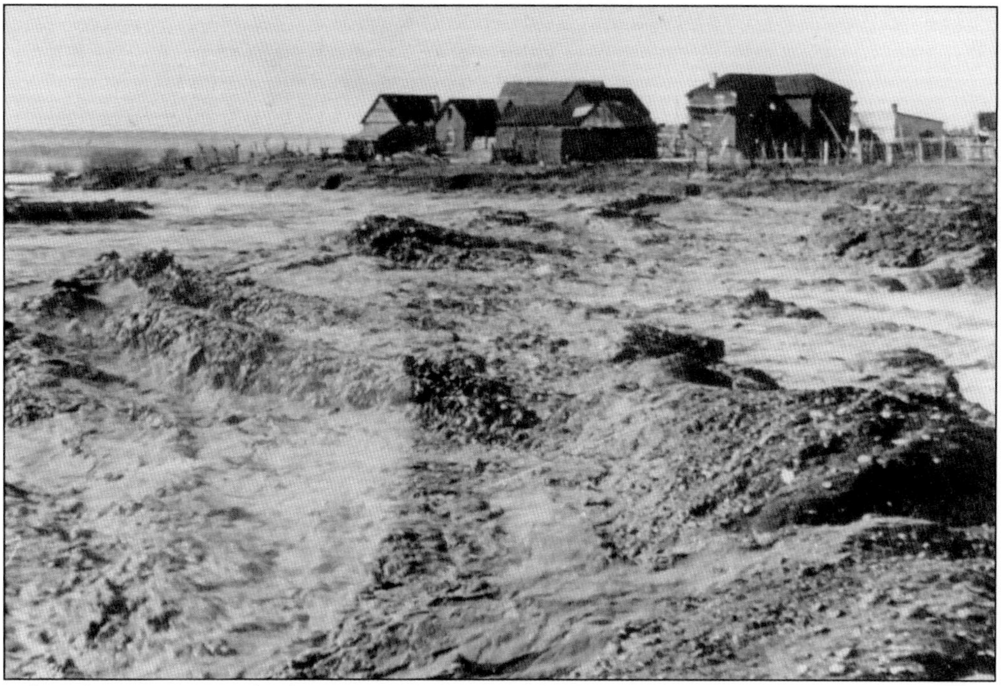

When the Lyman Dam broke in 1915, the water rushed into St. Johns at a terrific speed, taking out the majority of homes on the river. (Courtesy Arizona State University, Department of Archives and Special Collections.)

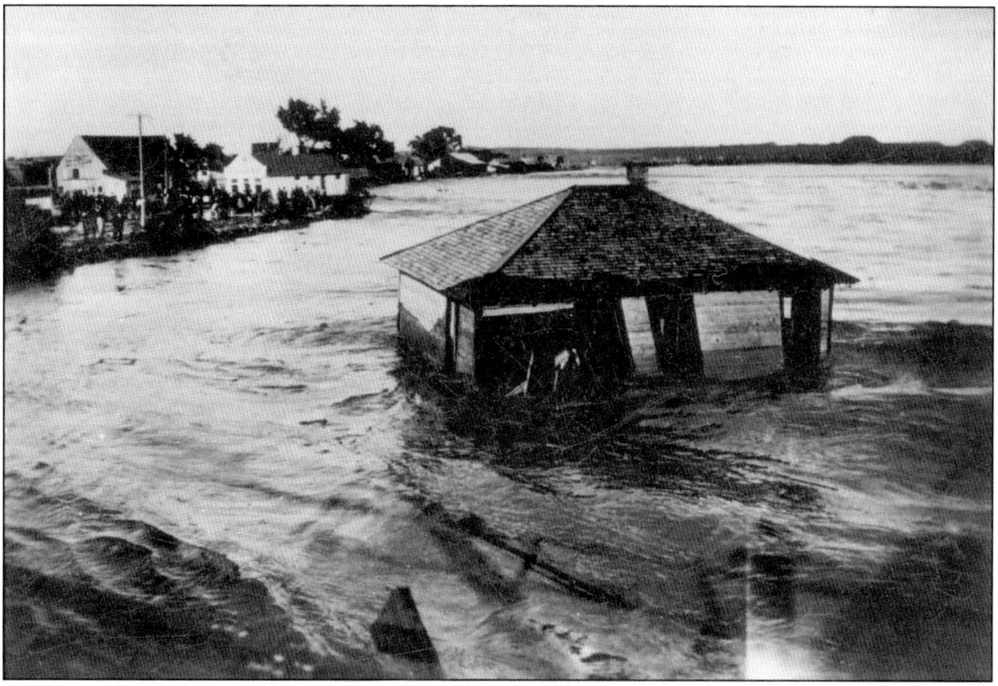

In this picture, citizens of St. Johns gather on the riverbank in the middle of Commercial Street and watch as a neighbor's house floats by. (Courtesy Arizona State University, Department of Archives and Special Collections.)

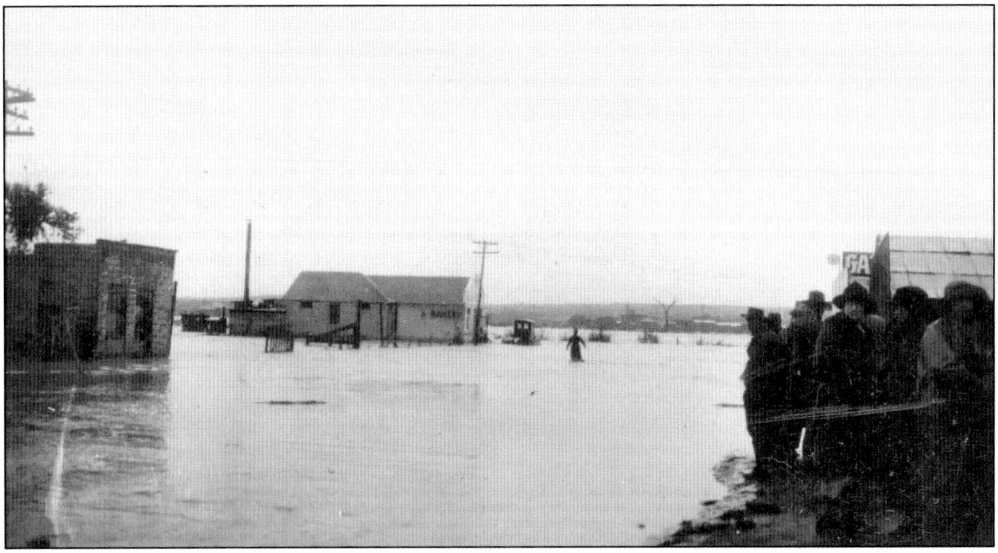

This picture shows standing water from the dam break down Commercial Street. (Courtesy Arizona State University, Department of Archives and Special Collections.)

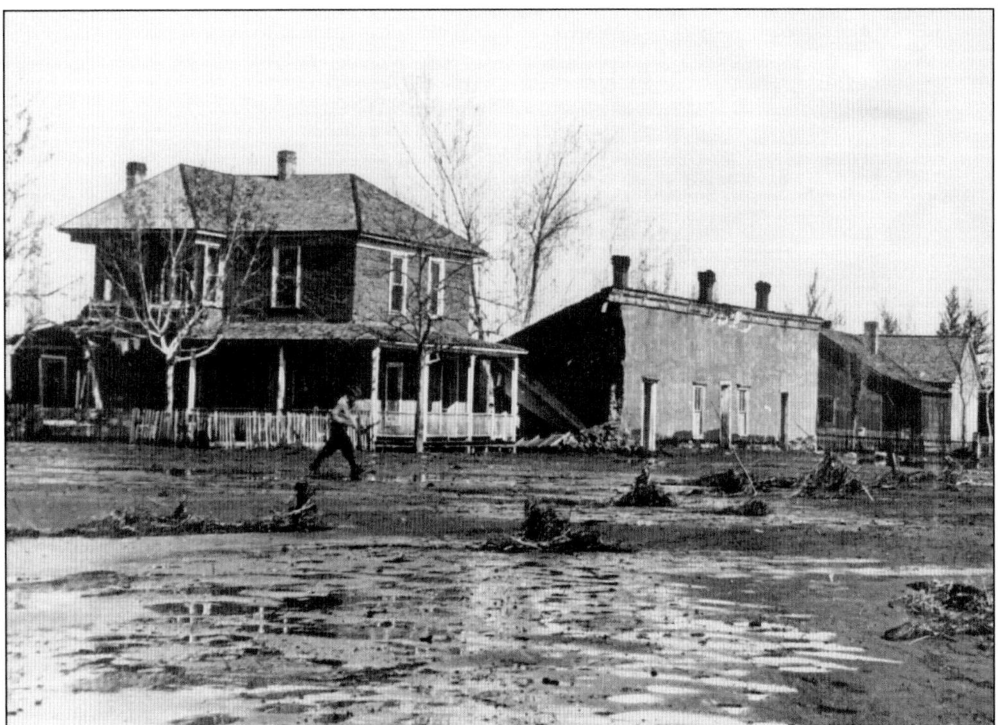

Here the water is finally beginning to subside, and an unidentified man runs through the frame. (Courtesy Arizona State University, Department of Archives and Special Collections.)

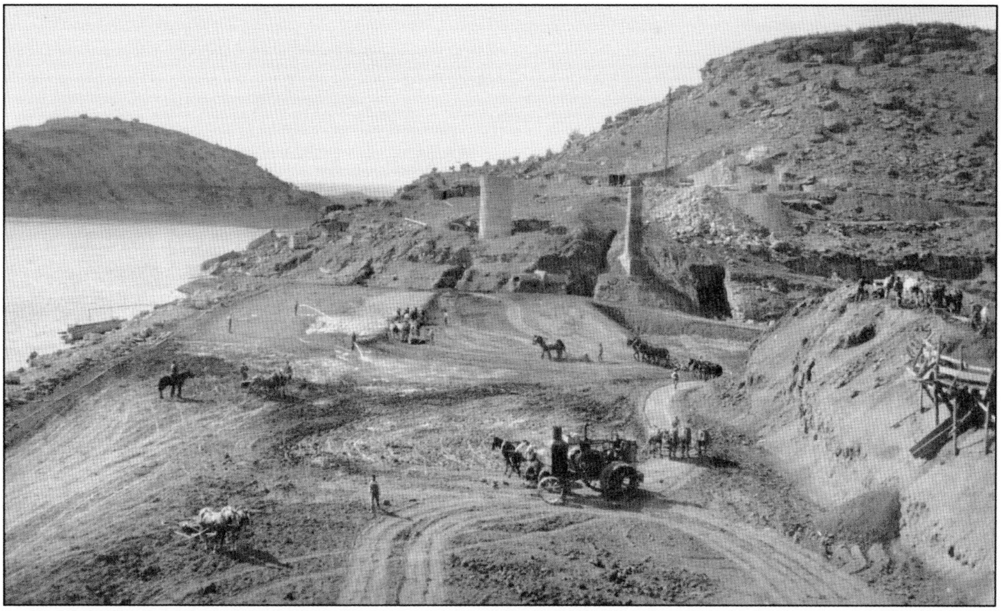

After the dam broke, some people gave up and moved away, but the majority closed ranks and decided to rebuild the dam, shown here. Because no other suitable site could be found along the river, it was decided to rebuild at the same location. (Courtesy Arizona State Library, Archives and Public Records, Archives Division, No. 97-0527.)

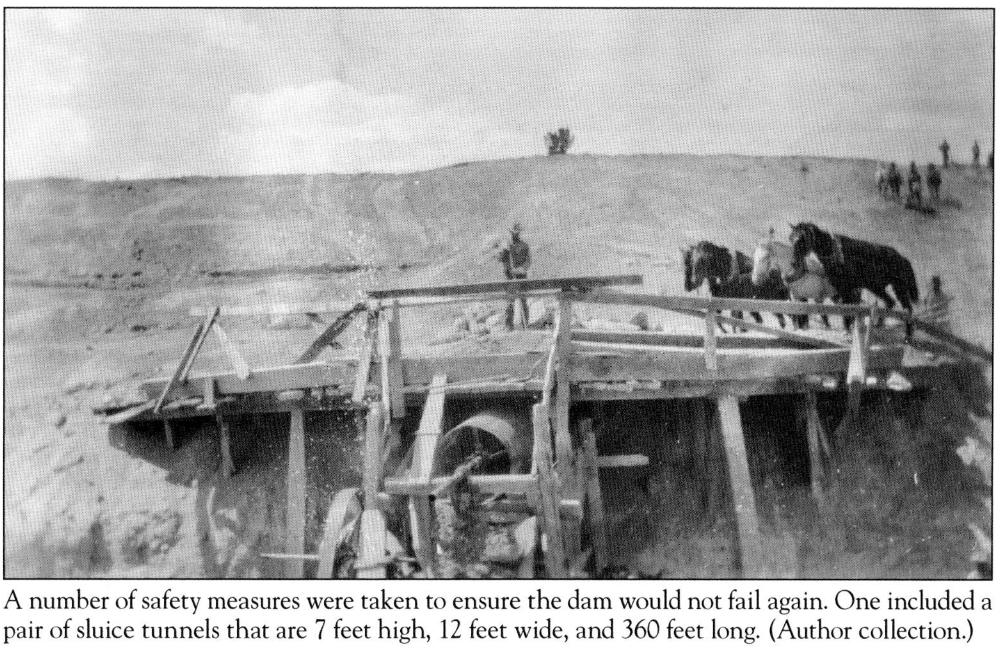

A number of safety measures were taken to ensure the dam would not fail again. One included a pair of sluice tunnels that are 7 feet high, 12 feet wide, and 360 feet long. (Author collection.)

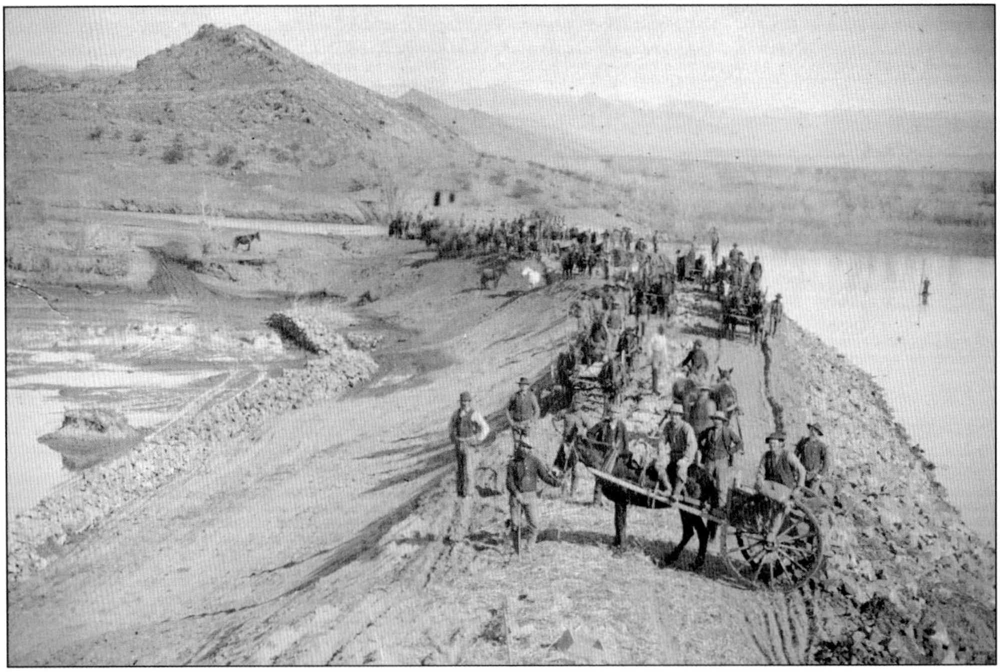

It was determined that the failure of the first dam was due to a little spring buried at the south end of the dam. To ensure the dam wouldn't fail again, a deep trench was dug half the length of the dam, and creosote pilings were driven closely in to form a wall of wood from the base of the dam down to the bedrock, sealing the little spring and diverting the seepage to the reservoir side of the dam. Hand-placed limestone (below) was used to control erosion. (Both courtesy St. Johns Historical Society and Museum.)

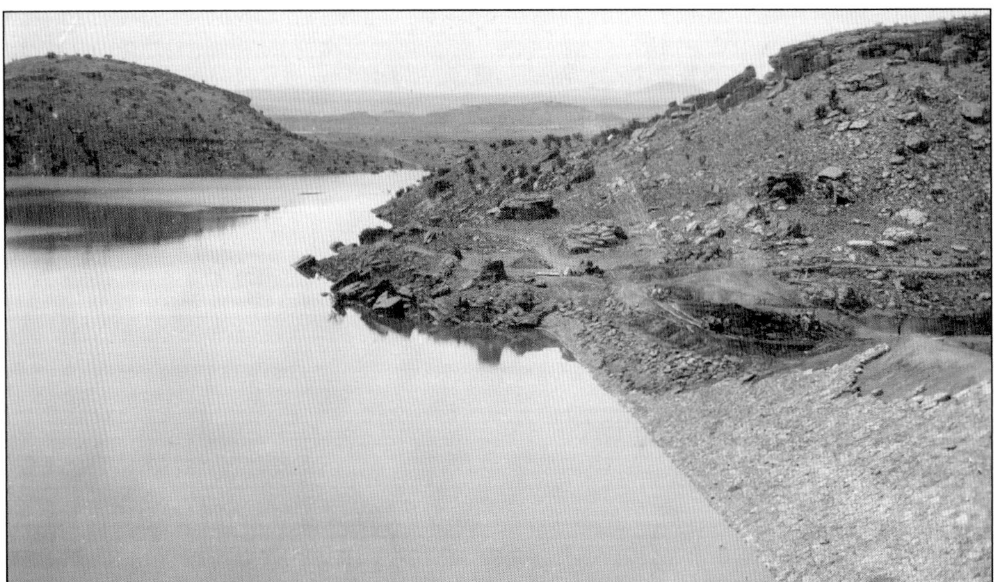

Four

EDUCATING ST. JOHNS

The first school to be built not just in St. Johns, but in all of Apache County, was constructed in the early 1880s and would come to be known as "the White School House on the Hill." Big, bright, and beautiful, it appeared to rise up and salute those entering St. Johns.

The St. Johns Stake Academy was the only place in St. Johns where children could receive a secondary education. The academy first opened in 1889 with John W. Brown as the principal and 13 students. Classes were initially conducted in the Mormon tithing office until authorities authorized the building of the academy. The new structure took 10 years to build, cost $14,000, and was dedicated December 16, 1900, by Apostle Joseph F. Smith. The academy was only a two-year education that had a rather high tuition. In the spring of 1921, the church closed the entire academy and the town began to build a high school, which was finished in 1926.

The first high school in St. Johns, known then as it is now as simply St. Johns High School, was opened in 1926, and the Redskin was chosen as the mascot. The class of 1925 was the first to receive a four-year education and graduate (they went to school in the academy while the high school was still under construction). Sports included basketball, baseball, and track. Basketball was played year-round, and they traveled to games in an open truck. Snowflake was their chief rival. The team had to leave the day before the game and travel all day by wagon, play in the morning on a dirt court, then spend the rest of the day traveling back to St. Johns. There were eight players on the team, one the acting coach. Since the school's inception, the Redskins have won 26 state championships in sports, and in 2000, the school was awarded the School of the Century for having more basketball championships than any school in the state for the entire 20th century. One of the most impressive winning streaks from the Redskins is the 21 consecutive wins achieved in the Academic Decathlon.

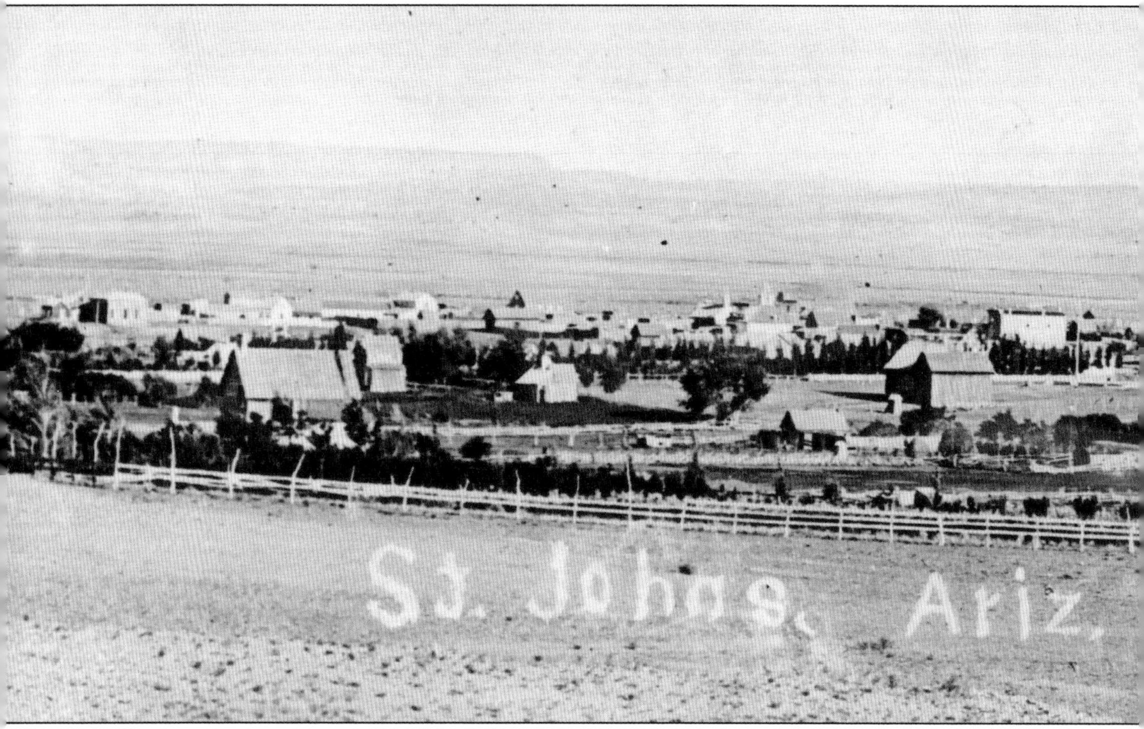

This panoramic photograph of St. Johns was taken by Welcome Chapman in 1890 and is one of few in existence where the White School House on the Hill can be clearly seen. Welcome Chapman arrived in St. Johns in 1884 and supplemented his income by taking pictures. His main

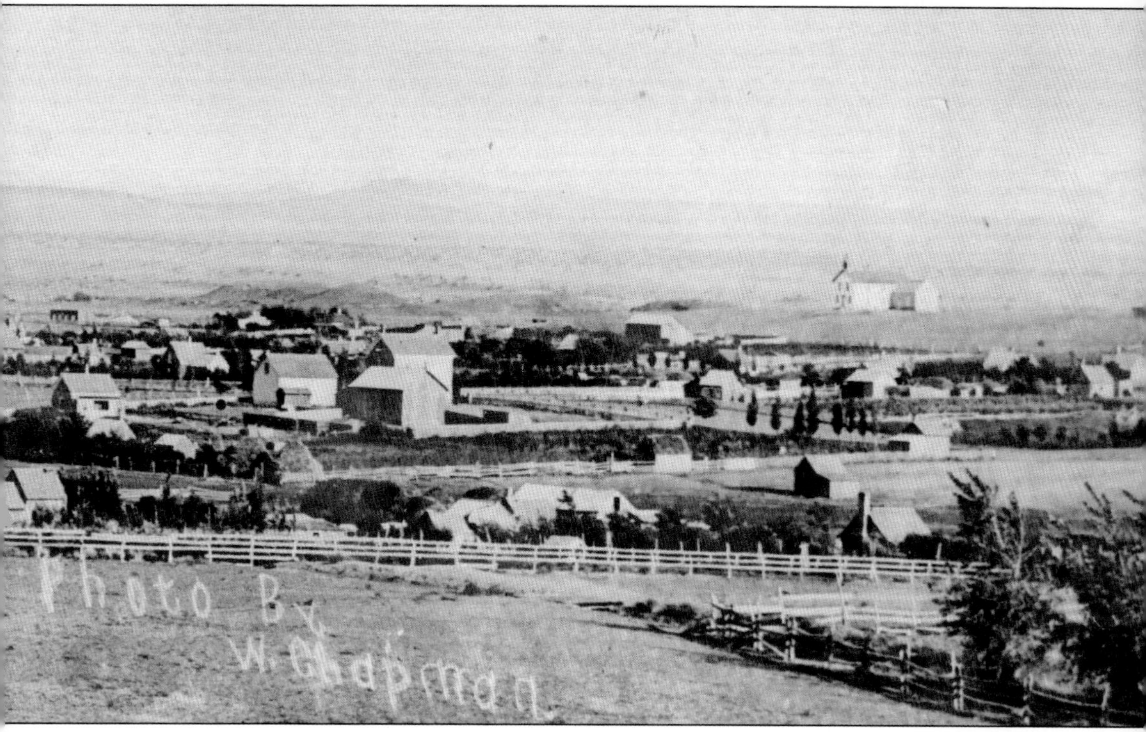

source of income was making headstones and hearthstones from sandstone he quarried outside St. Johns. He even made his own headstone. (Courtesy St. Johns Family History Center.)

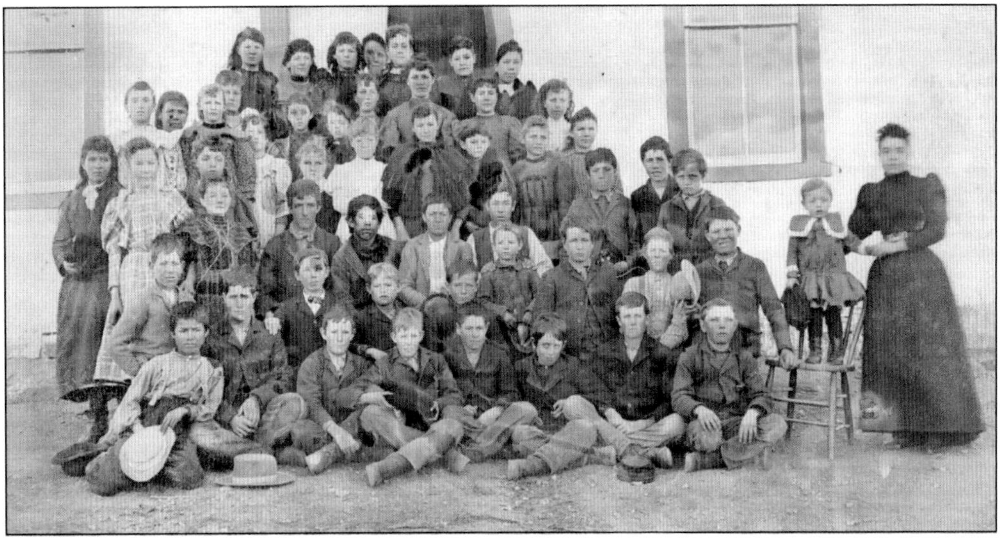

The photograph above, taken in the early 1880s, is the earliest known picture of the students at the White School House. Below is another picture of the students taken in 1890. The only person identified is the teacher, Miss Sharp, at the extreme right in the back. (Both courtesy St. Johns Family History Center.)

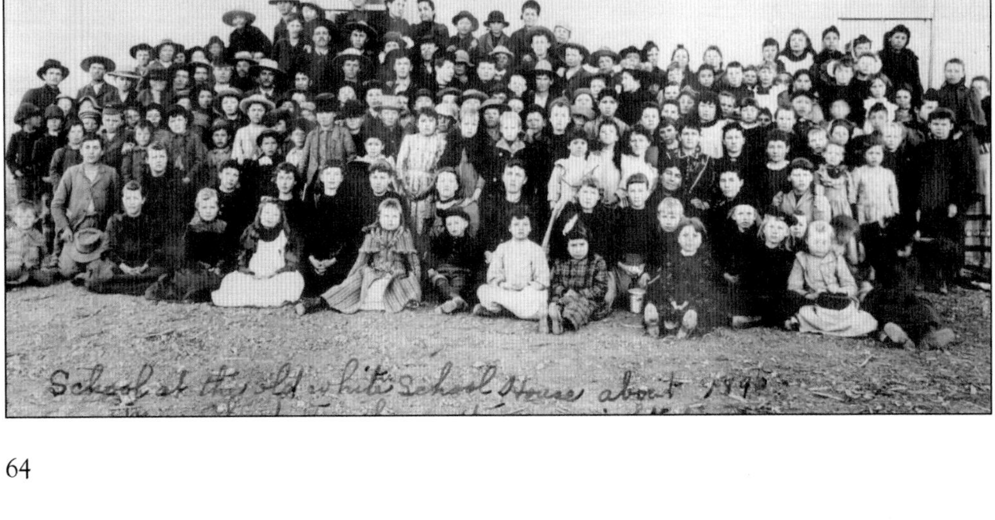

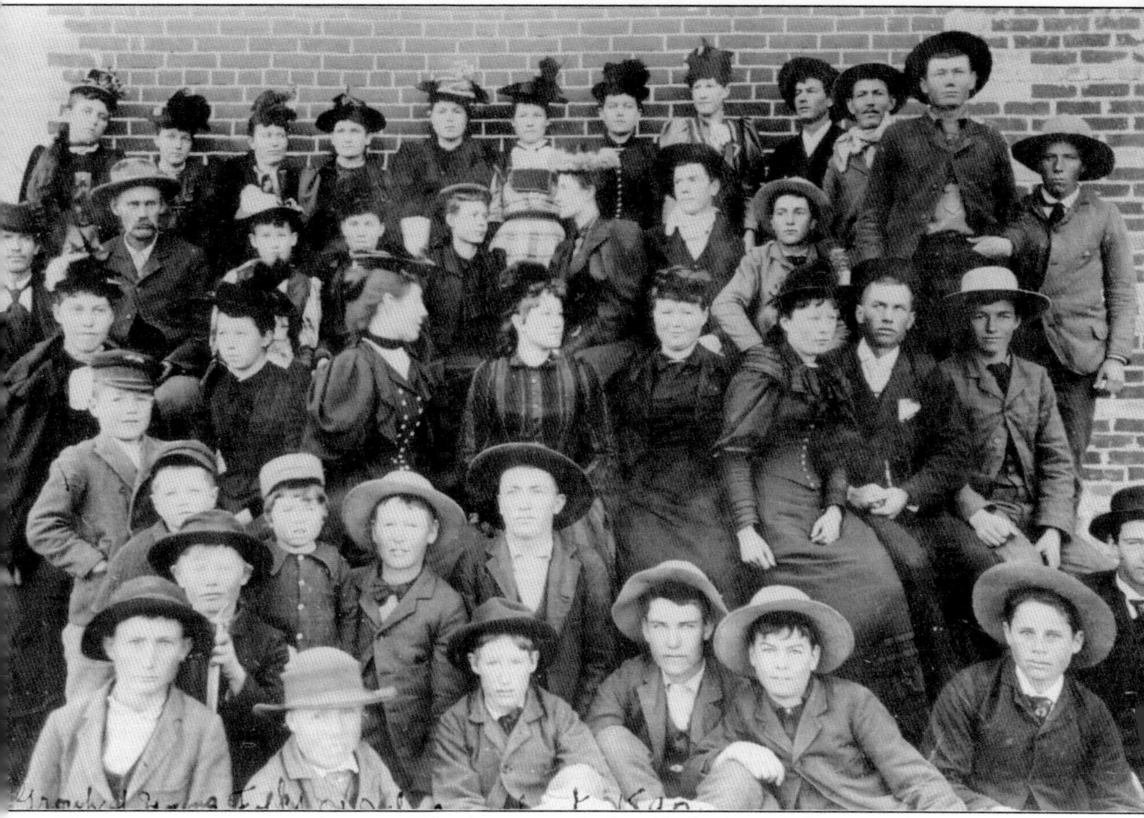

This group picture was taken in 1892 of a group of school kids. From left to right are (first row) Emer Plumb, Will Jenson, Andy Gibbons, Maxie Black, Frank LeSueur, John Jones, and Norman Freeman; (second row) Joy Patterson, Jay Patterson, Charley Bloom (in front of Jay), Ray LeSueur, Will Sherwood, and Eugene Chapman; (third row) Lucy Davis, Hattie Butler, Lou Sherwood, Naomi Gibbons, Stella Sherwood, Hannah Peterson, Alma Davis, and Pete Peterson; (fourth row) Warren Mallory, Tom Peterson, Annie Butler, unidentified, Maud Sherwood, Lottie Sherwood, George Waite, and Welcome Chapman Jr.; (fifth row) Lavine Berry, Louie Freeman, Amanda Kempe, Pearl Walters, Maud Noble, Sarah Butler, Vinnie Plumb, Mary Thomas, Frank Thomas, Eph Stradling, Louis Yergenson, and Henry Butler. (Courtesy St. Johns Family History Center.)

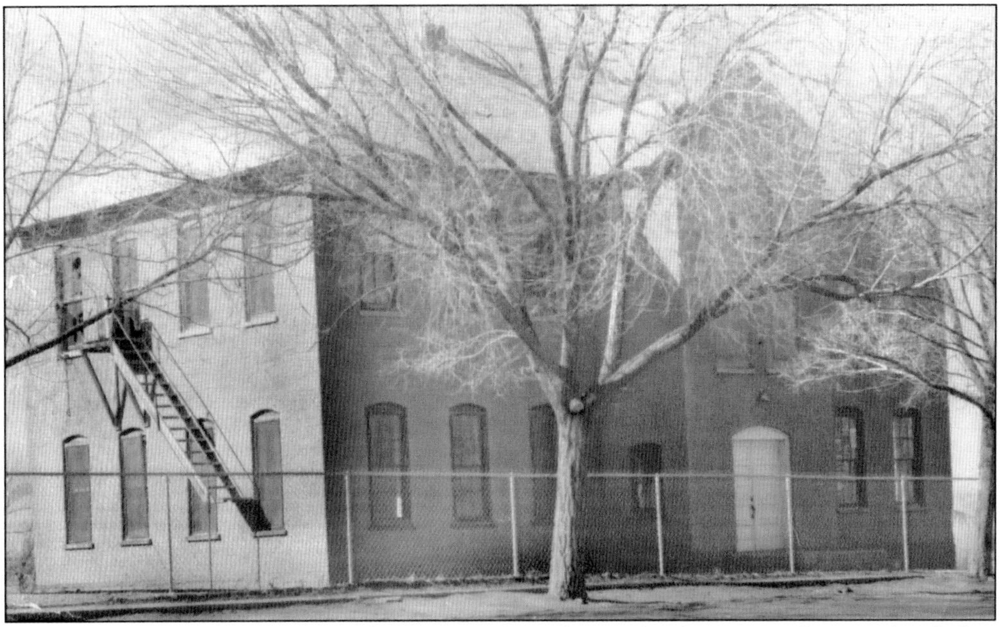

By 1909, the town of St. Johns had outgrown the White School House and it was decided to divide the school district, leaving part of the town in school at the White School and building a new brick schoolhouse for the other part. That school is pictured here, boarded up and ready to be torn down. (Courtesy St. Johns Historical Society and Museum.)

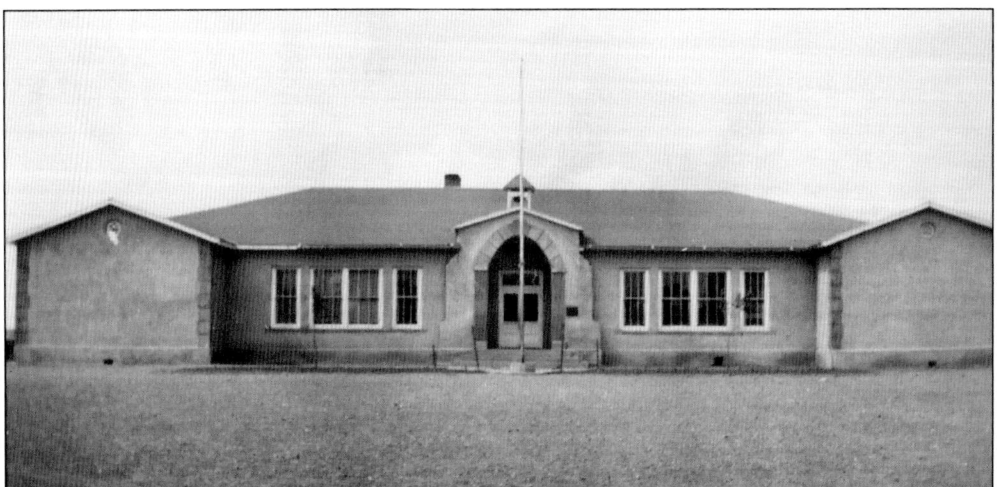

After a new courthouse was built, the part of town that had remained at the White School House was moved into the old courthouse and newly renovated Coronado Elementary School, shown here. (Courtesy St. Johns Family History Center.)

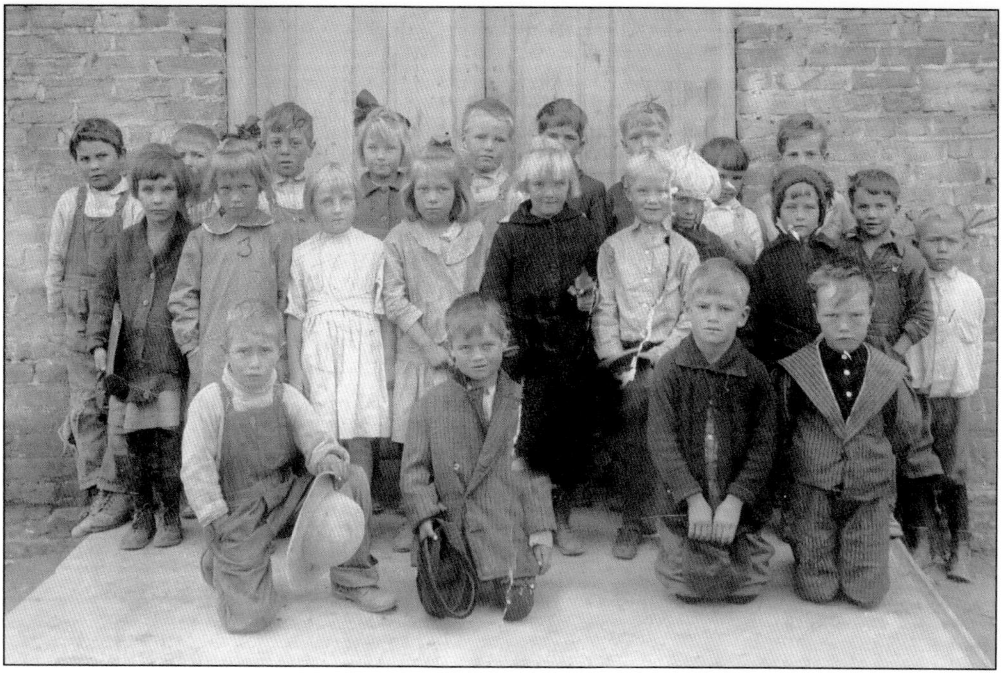

These groups of kids (seven-year-olds, above, and nine-year-olds, below) went to the new brick schoolhouse in 1912. (Both author collection.)

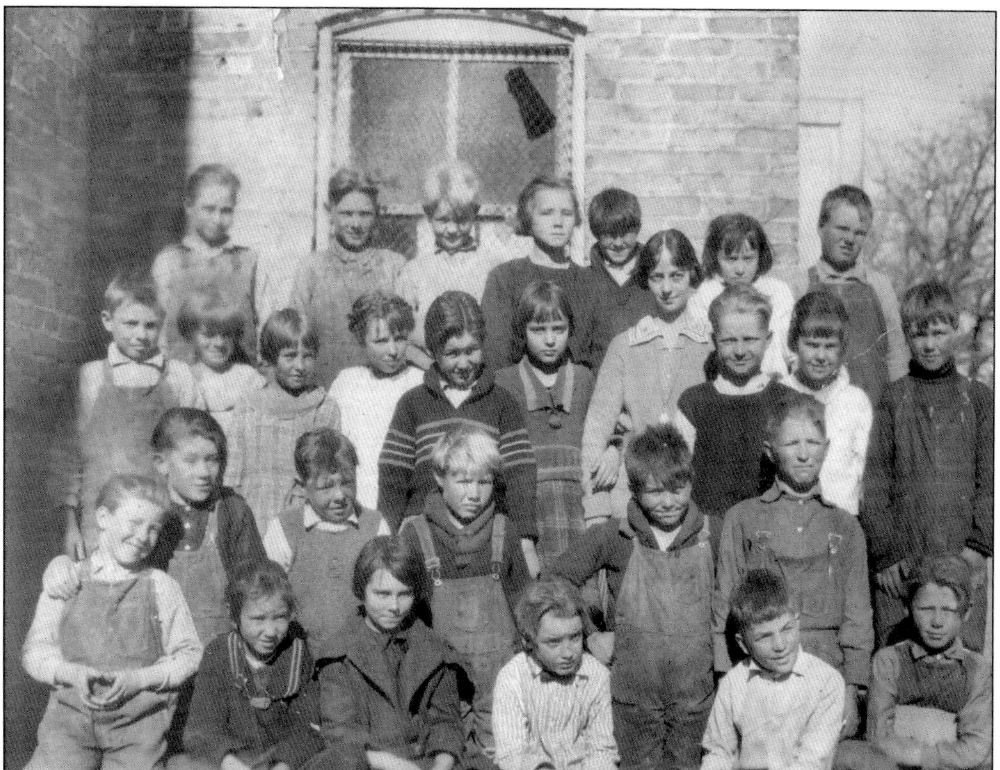

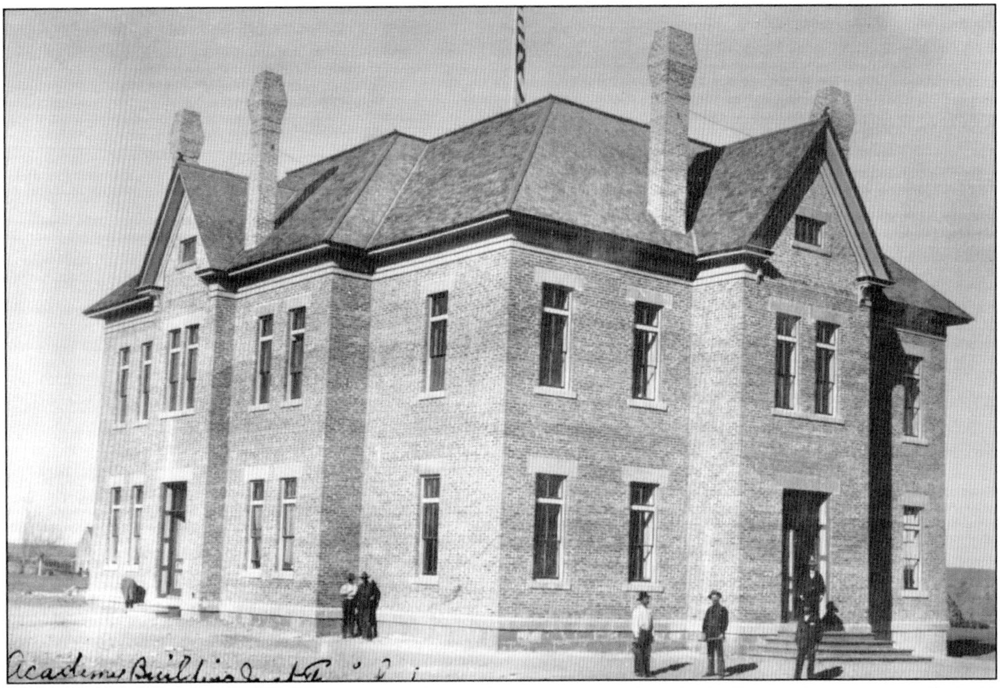

The St. Johns Stake Academy is shown here the day it was finished. Henry Overson and N. P. Johnson (workmen), Charles P. Anderson, and Joseph B. Patterson (the superintendent of the building) are in the door. (Courtesy St. Johns Family History Center.)

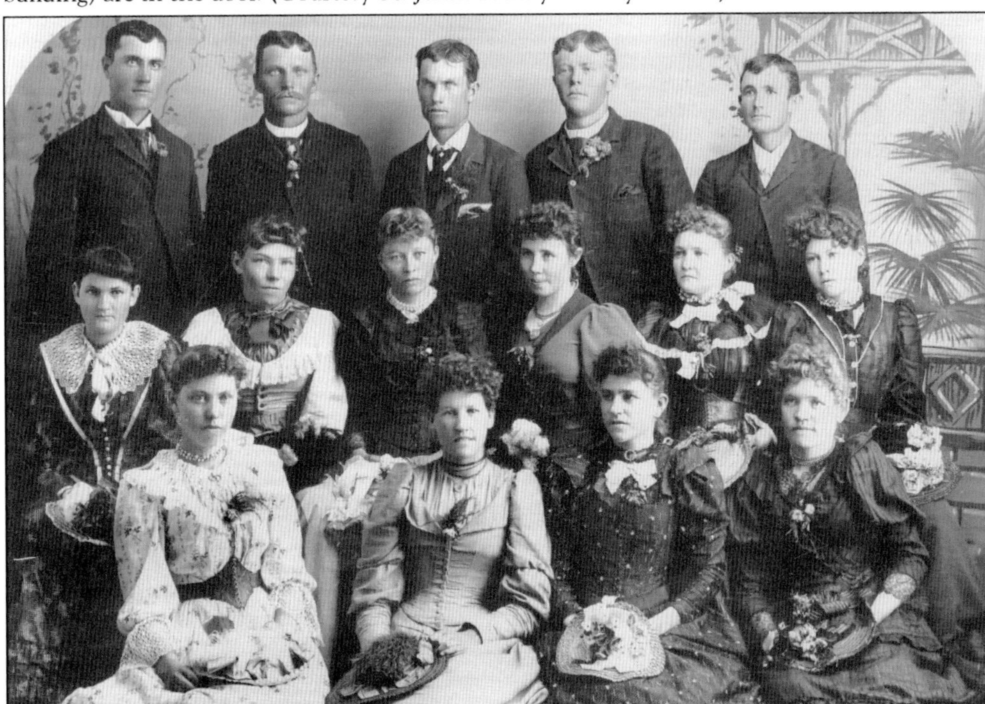

This picture shows a group of early academy graduates. (Courtesy St. Johns Historical Society and Museum.)

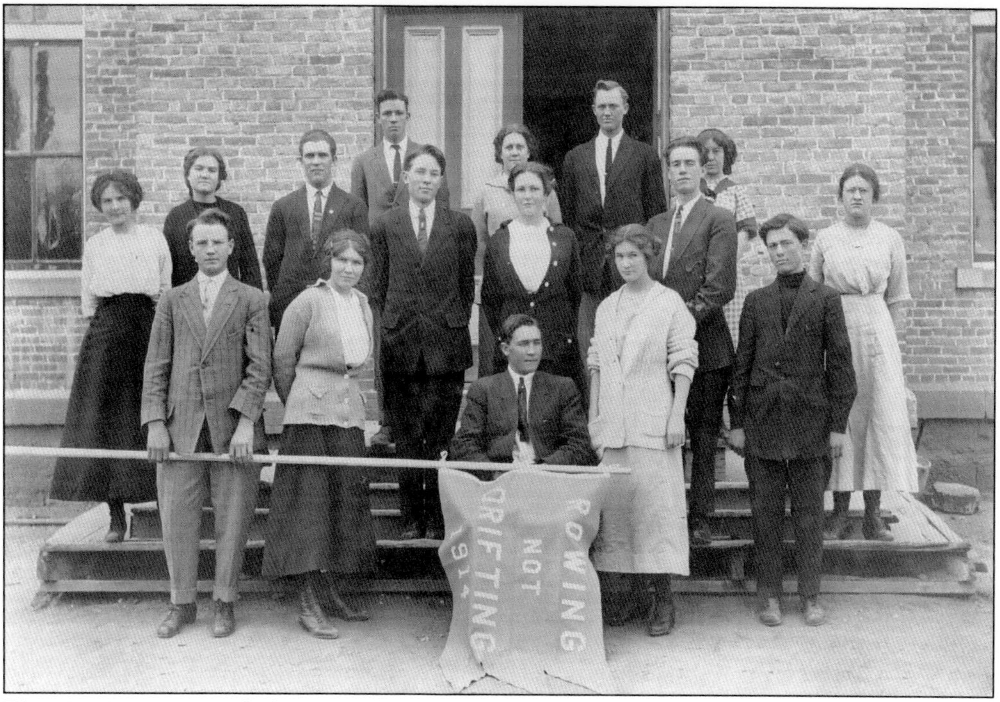

The 1914 "rowing not drifting" academy graduates shown here, from left to right, are (first row) Matt Morgan, Amy Slade, Albert Jarvis (seated), Mona Patterson, and J. Smith; (second row) Hazel Thompson, Clara Hall, Wilford Brinkerhoff, Gilbert Udall, Joyce Udall, Stan Hamblin, and Pearl Jarvis; (third row) Zech Farr, Miss Fredrickson, and Arch Isaacson. (Courtesy St. Johns Historical Society and Museum.)

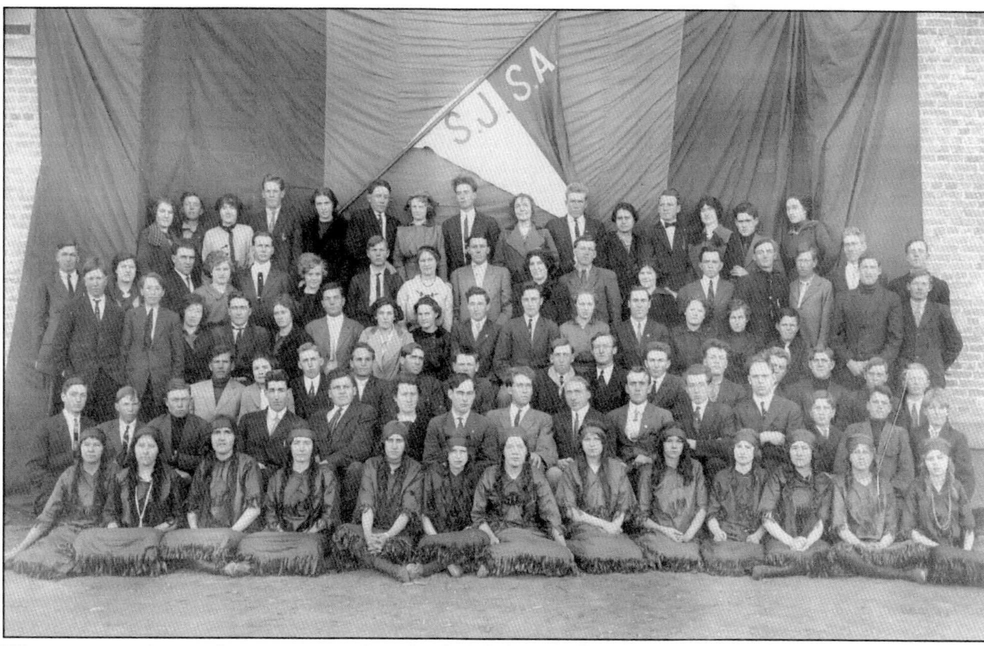

This picture shows the entire student body of the academy around 1910. (Courtesy St. Johns Family History Center.)

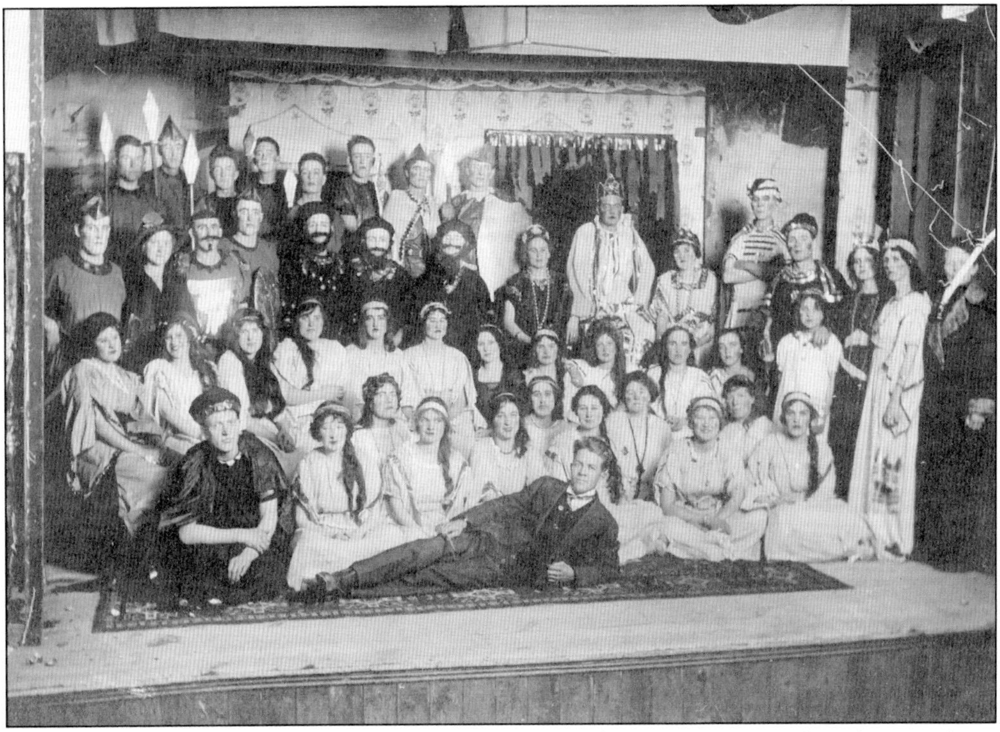

Plays, or "opera" as it was referred to, was a popular form of entertainment, and academy students worked hard to put on two to four opera presentations a year, as shown in both of these pictures. (Both courtesy St. Johns Historical Society and Museum.)

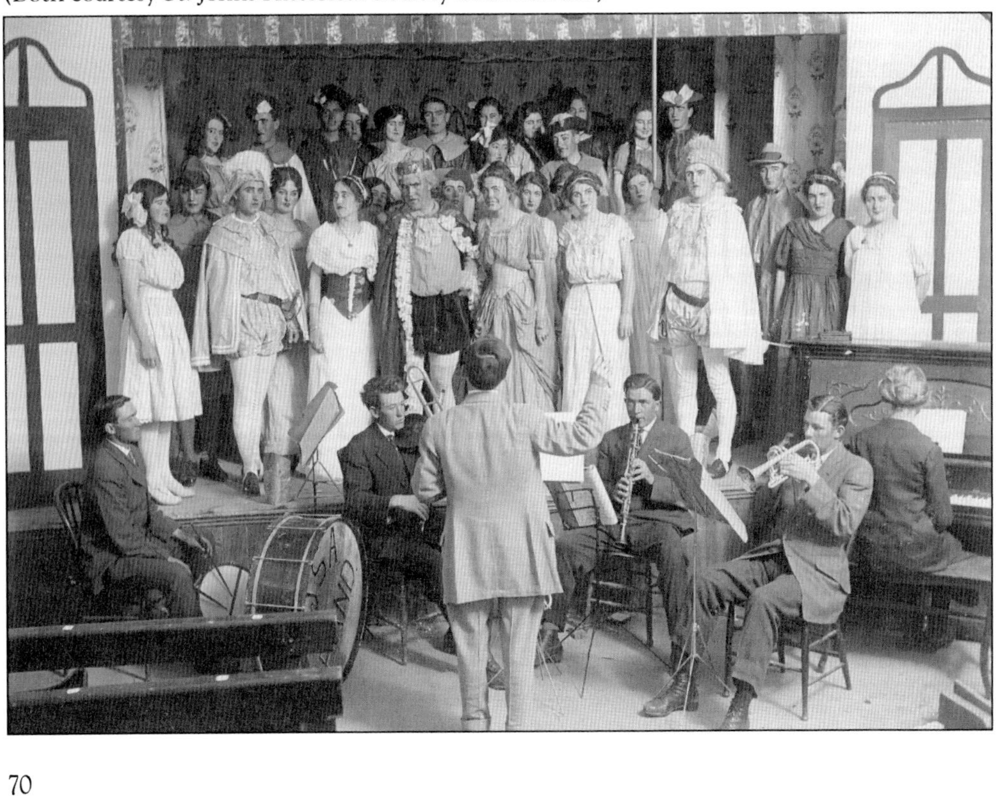

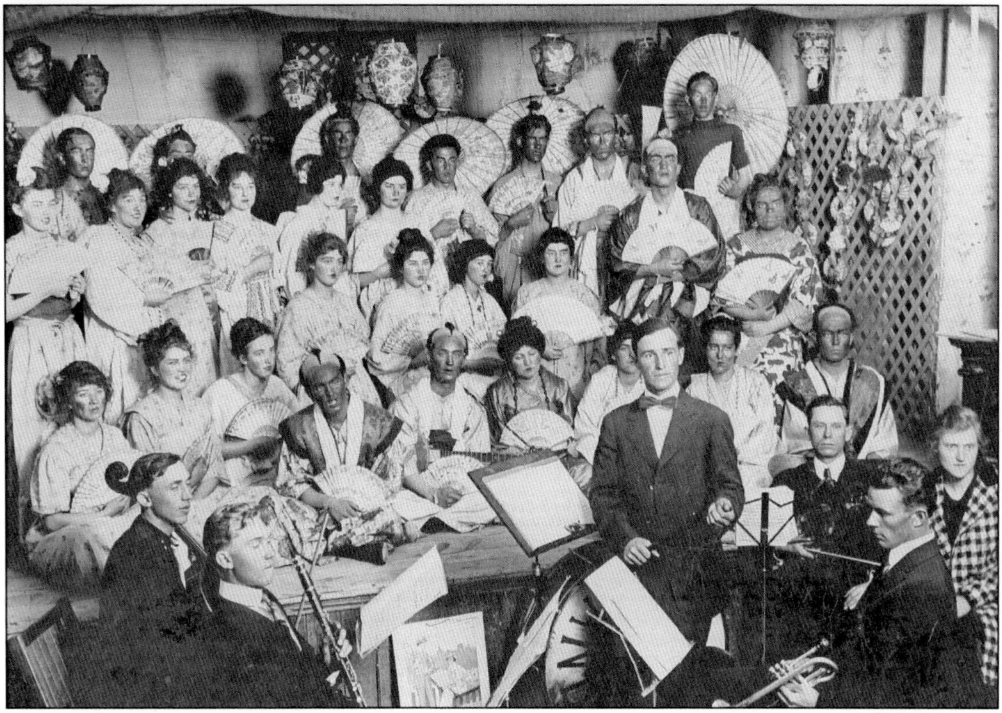

These pictures show the 1912 academy opera production of the *Mikado*. (Both courtesy St. Johns Historical Society and Museum.)

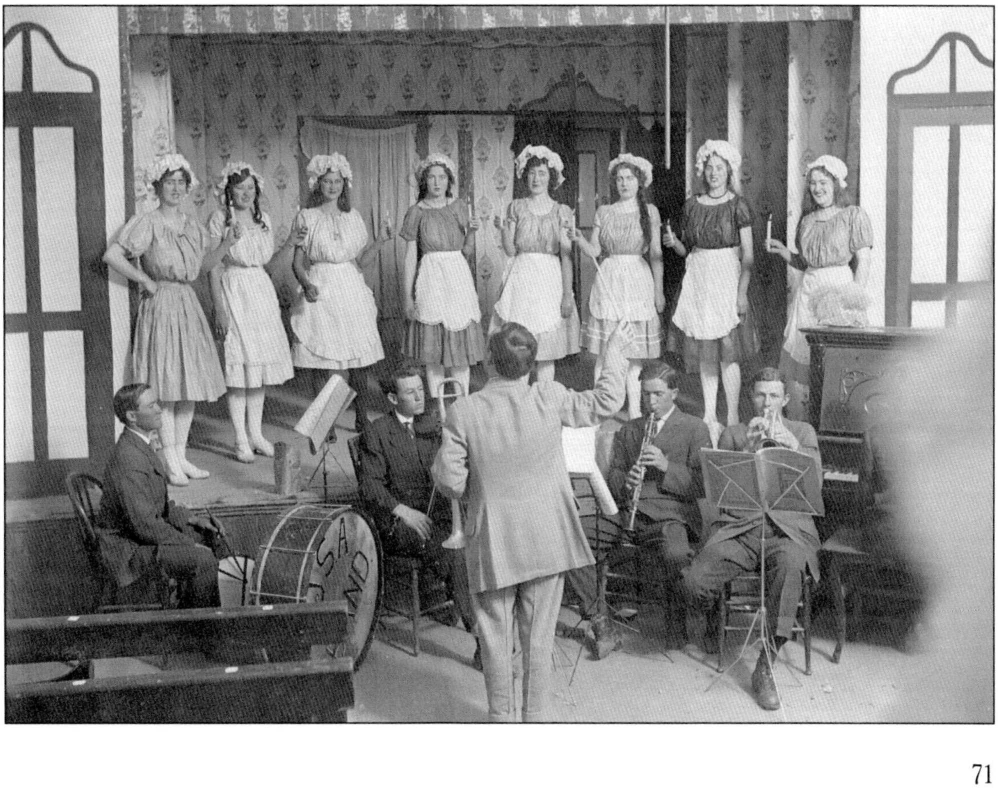

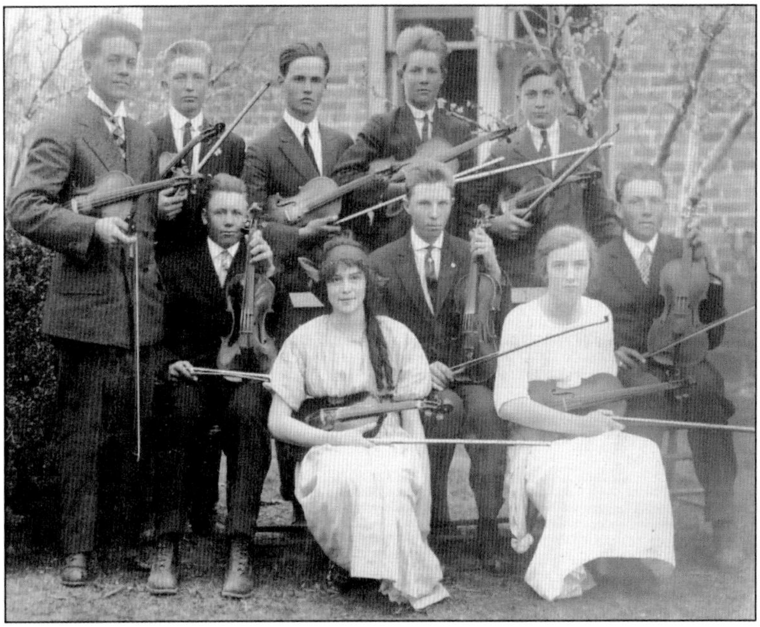

Pictured here is the St. Johns Stake Academy Orchestra. From left to right they are (first row) Genievene Gibbons and Esther Brown; (second row) Parley Heap, Lloyd Overson, and Edgar Mineer; (third row) A. C. Willardson (teacher), Tom Isaacson, Emer Hatch, Victor Overson, and Ernest Danenbaum. (Courtesy St. Johns Family History Center.)

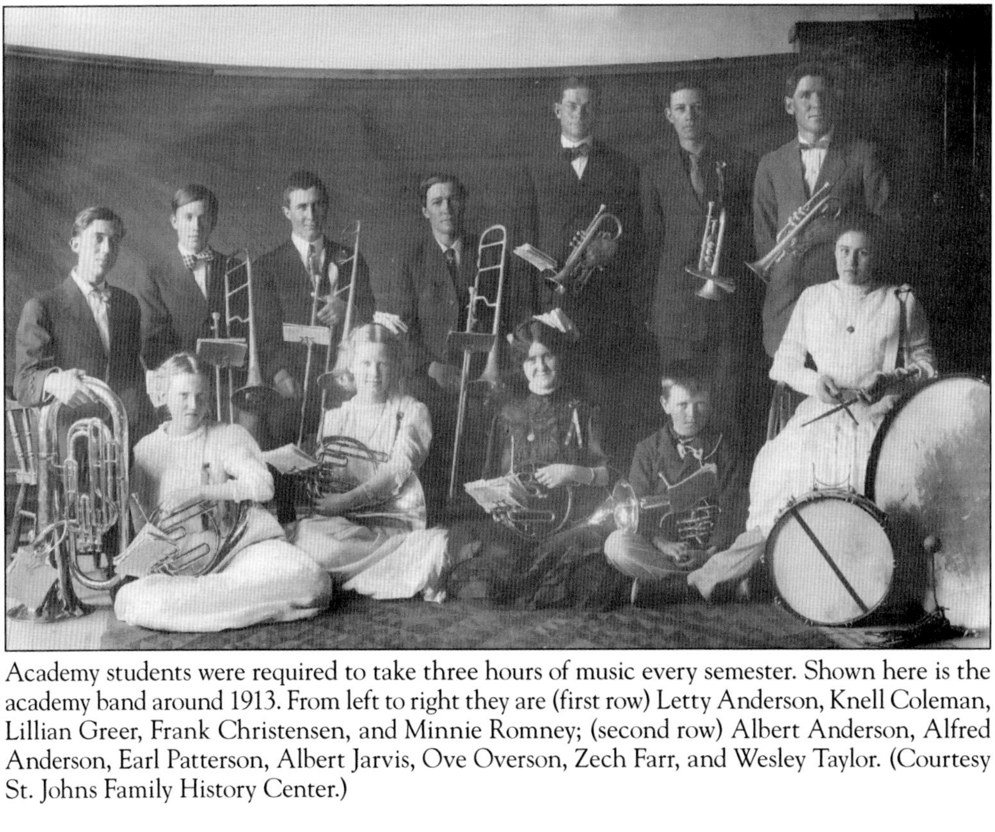

Academy students were required to take three hours of music every semester. Shown here is the academy band around 1913. From left to right they are (first row) Letty Anderson, Knell Coleman, Lillian Greer, Frank Christensen, and Minnie Romney; (second row) Albert Anderson, Alfred Anderson, Earl Patterson, Albert Jarvis, Ove Overson, Zech Farr, and Wesley Taylor. (Courtesy St. Johns Family History Center.)

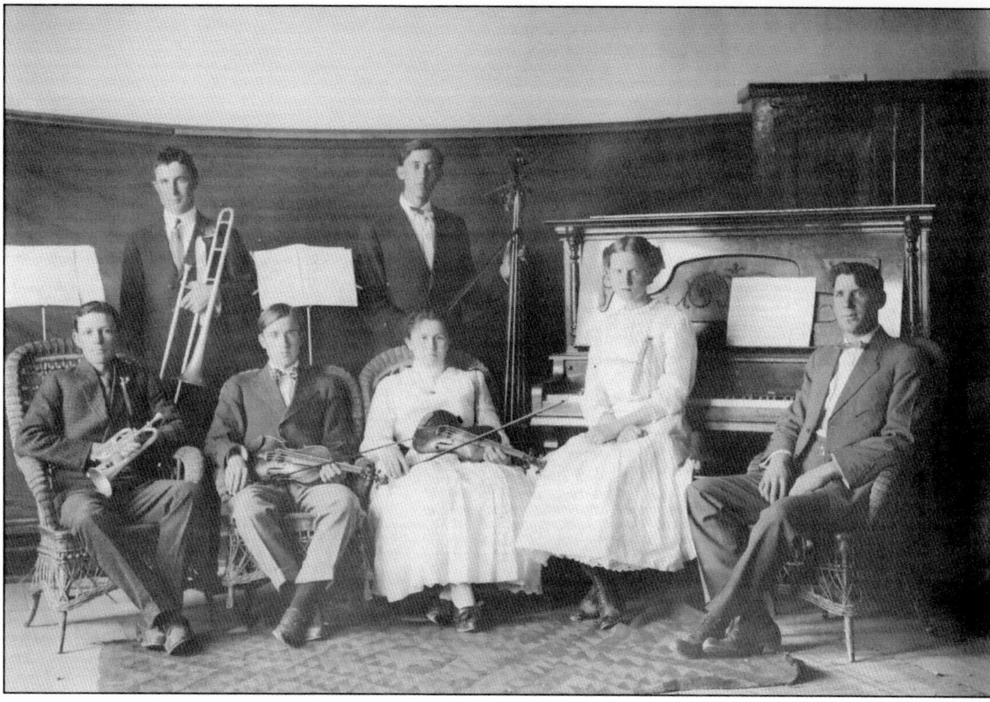

This photograph shows the academy band in 1914. The members are, from left to right, (seated) Zech Farr, Alfred Anderson, Mimi Pomeroy, Letty Anderson, and Wesley Taylor; (standing) Earl Patterson and Albert Anderson. (Courtesy St. Johns Family History Center.)

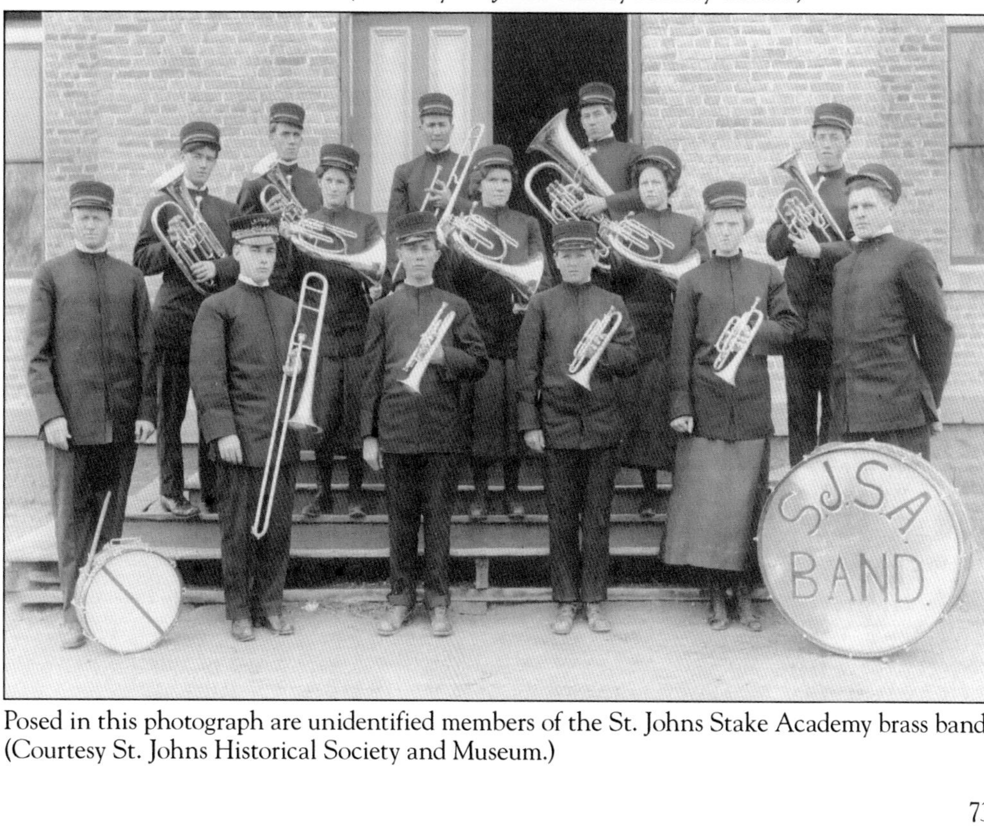

Posed in this photograph are unidentified members of the St. Johns Stake Academy brass band. (Courtesy St. Johns Historical Society and Museum.)

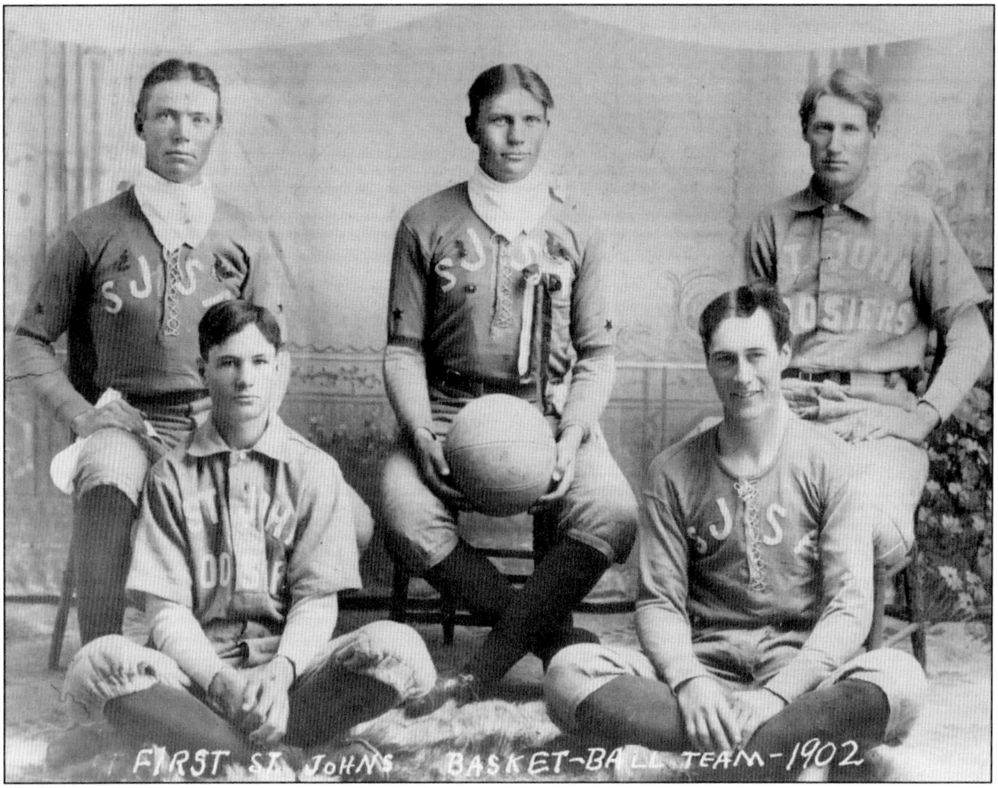

This picture shows the first St. Johns basketball team, formed in 1902 as the Hoosiers, in the only year that team name exists. The team members are, from left to right, (first row) Joy Patterson and Jarvis Gibbons; (second row) James Overson, Lyman Overson, and A. S. Gibbons. (Courtesy St. Johns Historical Society and Museum.)

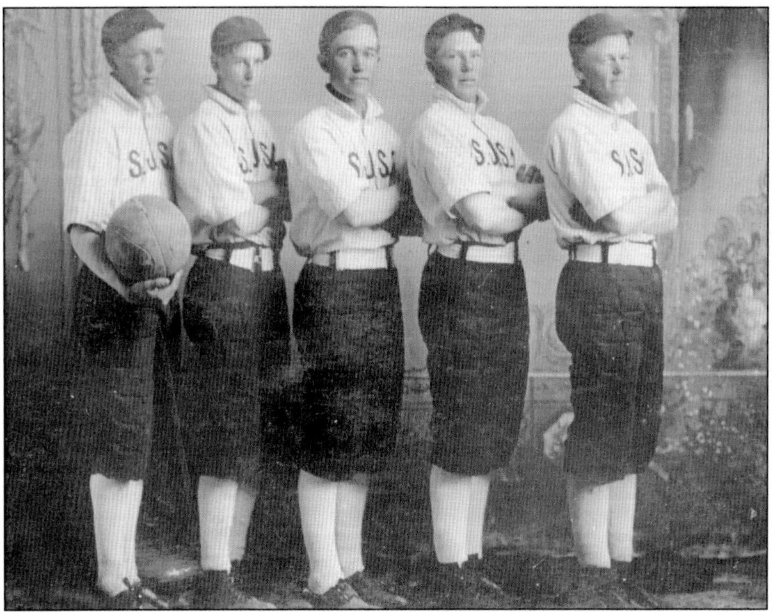

The 1910 academy basketball team was, from left to right, center Levi Udall, guard Berry Jolly, forward John H. Udall, guard Linton Morgan, and forward Ward Heap. (Courtesy St. Johns Family History Center.)

Pictured here are the 1919 state basketball champions. (Courtesy St. Johns Historical Society and Museum.)

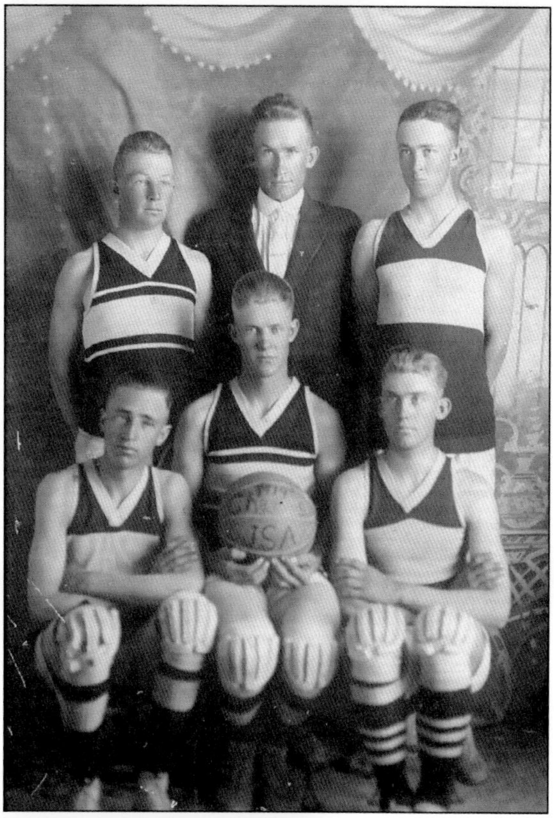

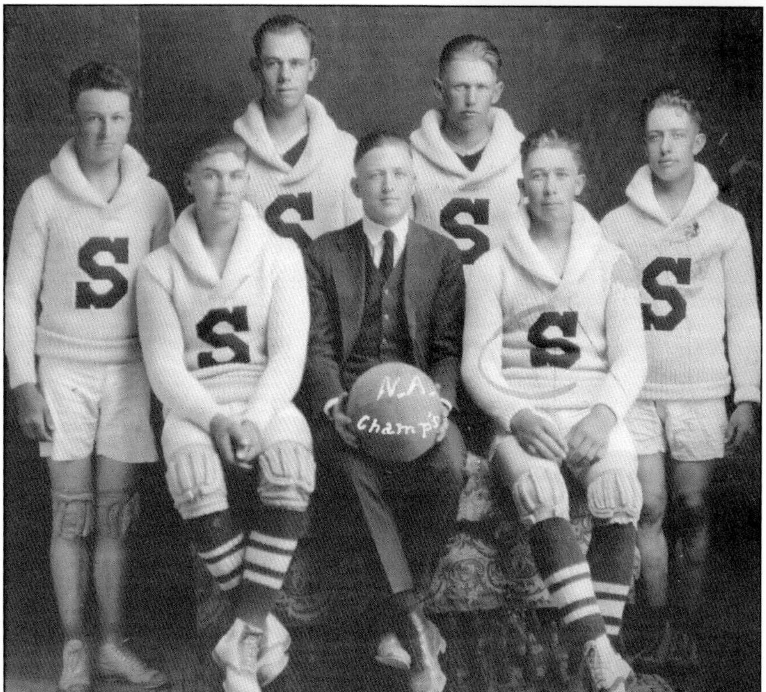

This photograph shows the 1922 academy basketball champs. From left to right they are (seated) Ove Overson, principal and coach John Napier, and Clyde Davis; (standing) Silas Jarvis, Alma Naegle, Joe Christensen, and Bates Gibbons. (Courtesy St. Johns Historical Society and Museum.)

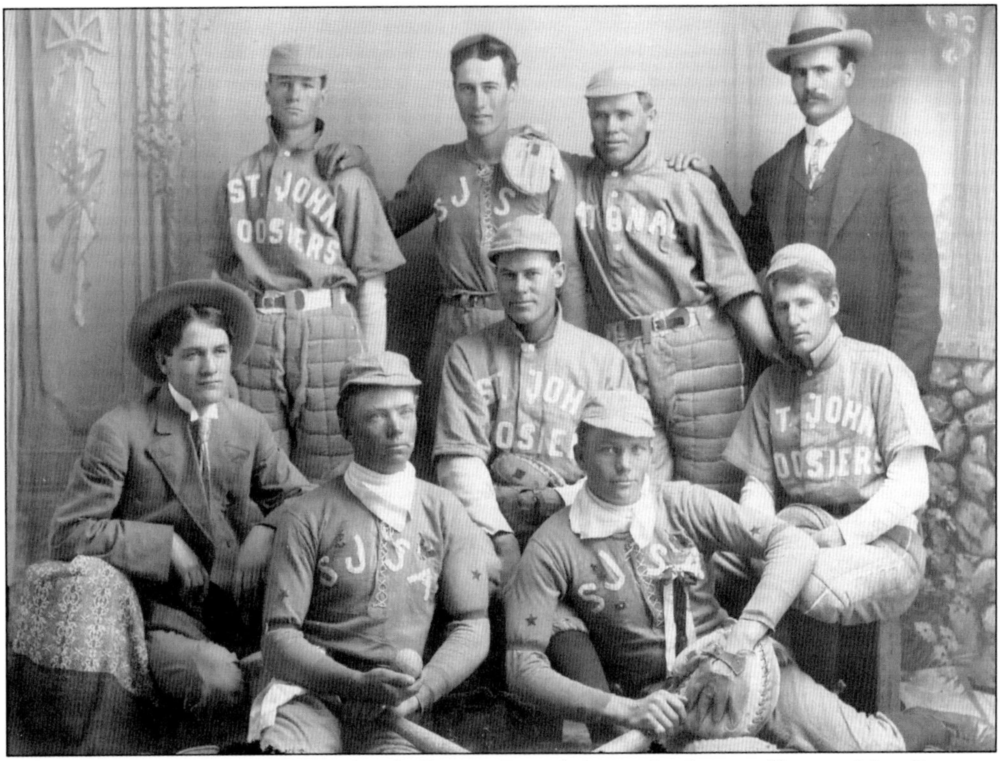

Pictured here is the 1902 academy baseball team. From left to right they are (first row) Jim Overson and Lyman Overson; (second row) Joy Patterson, C. Gibbons, and A. S. Gibbons; (third row) Jay Patterson, June Gibbons, Henry Jones, and B. Gibbons. (Courtesy St. Johns Historical Society and Museum.)

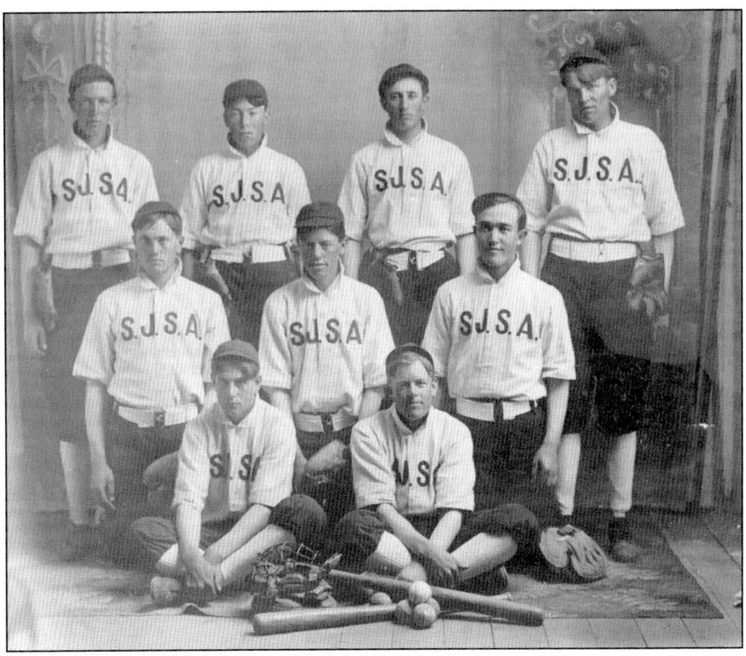

The 1910 academy baseball team, from left to right, includes (first row) Berry Jolly and Ward Heap; (second row) Bert Waite, Elmer Christensen, and John H. Udall; (third row) Levi Udall, Elmer Mineer, Gerald Berry, and Allie Mineer. (Courtesy St. Johns Historical Society and Museum.)

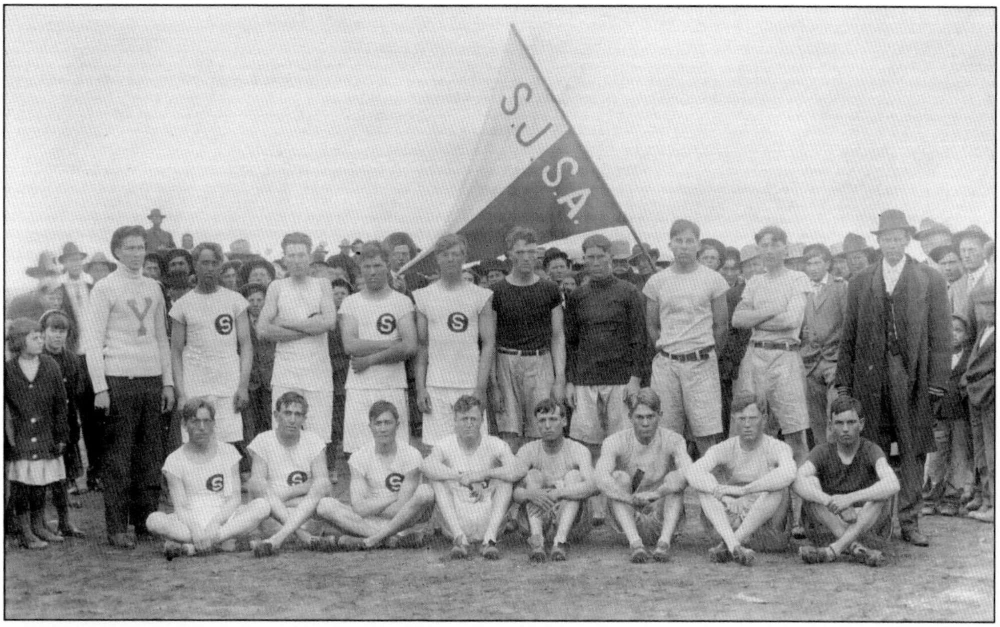

The academy track team is pictured here with what appears to be a good portion of the town. Track, according to one student, was one of the best sports in town, and the townspeople "yelled like thunder," cheering on their team. (Courtesy St. Johns Family History Center.)

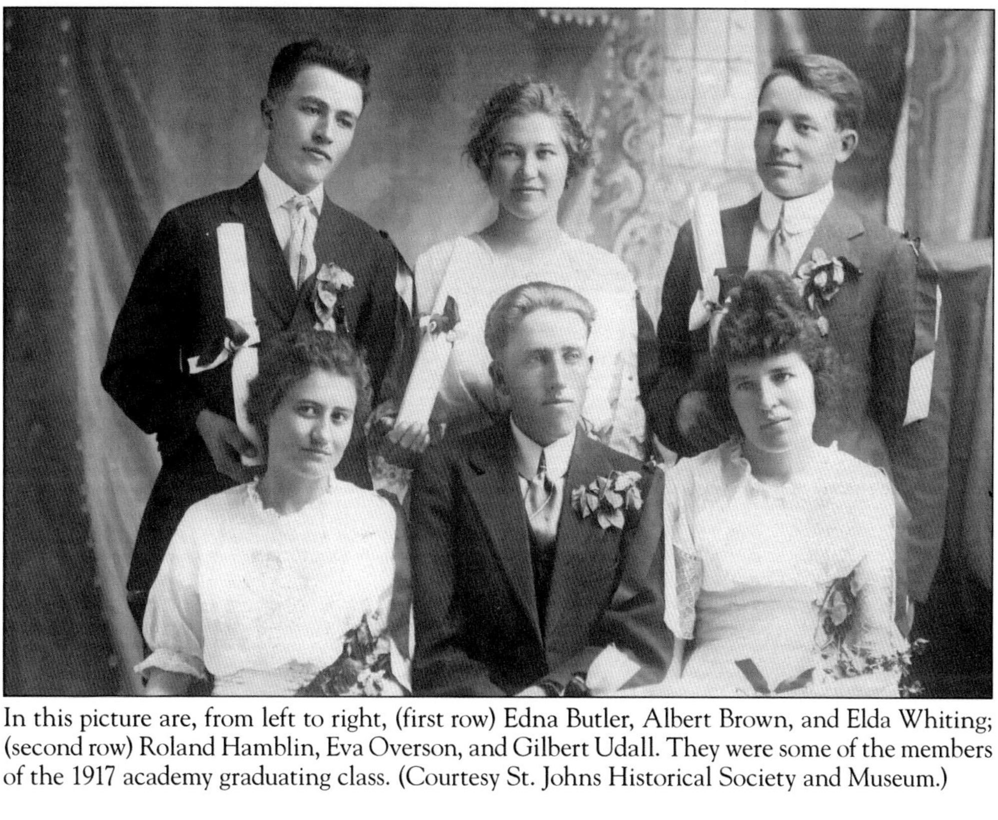

In this picture are, from left to right, (first row) Edna Butler, Albert Brown, and Elda Whiting; (second row) Roland Hamblin, Eva Overson, and Gilbert Udall. They were some of the members of the 1917 academy graduating class. (Courtesy St. Johns Historical Society and Museum.)

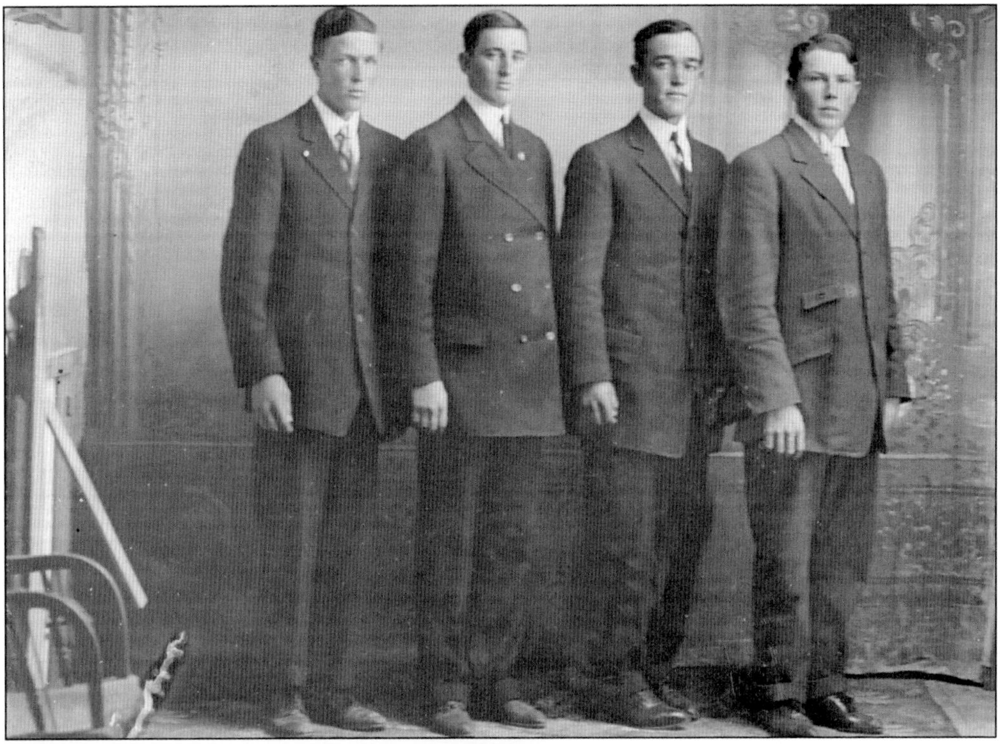

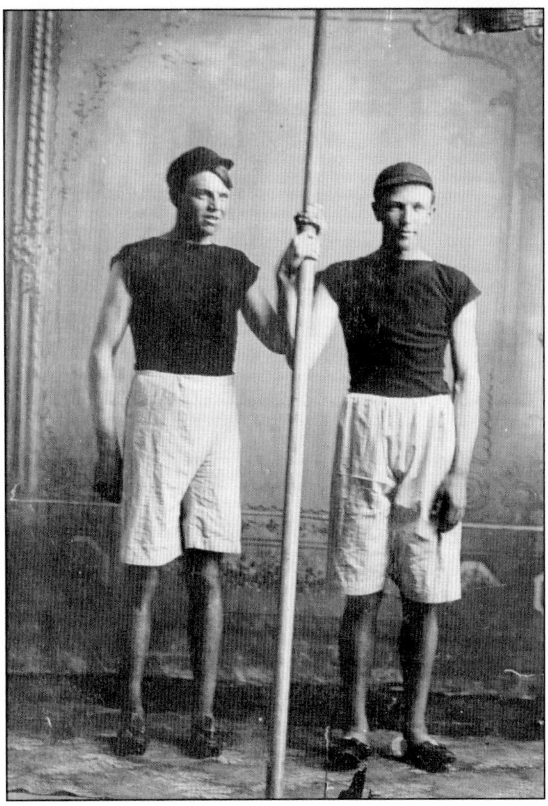

Academy students shown here are, from left to right, Levi Udall, unidentified, John H. Udall, and Allie Mineer. (Courtesy St. Johns Historical Society and Museum.)

Pictured here are pole-vaulters Allie Mineer (left) and Levi Udall. (Courtesy St. Johns Family History Center.)

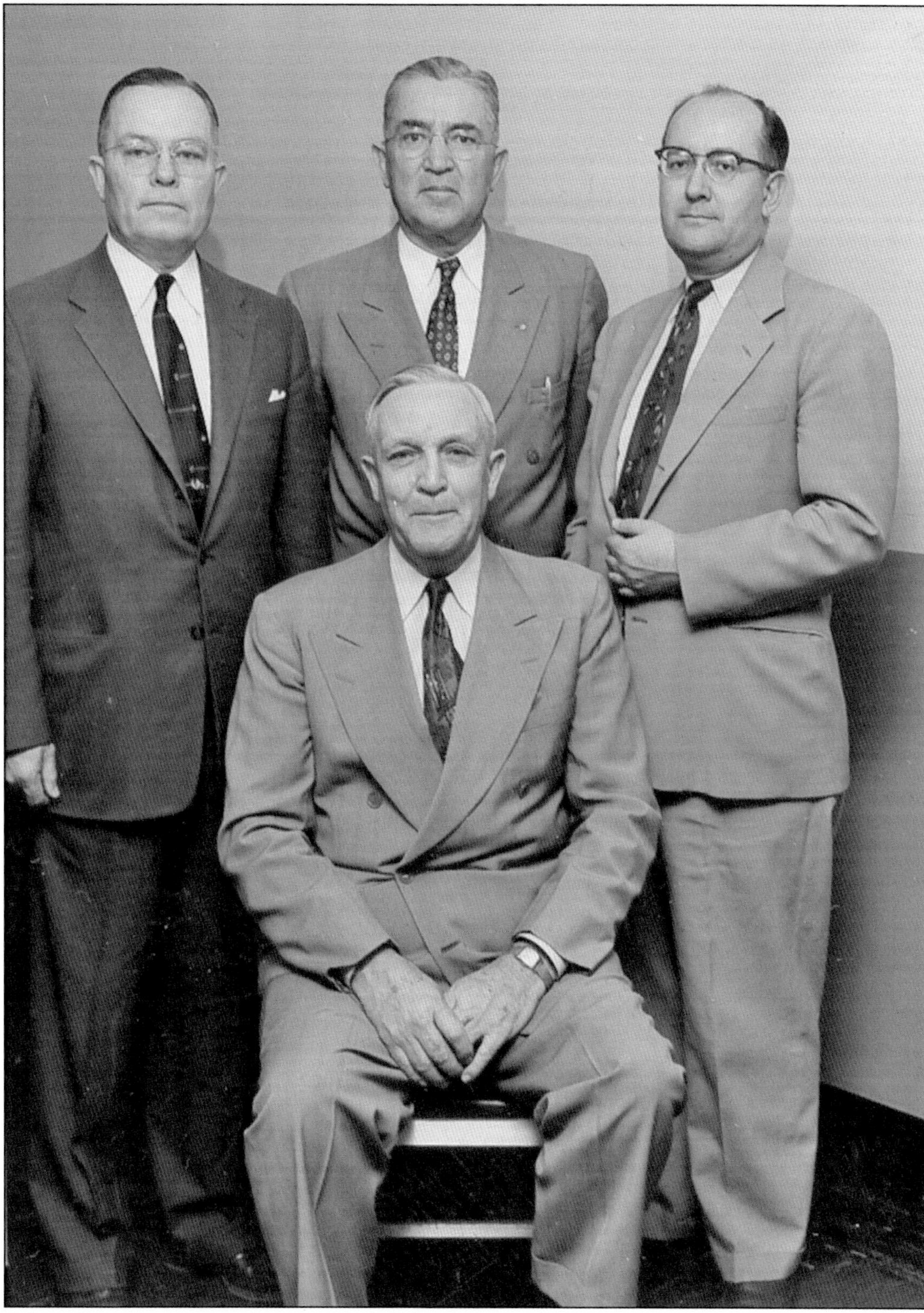

When this picture was taken, Levi Udall (seated) was the chief justice for the Arizona Supreme Court, brother Don (back left) was the superior court judge in Navajo County, brother Jesse (back center) was the superior court judge in Graham County, and their nephew J. Nicholas "Nick" Udall (back right) was a superior court judge in Maricopa County. All these men were born in St. Johns and all but Nick graduated from the St. Johns Stake Academy. (Author collection.)

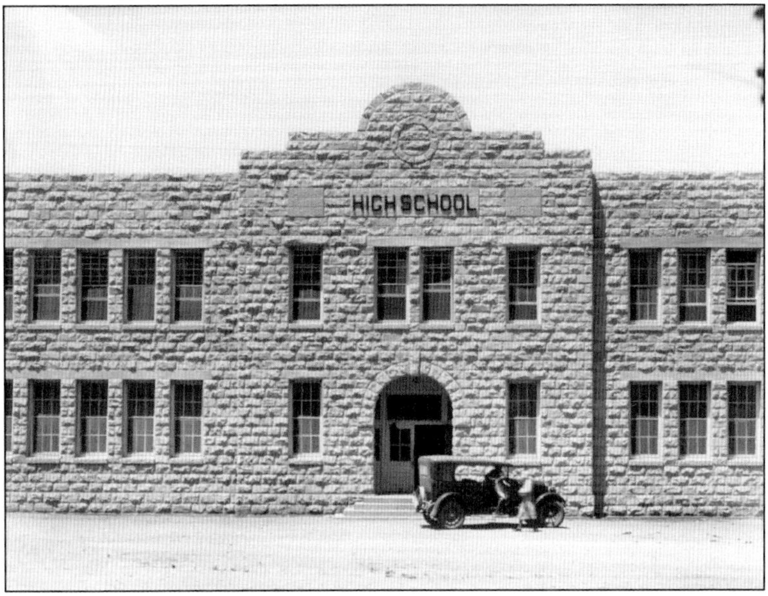

The St. Johns High School, shown here, was built when the academy closed in 1921 and was finished in 1926. It is now used as an annex building for the courthouse. (Courtesy St. Johns Family History Center.)

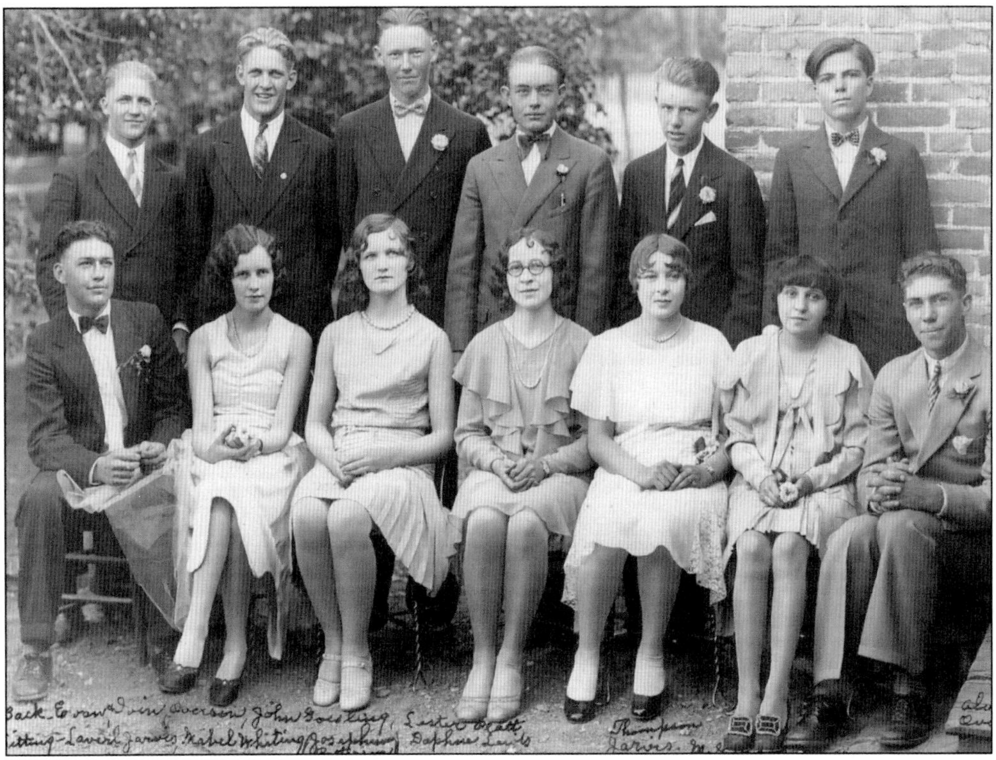

Pictured here is the 1929 St. Johns High School graduating class. From left to right they are (first row) Laverl Jarvis, Mabel Whiting, Josephine Patterson, Daphne Lewis, Leola Jarvis, Margaret Garcia, and Alvin Overson; (second row) Evan Overson, Ivan Overson, Johnny Goesling, Lester Platt, Alva Thompson, and unidentified. (Courtesy St. Johns Family History Center.)

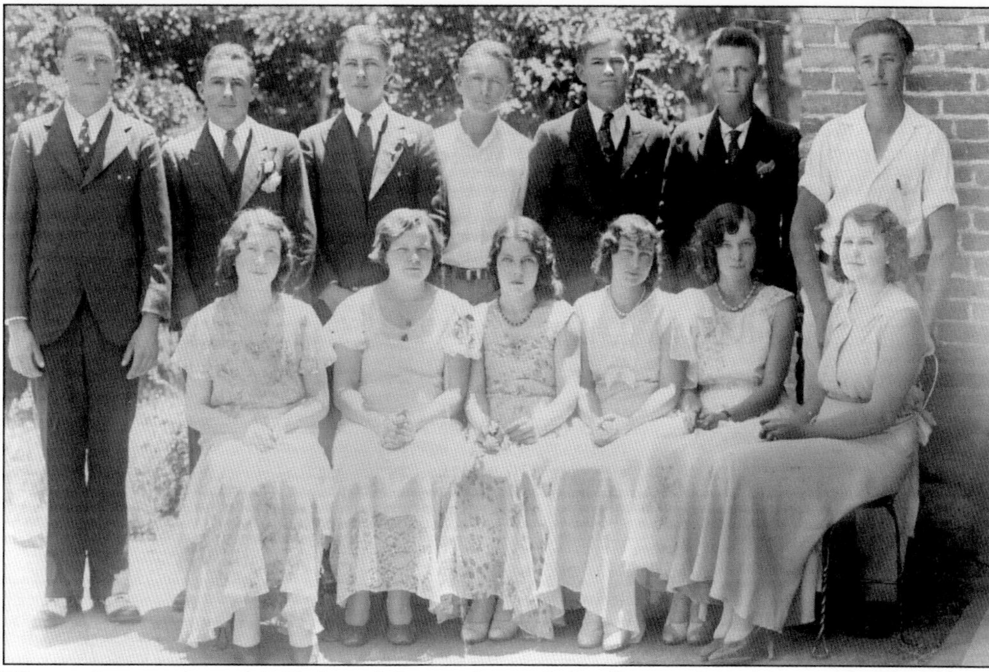

The graduating class of 1931, from left to right, includes (first row) Kathleen Hamblin, Estelle Whiting, Katy Raban, Calla Plumb, Ida Davis, and Monita Whiting; (second row) Joy Waite, Homer Richey, Ray Waite, Sherwood Udall, Philip Greer, Clyde Rothlisberger, and Ben Gibbons. (Author collection.)

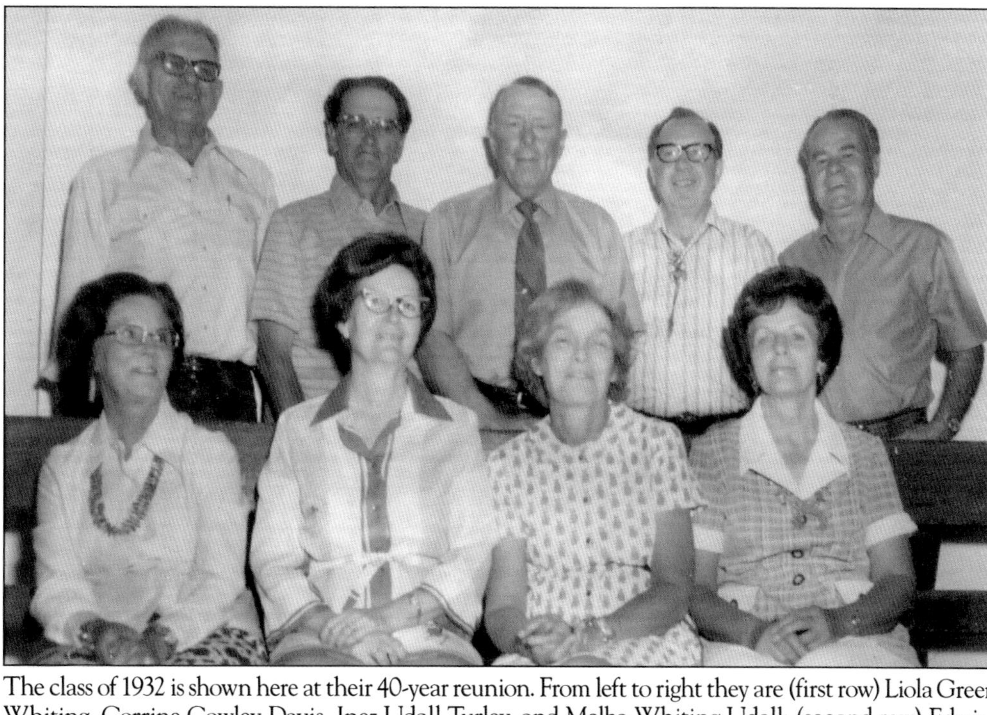

The class of 1932 is shown here at their 40-year reunion. From left to right they are (first row) Liola Greer Whiting, Corrine Cowley Davis, Inez Udall Turley, and Melba Whiting Udall; (second row) Edwin Whiting, Kenneth Pulsipher, Earl Jarvis, Lister Mineer, and Errol Brown. (Author collection.)

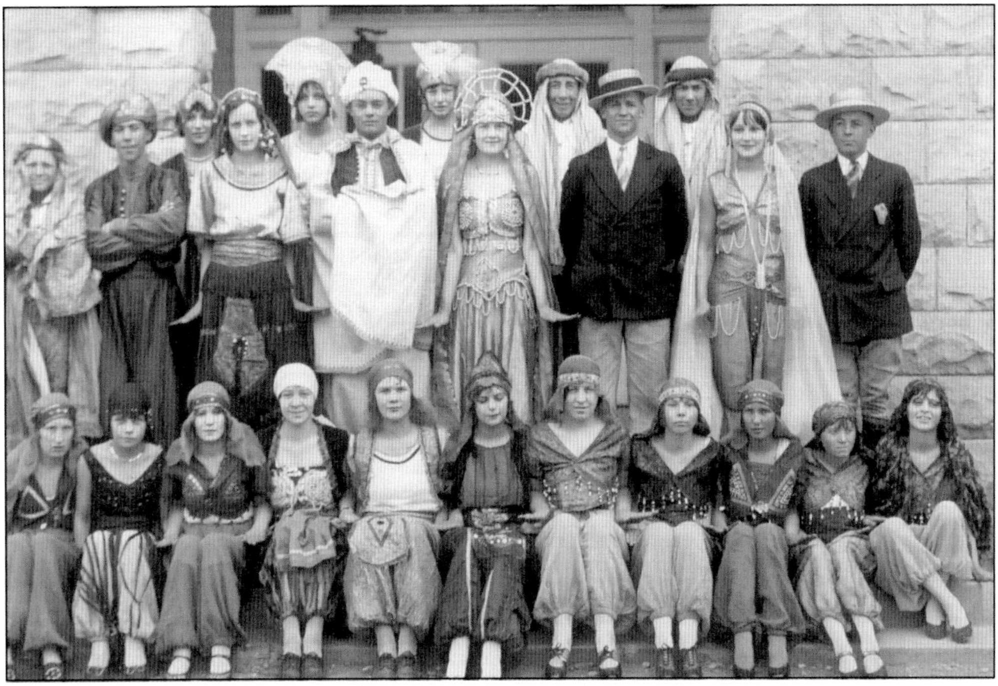

Even though the academy had closed, students continued to do opera productions, such as *Crocodile Island* in 1931 (above) and *Sky High* in 1930 (below). (Both author collection.)

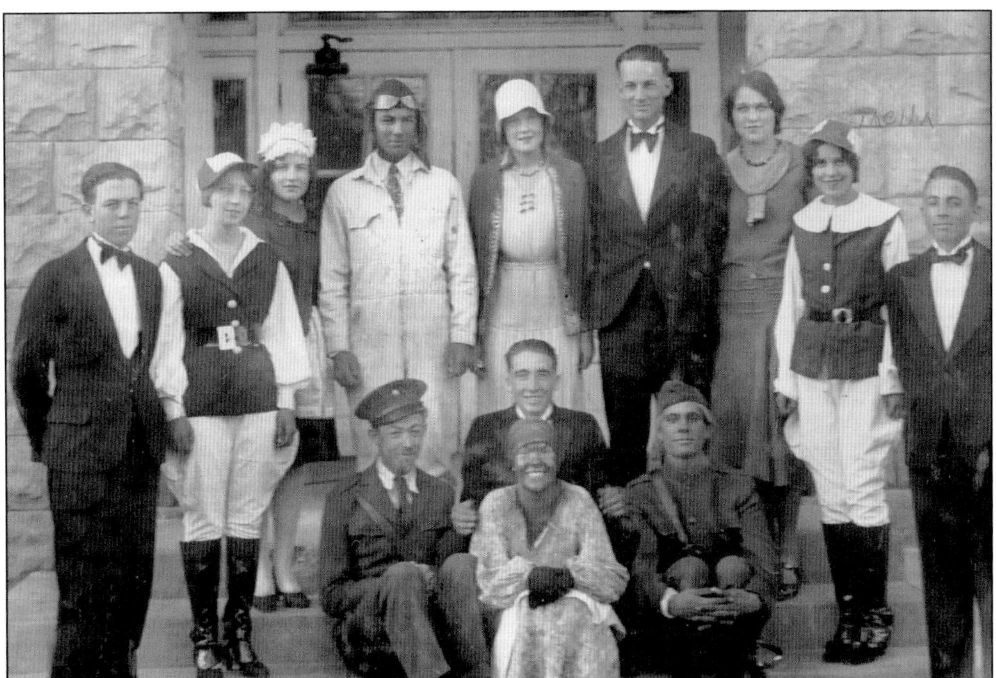

Pictured here are Melba Whiting and an unidentified man gearing up for the 1930 opera production of *The Colonial Days*. (Author collection.)

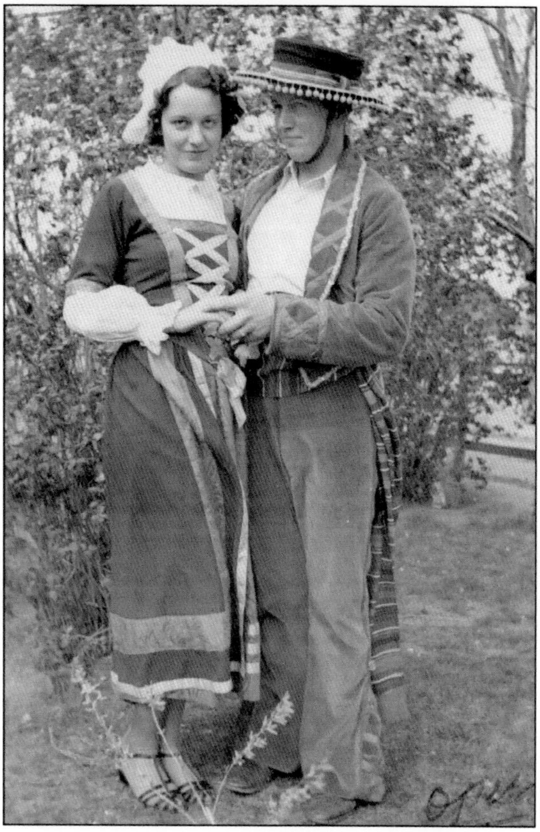

Shown here is a group of girls in a drill for entertainment "Co.B." From left to right they are (first row) Naomi Gibbons (leader), Leila Kempe, Pearl Davis, Annie Butler, Sarah Butler, and Mattie Holgate; (second row) Anna Sorensen, Annie Anderson, Annie Jarvis, Amber Walters, and Louie Freeman. (Courtesy St. Johns Family History Center.)

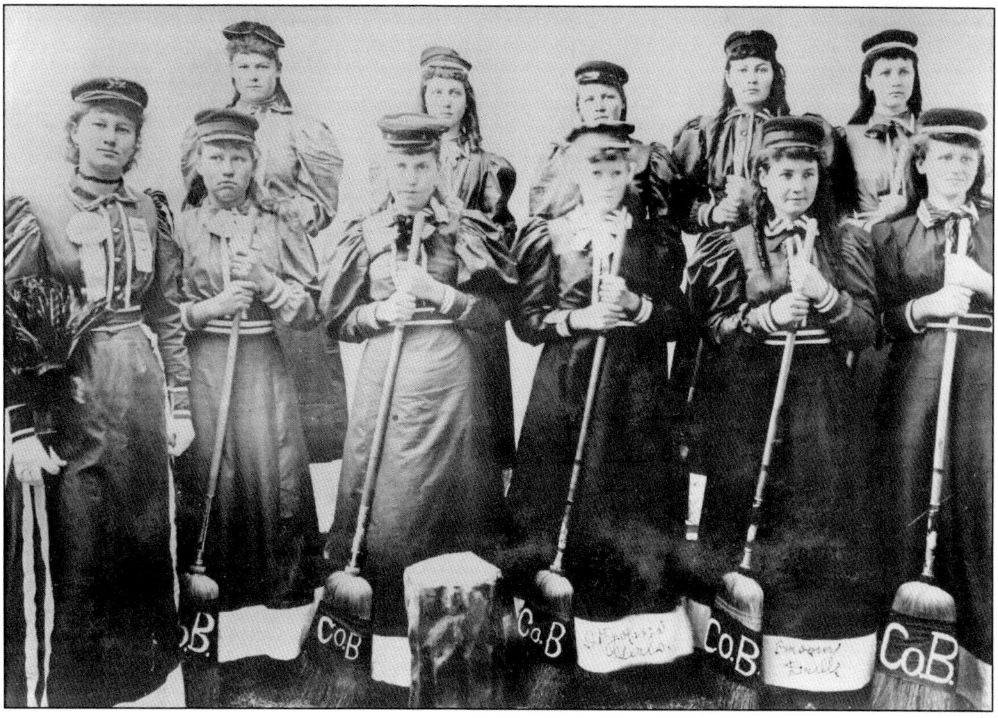

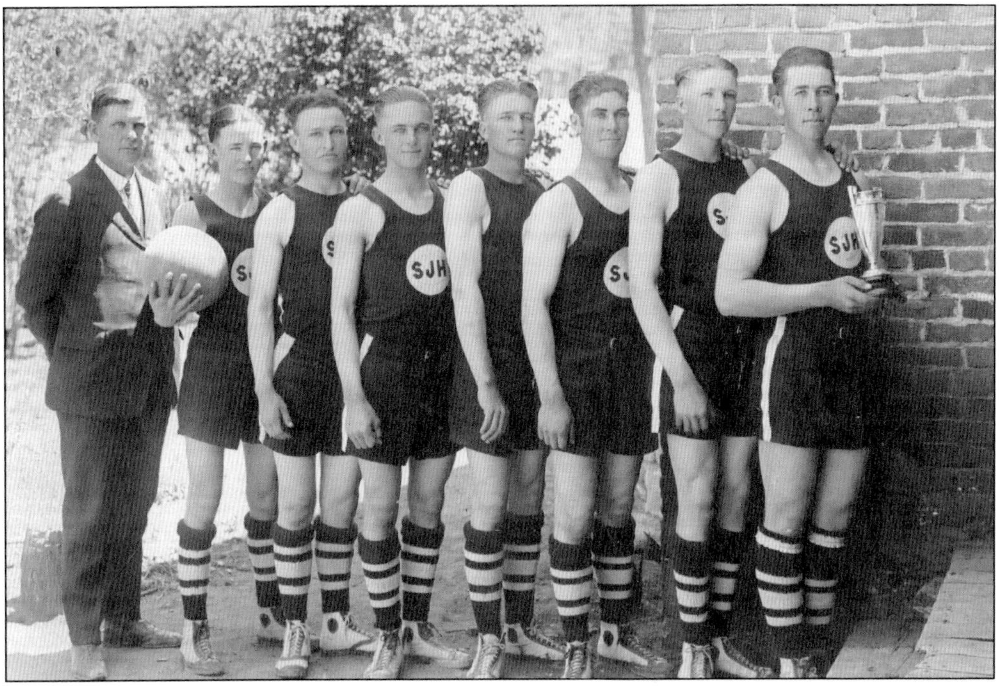

This picture shows the 1925 Northern Arizona basketball champions. From left to right they are coach Libbert, Lawson Hamblin, Silas Jarvis, Harry Overson, Pratt Overson, Ove Overson, Wilford Overson, and Clyde Davis. (Courtesy St. Johns Family History Center.)

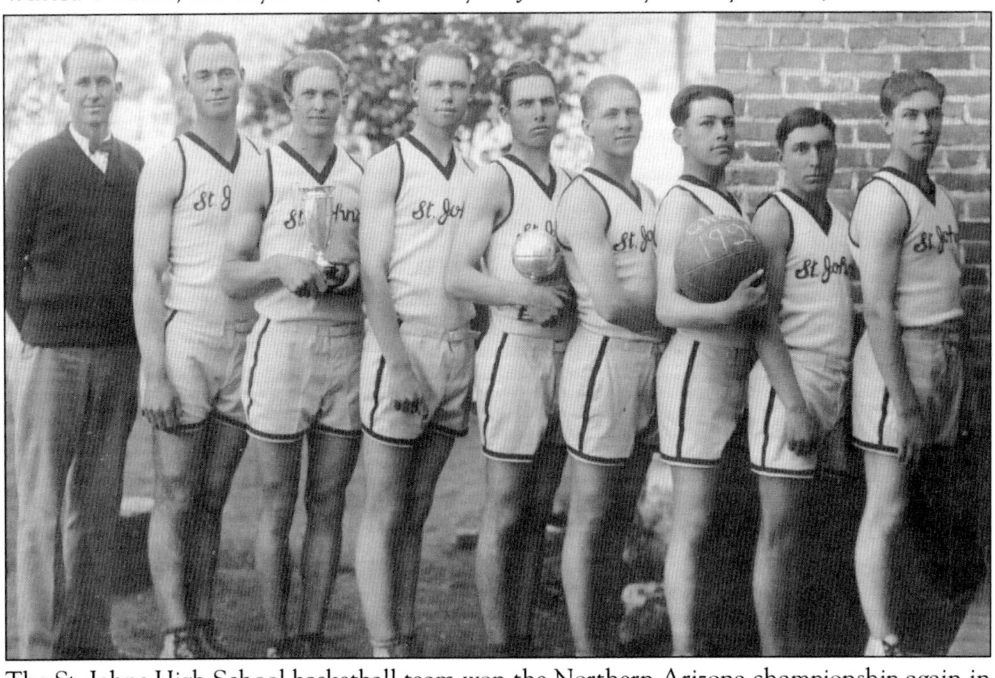

The St. Johns High School basketball team won the Northern Arizona championship again in 1927. Pictured from left to right are coach Dean Nutting, Roy Naegle, Ivan Overson, Cecil Naegle, Marvin Stradling, Evan Overson, Laverl Jarvis, Emilio Garcia, and Alvin Overson. (Courtesy St. Johns Historical Society and Museum.)

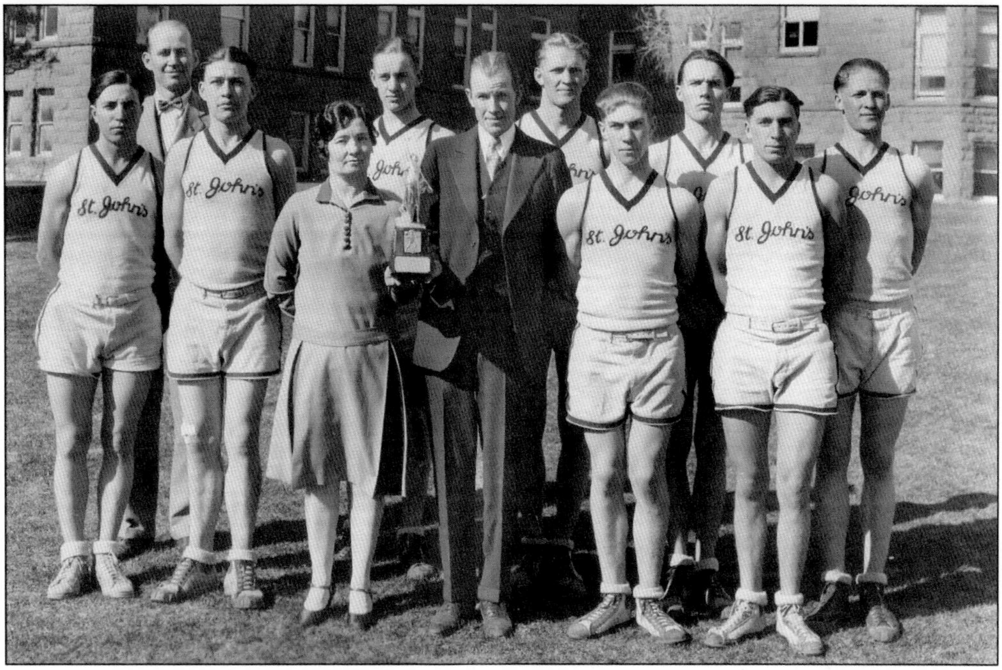

The St. Johns High School basketball team won their first Arizona state championship in 1928. The team, shown here from left to right, includes (first row) Joe Garcia, Laverl Jarvis, Mrs. Denman, coach Denman, Alvin Overson, and Emilio Garcia; (second row) Dean Nutting (standing behind Garcia and Jarvis), Kay Berry, Marvin Stradling, Evan Overson, and unidentified. (Courtesy St. Johns Historical Society and Museum.)

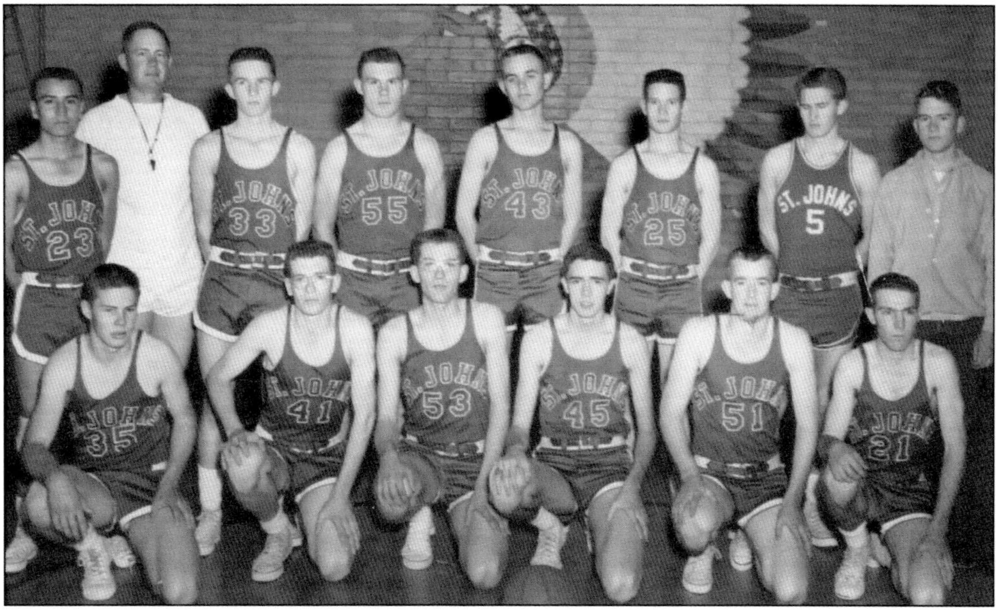

Born and raised in St. Johns, Verl Heap played semipro ball before coming back to St. Johns to teach and coach basketball. Coach Heap, shown here with the 1960 state basketball champions, was the coach for eight of the nine basketball championships won by the Redskins. (Courtesy St. Johns Historical Society and Museum.)

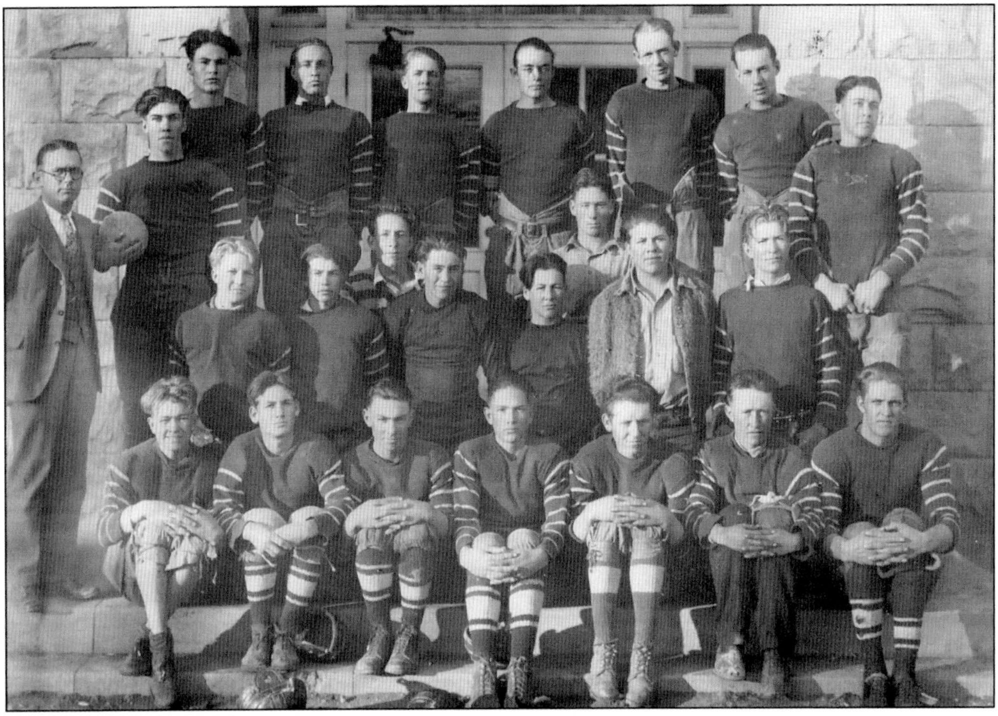

Shown here is an early St. Johns football team. In 1928, football was introduced at a special assembly where the coach explained the game to everybody. (Courtesy St. Johns Family History Center.)

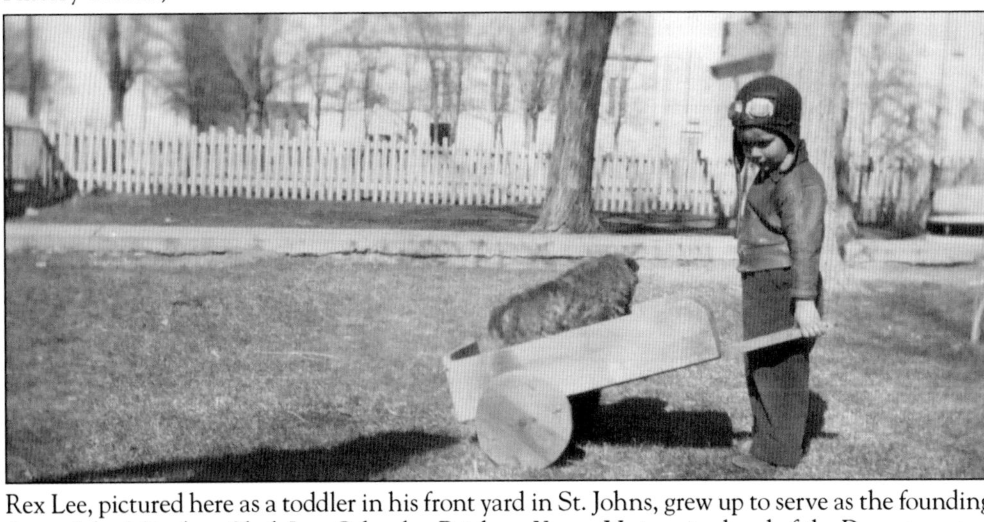

Rex Lee, pictured here as a toddler in his front yard in St. Johns, grew up to serve as the founding dean of the J. Reuben Clark Law School at Brigham Young University, head of the Department of Justice Civil Rights Division under Pres. Gerald Ford, and solicitor general to the U.S. Supreme Court under Pres. Ronald Reagan, arguing a remarkable 59 cases in front of the Supreme Court. Lee later became the president of Brigham Young University from 1989 to 1995. He died of cancer in 1996 from the result of being a "downwinder." From 1951 to the middle of 1962, the United States exploded 86 nuclear devices in Nevada, releasing a significant amount of radioactive material into the atmosphere. St. Johns is downwind from the site, thus a disproportionate number of its citizens have died of cancer. (Author collection.)

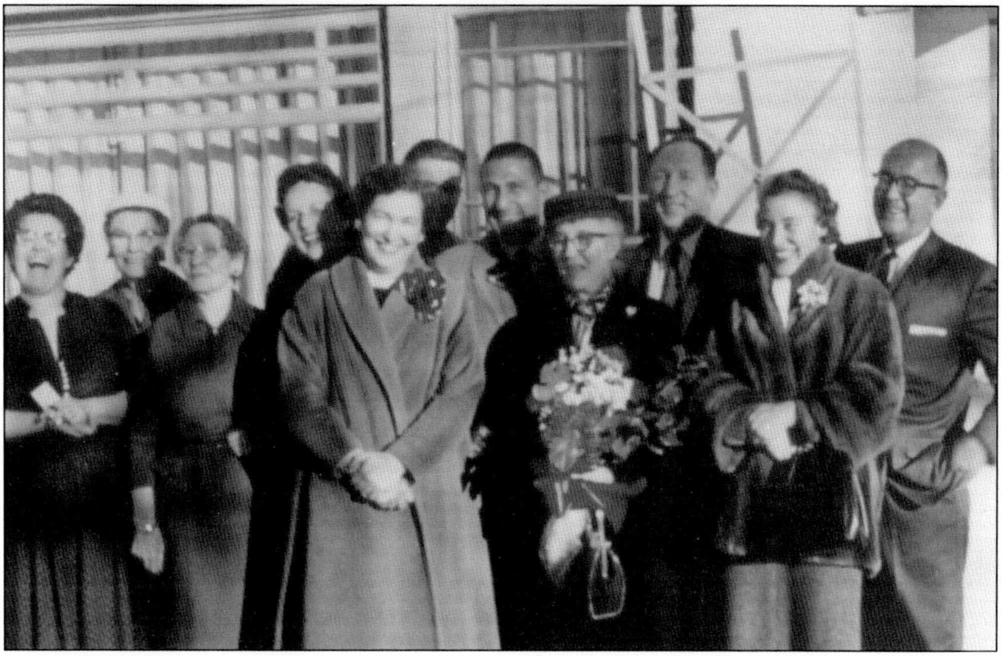

This photograph was taken in St. Johns outside the Udall family home, the Elm, shortly after Stewart Udall was named the secretary of the interior by Pres. John F. Kennedy. Pictured from left to right are (first row) Inez Udall Turley, Louise Udall, and Elma Udall; (second row) Gwen Udall, Maud Udall, Dora Udall, Melba Udall, Sherwood Udall, Stewart Udall, Keith Udall, and Nicholas Udall. (Author collection.)

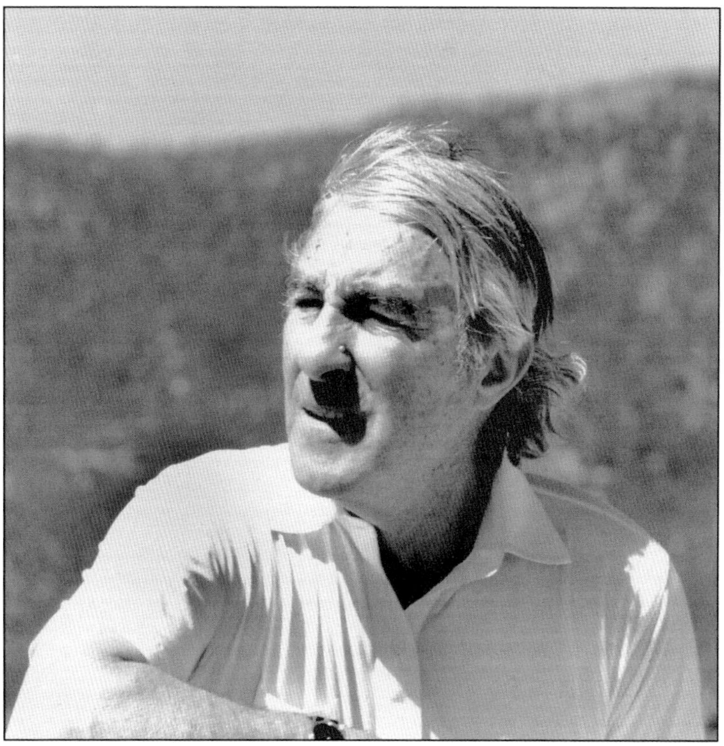

Born in St. Johns, Stewart L. Udall was elected to four terms as a congressman from Arizona before being appointed the secretary of the interior by Pres. John F. Kennedy, a position he held through Pres. Lyndon B. Johnson's administration. As a private attorney, he helped force the U.S. government to compensate people "downwind" from the Nevada nuclear test site who have family that died from the cancer the tests caused. (Courtesy Arizona Historical Foundation.)

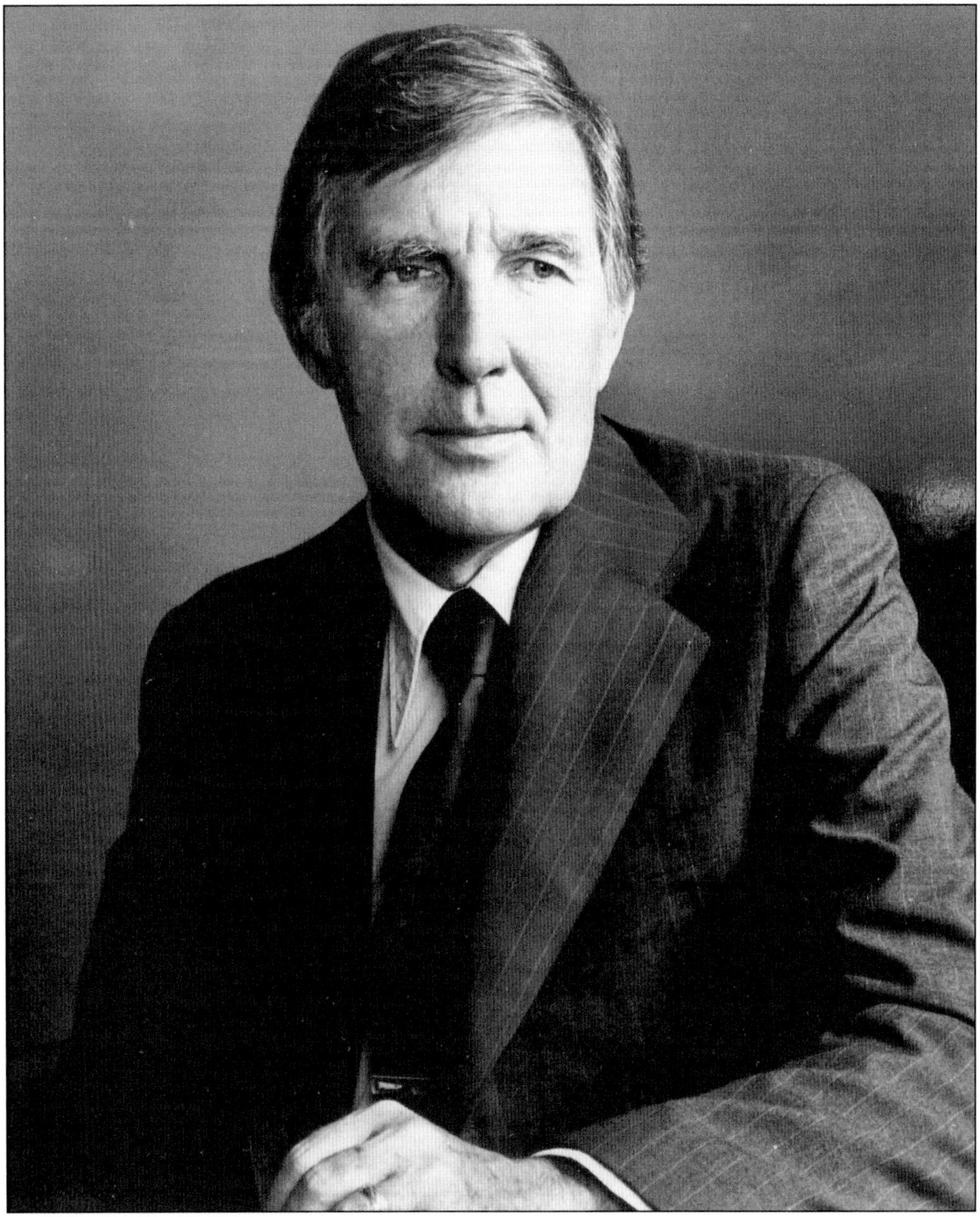

Born and raised in St. Johns, Morris "Mo" King Udall is one of Arizona's most celebrated citizens. Despite the fact he had only one eye (he lost the other to a friend's pocketknife at the age of six), he played basketball for the Denver Nuggets before returning to Arizona to practice law. After his brother Stewart vacated his congressional seat to serve in President Kennedy's cabinet, Mo was elected to Congress for the next 30 years. He often referred to St. Johns during his unsuccessful bid for the presidency by saying such things as "St. Johns is so small, you can't even lust in your own heart." (Courtesy Arizona Historical Foundation.)

Five

PRIDE AND PERSEVERANCE

People driving through St. Johns might just wonder how such a town could ever exist in such a place and why anyone would ever choose to live there. The best explanation comes from J. Golden Kimball, a general authority in the Mormon Church, who said in a central conference address given in Salt Lake City, "I would like to take you on a trip down to Arizona, in the St. Johns Country. I preached faith there once, but I want to tell you I haven't enough faith to stay in such an undesirable country. You talk about good people, you talk about righteous people; I can tell you there are people in this city who are not worthy to unlatch their shoestrings. That hard country, and their obedience to God, has made those men of great characters. You can't discourage them. They will build a dam across the Little Colorado River every five years, and if it washes out the next day, they'll live on dry bread and molasses. Yet that is their home; that is there country; there they worship God."

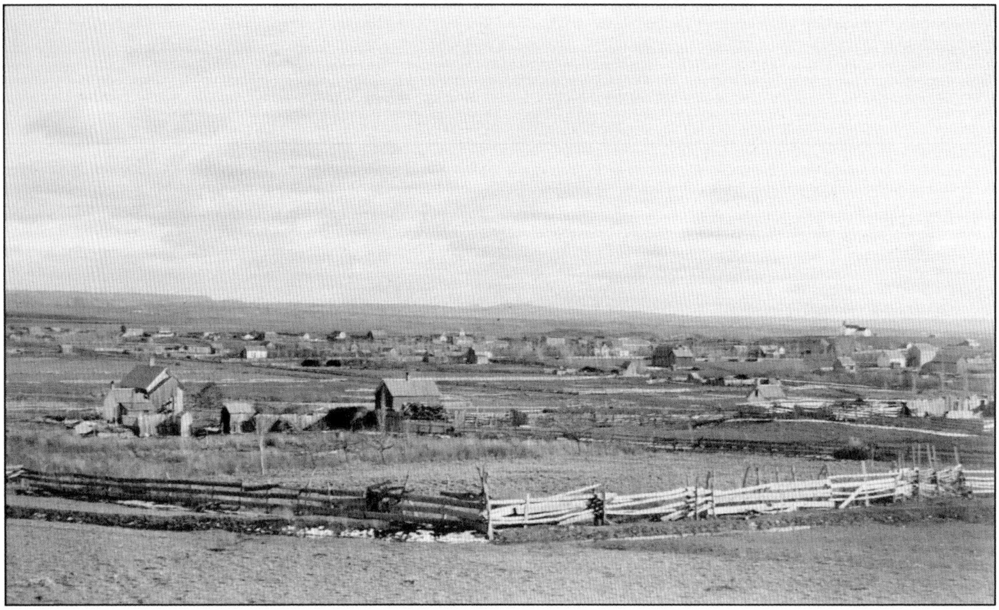

This picture was taken from the west end of town in the 1890s. (Courtesy St. Johns Historical Society and Museum.)

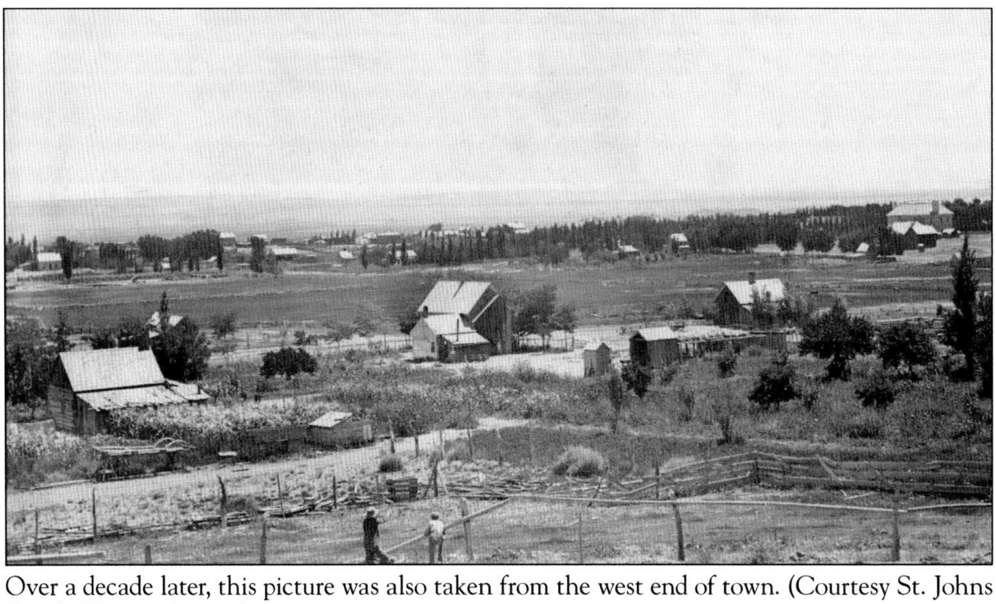

Over a decade later, this picture was also taken from the west end of town. (Courtesy St. Johns Family History Center.)

Typical of early St. Johns, a wagon is parked in front of the Barth Hotel. (Courtesy Ruth Patterson.)

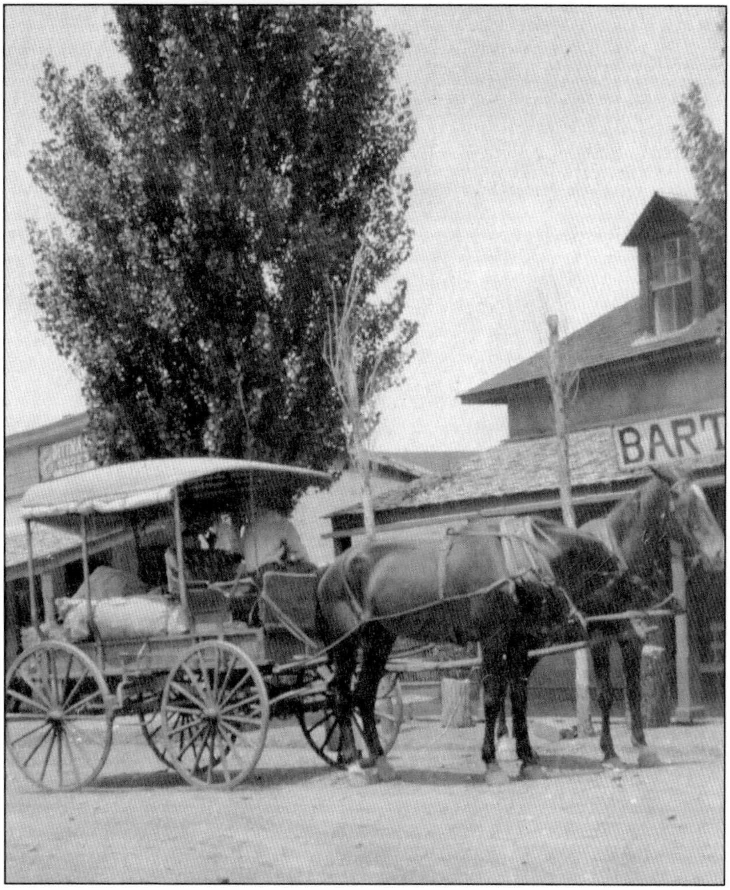

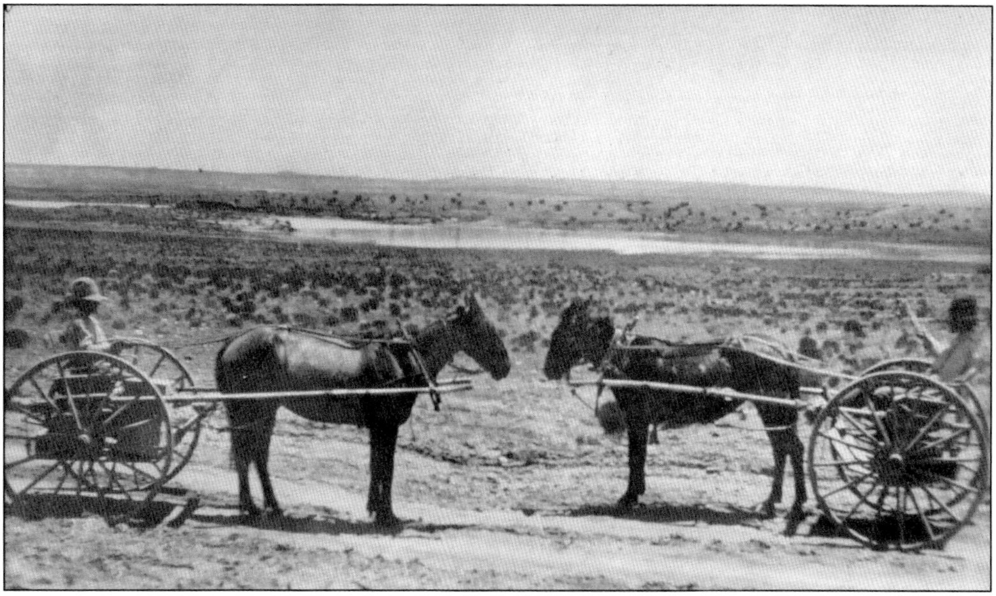

Here George (left) and Albert Jarvis are pictured at the Little Reservoir where they exchanged mail. (Courtesy St. Johns Family History Center.)

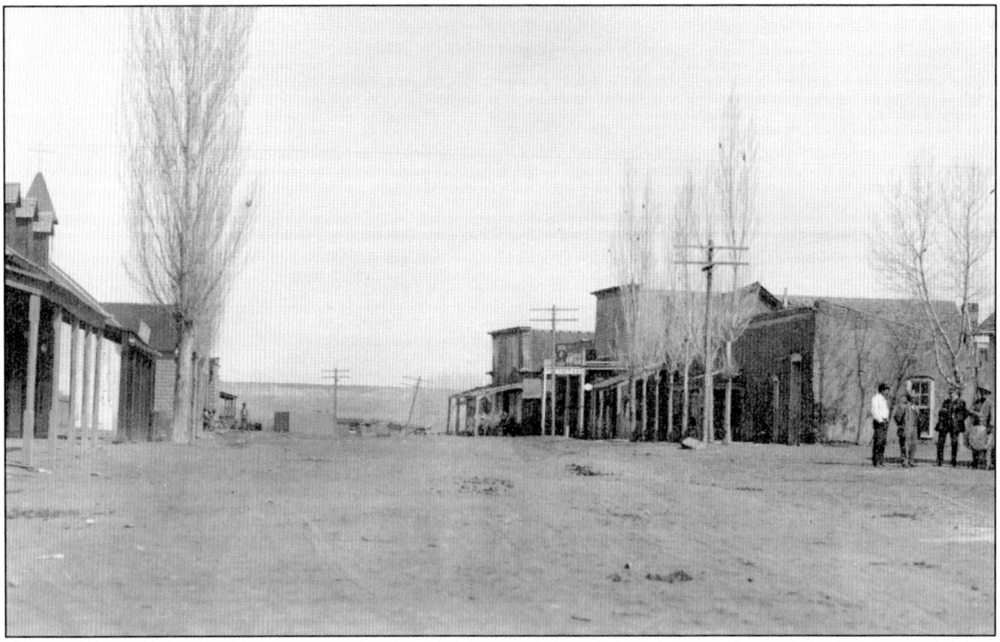

This very early view of Commercial Street, taken looking east, shows what appears to be a barren and dusty place. (Courtesy St. Johns Family History Center.)

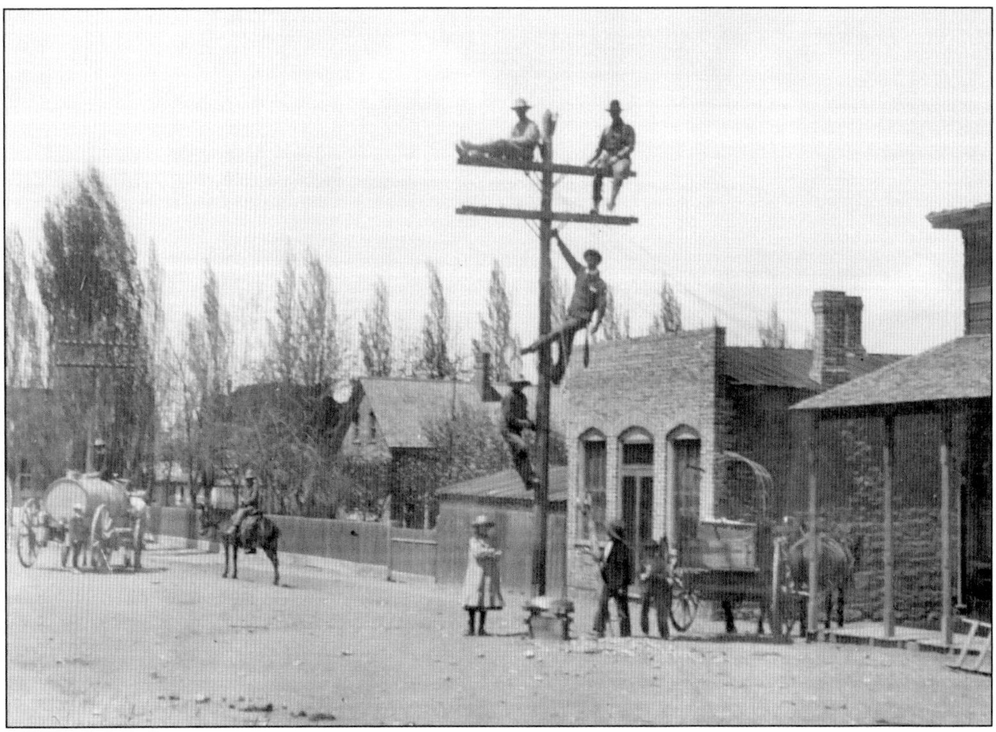

In 1898, the first telephone was installed in St. Johns in Charles Jarvis's office and photography gallery. On the ground to the right of the pole is Albert Jarvis; Charles Jarvis is on the other side of the pole near the wagon. On the pole, the person second from bottom is Martin Jensen; the others are unidentified. (Courtesy St. Johns Family History Center.)

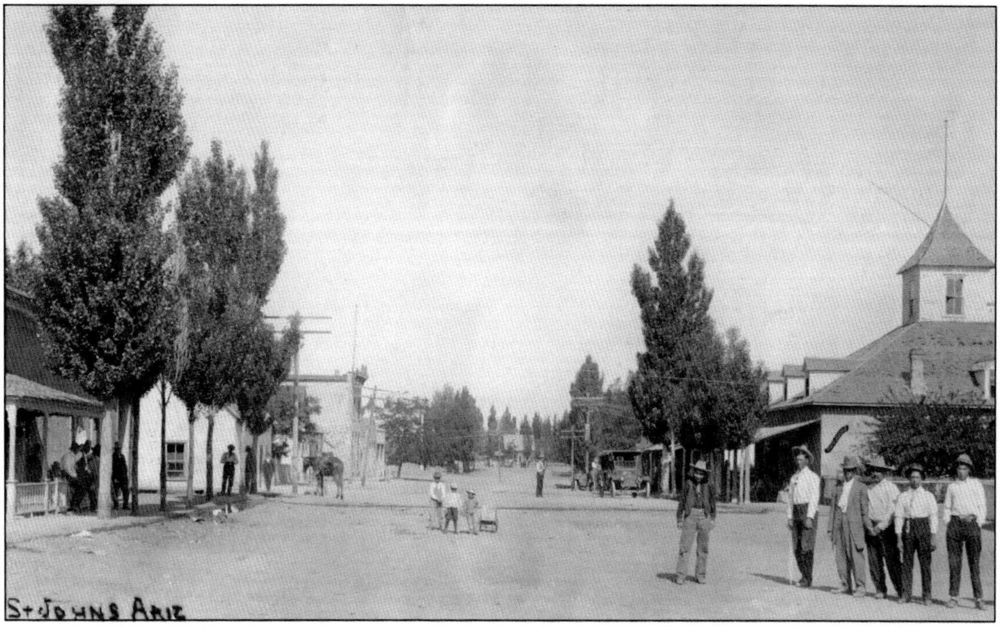

This picture, at the north side of Commercial Street, was taken around 1915 and shows the ditch that ran through the middle of the street. (Courtesy St. Johns Family History Center.)

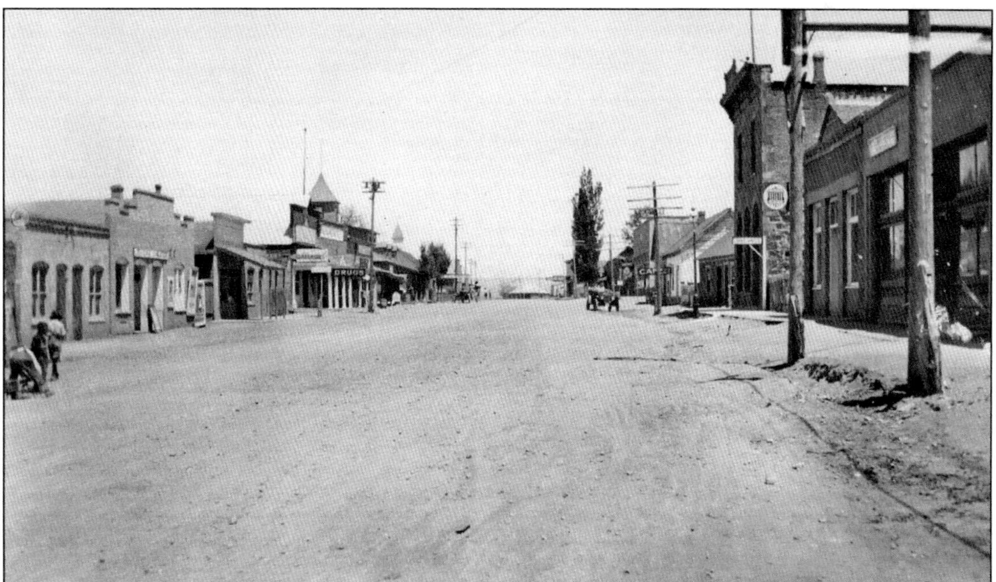

This 1920s picture shows Commercial Street looking east. (Courtesy Arizona State University, Department of Archives and Special Collections.)

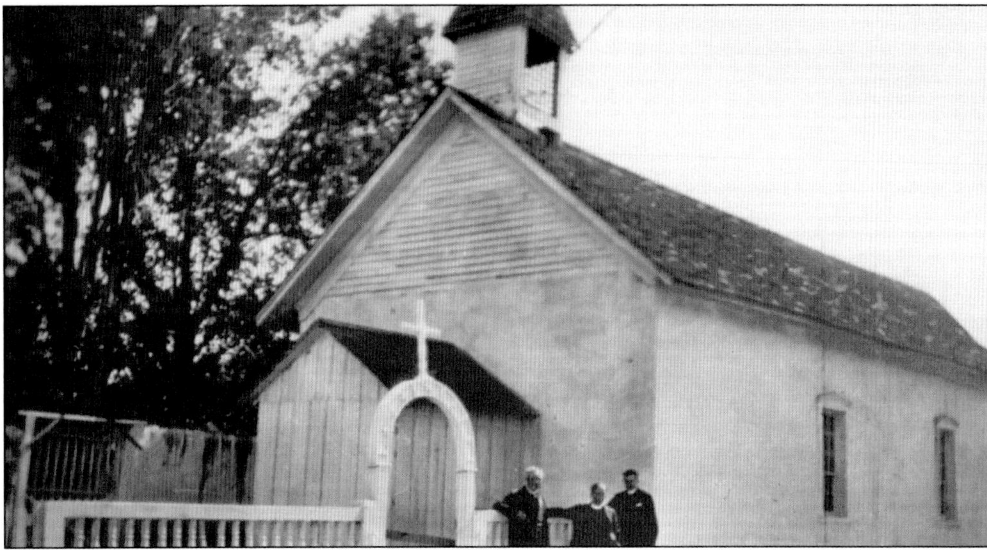

Fr. Luis Fernandez, shown here standing between two unidentified priests outside the first Catholic church in St. Johns, was the priest in St. Johns for 17 years and oversaw the building of the new Catholic church, which stands in St. Johns today, in the 1930s. (Courtesy Barbara Jaramillo.)

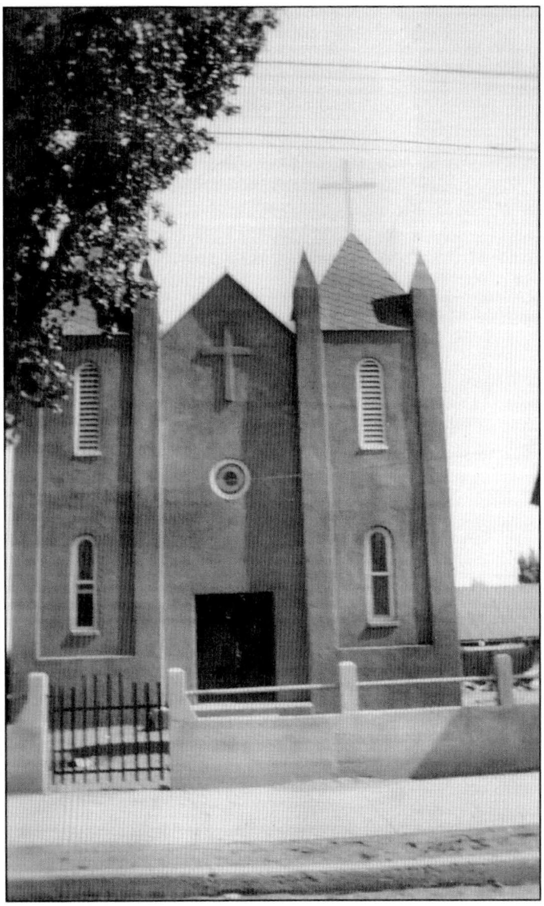

This picture shows the new San Juan de Baptista Catholic Church, built in the late 1930s. (Courtesy Barbara Jaramillo.)

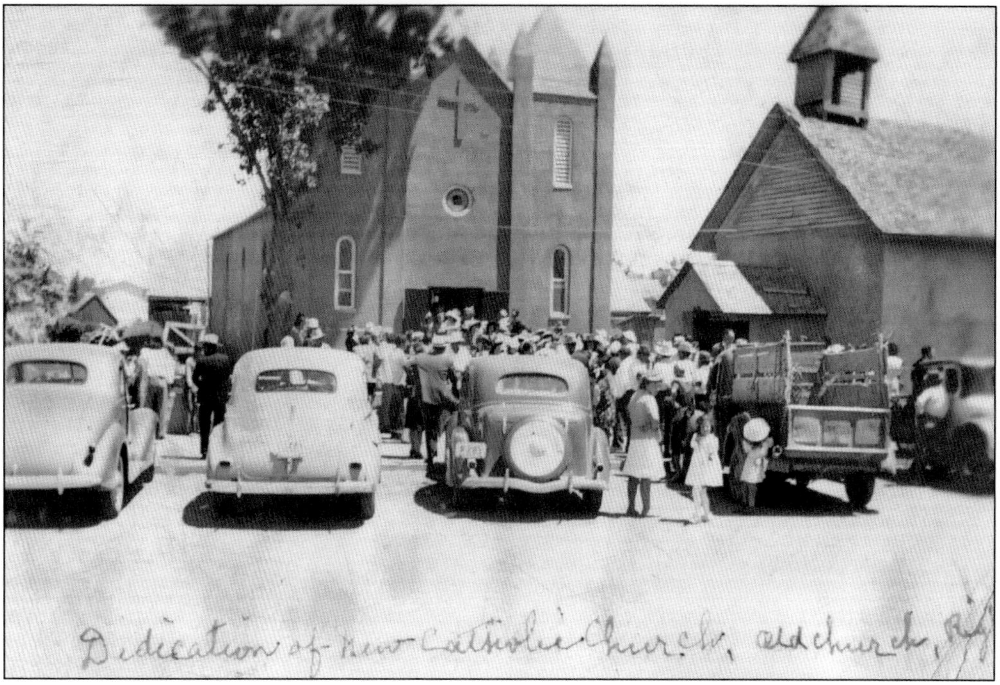

This picture was taken the day the new Catholic church was dedicated. (Courtesy Barbara Jaramillo.)

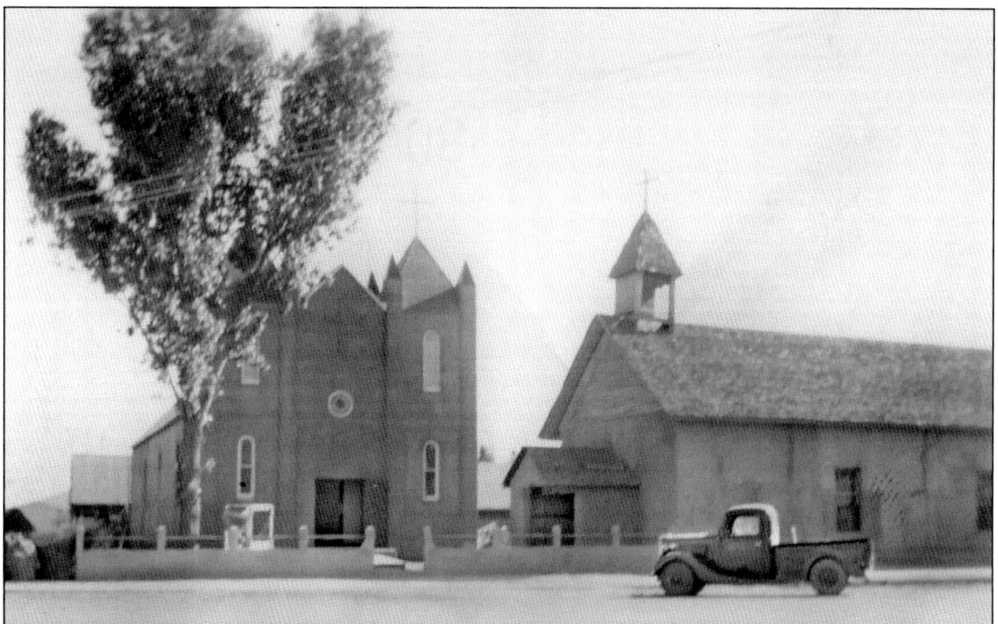

The new San Juan de Baptista Catholic Church (left) is shown here with the old one beside it. (Courtesy Barbara Jaramillo.)

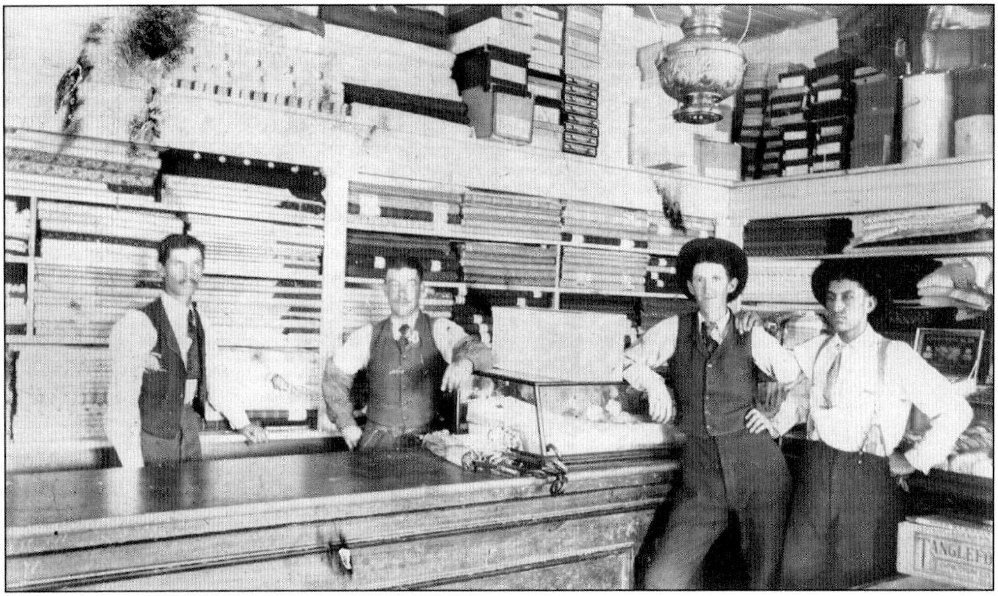

This photograph shows the inside of the Barth Mercantile in 1900. Pictured from left to right are Mahoy, Isaac Barth, St. George Creaghe, and Frank Ruiz. (Courtesy St. Johns Historical Society and Museum.)

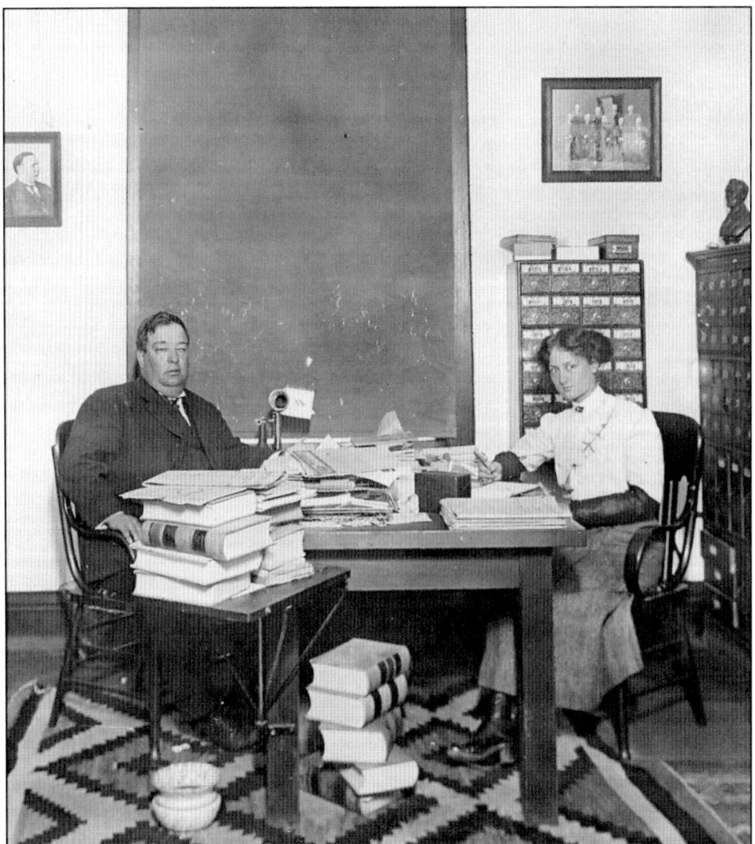

Sol Barth's eldest son Isaac is shown here with an unidentified woman inside his law office. (Courtesy St. Johns Historical Society and Museum.)

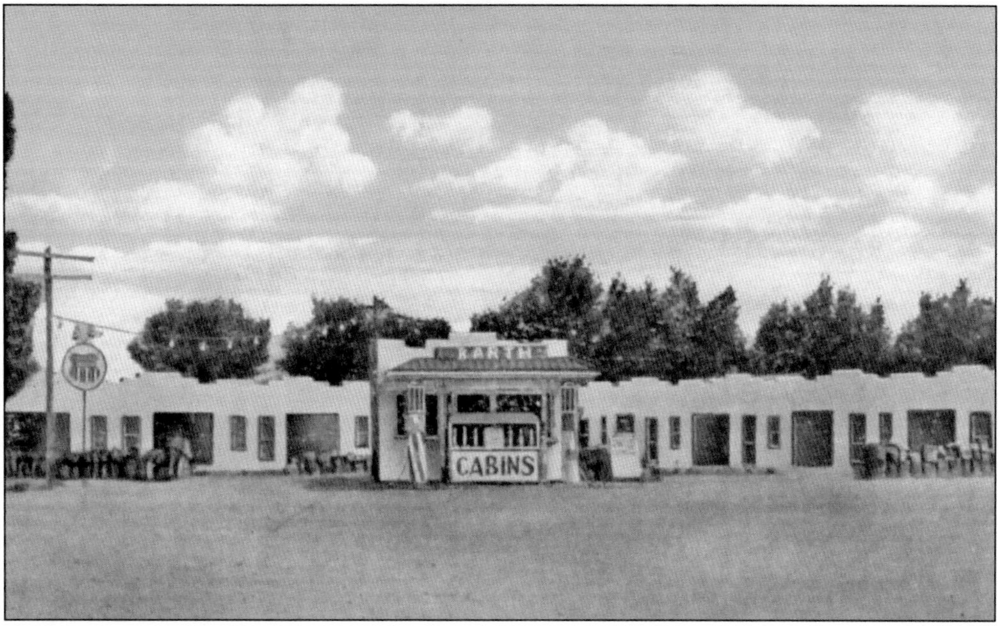

Barth Cottages and Motor Court, shown in this postcard, were built by the Barth family to lodge the weary traveler. (Courtesy Barbara Jaramillo.)

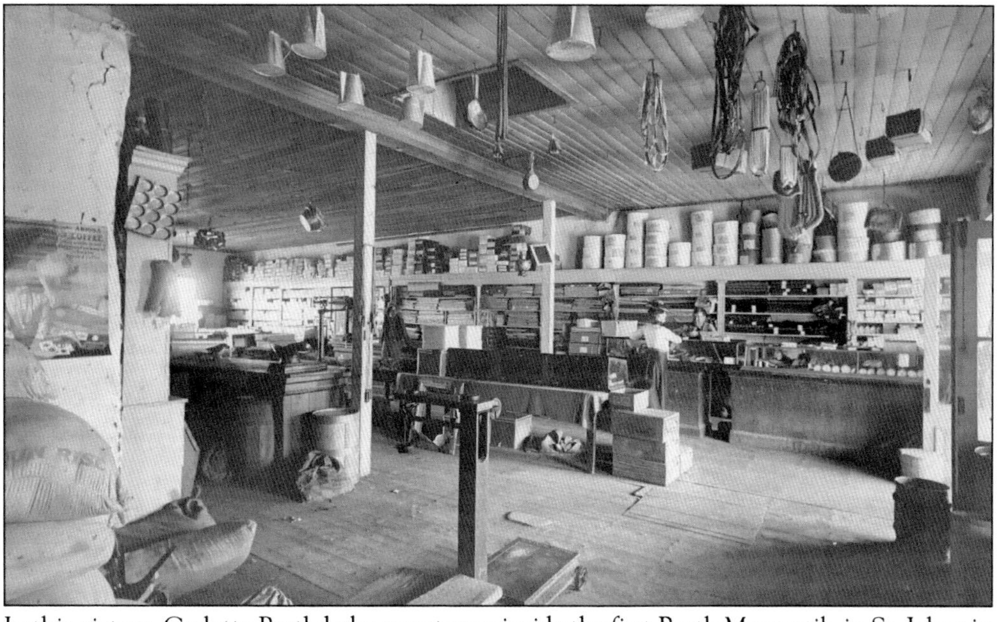

In this picture, Carlotta Barth helps a customer inside the first Barth Mercantile in St. Johns in the 1890s. (Courtesy St. Johns Historical Society and Museum.)

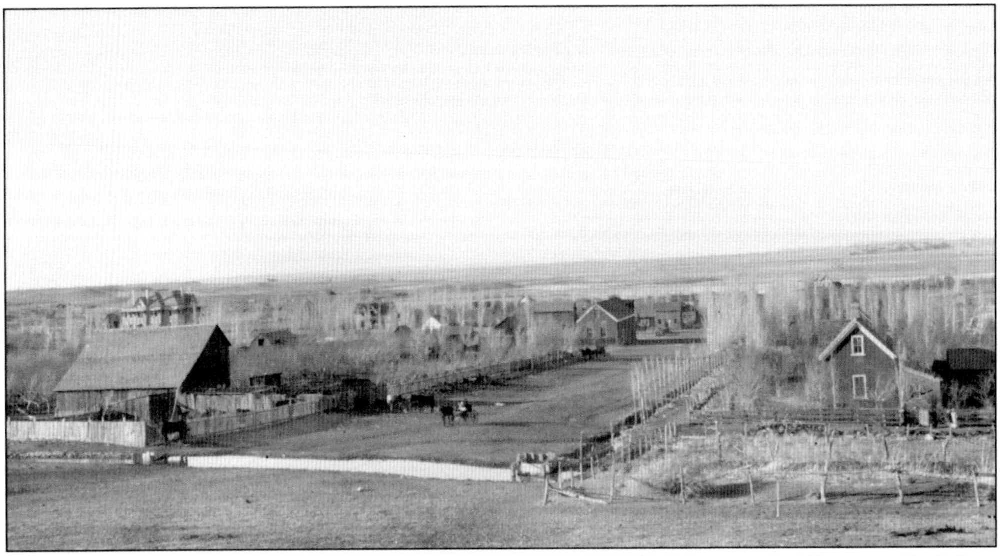

This picture was taken from the White School House in 1910 looking north. (Courtesy St. Johns Family History Center.)

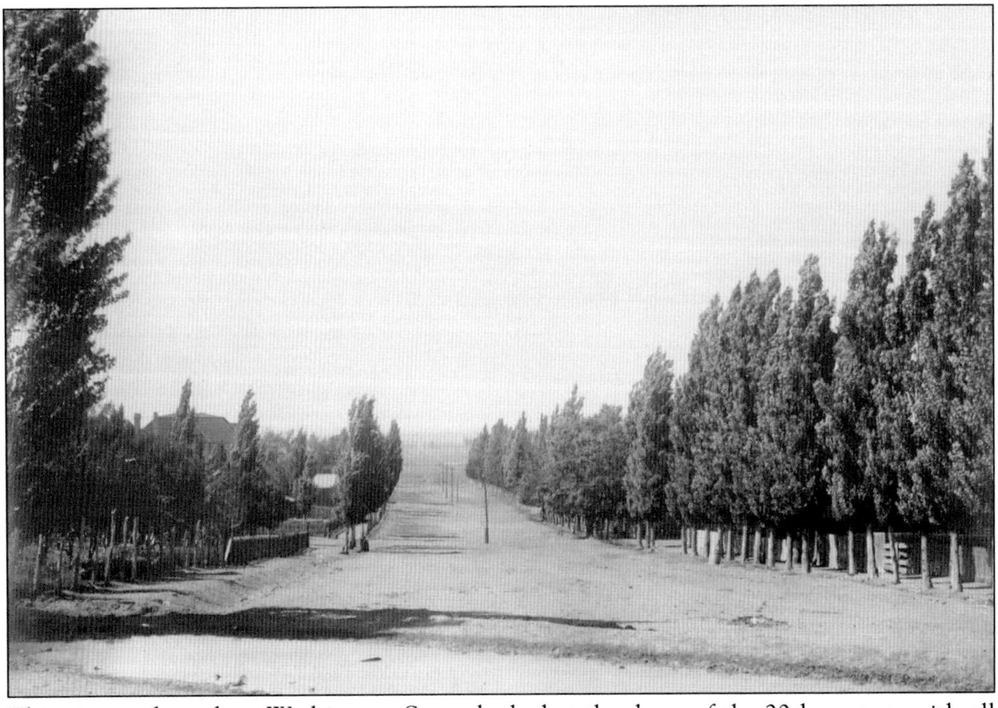

This picture shows how Washington Street looked at the dawn of the 20th century with all the poplar trees. Early settler Ralph Ramsey's son brought the Lombardy poplar seeds in his pouch to St. Johns and planted them along every ditch. (Courtesy St. Johns Historical Society and Museum.)

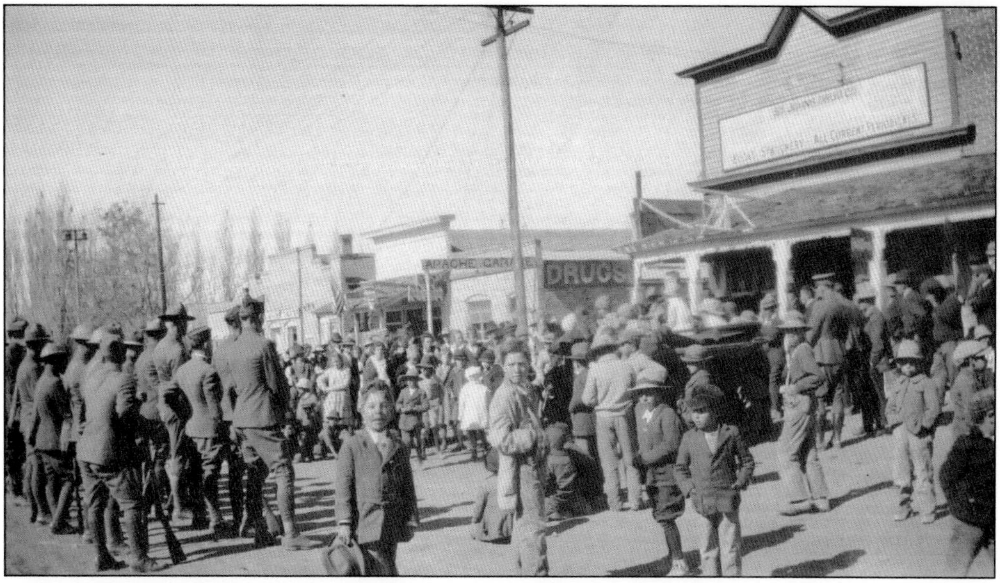

In this picture, a jubilant unidentified boy stares at the camera as the rest of the town celebrates the return of their sons, brothers, and friends from World War I. (Courtesy St. Johns Historical Society and Museum.)

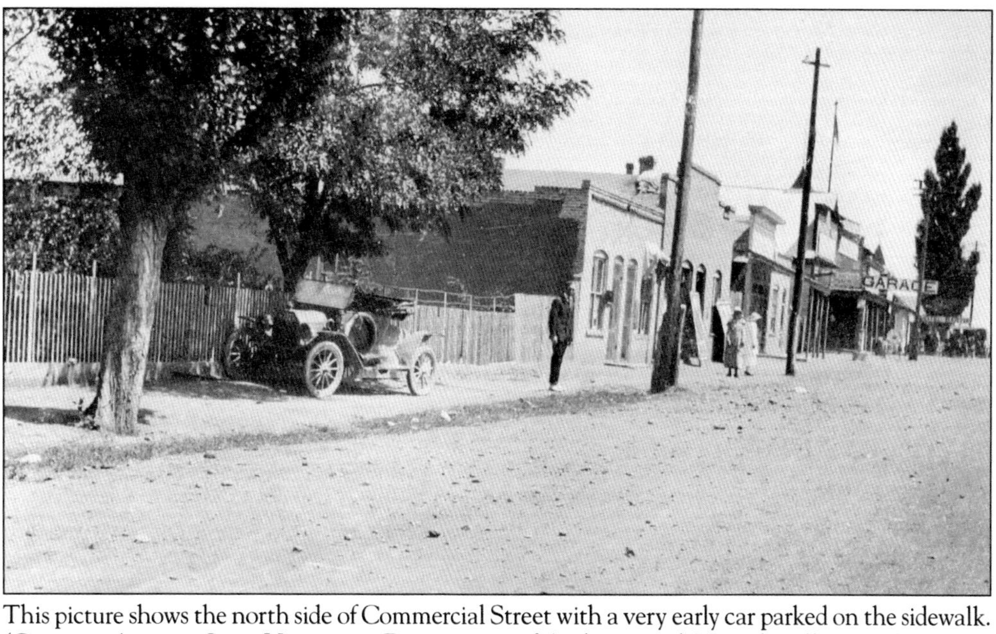

This picture shows the north side of Commercial Street with a very early car parked on the sidewalk. (Courtesy Arizona State University, Department of Archives and Special Collections.)

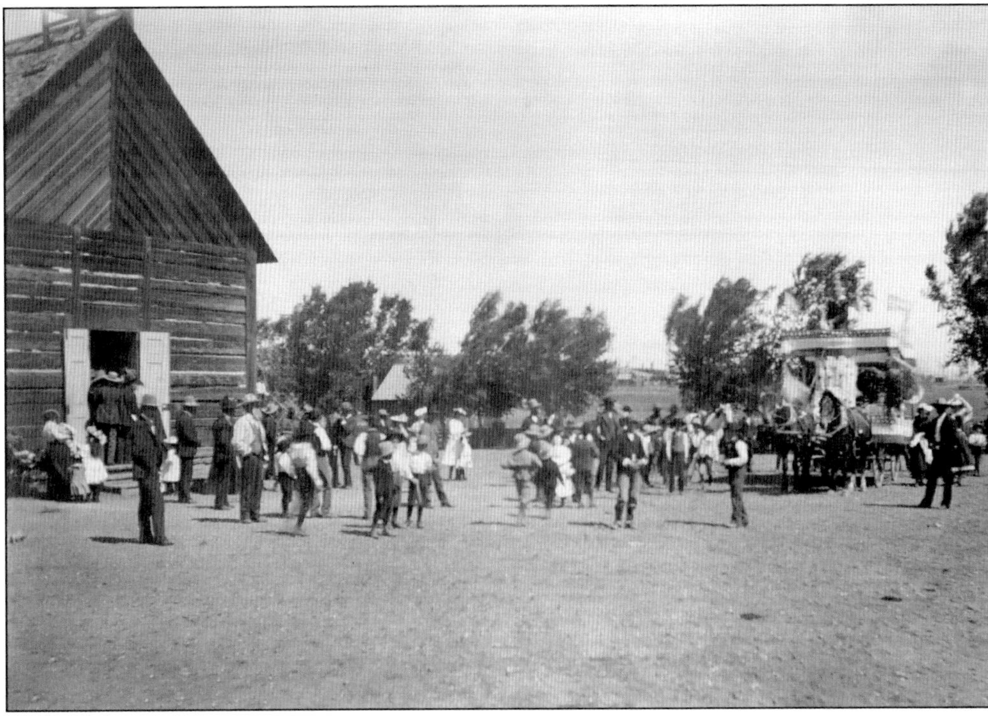

These pictures, taken in 1895, show the people of St. Johns in front of the Assembly Hall gathering for the Fourth of July parade. (Courtesy St. Johns Historical Society and Museum.)

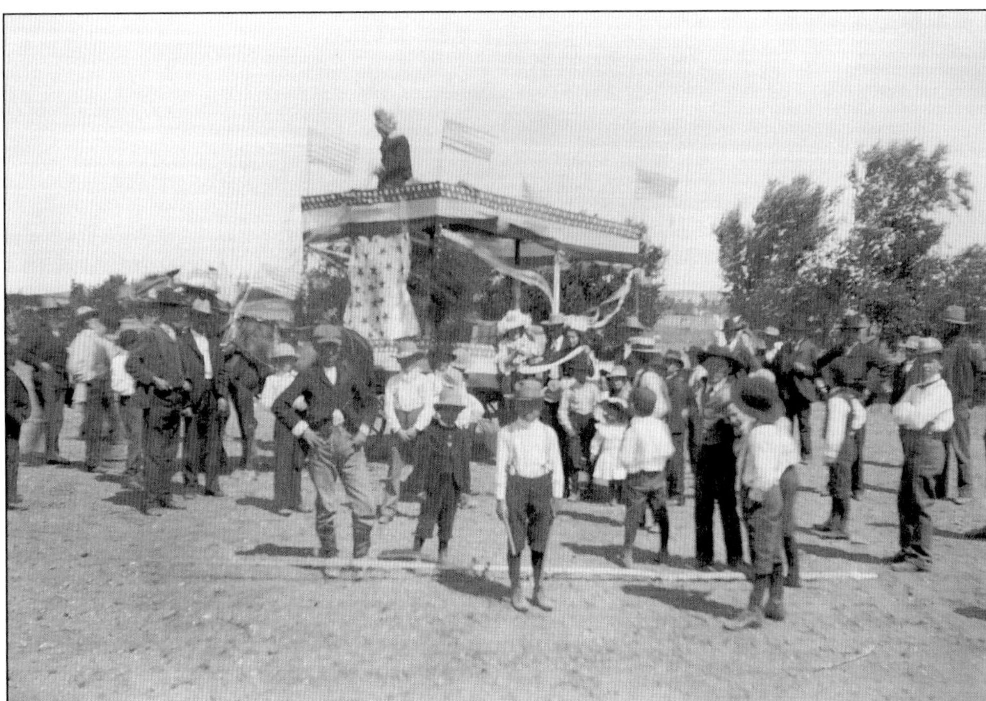

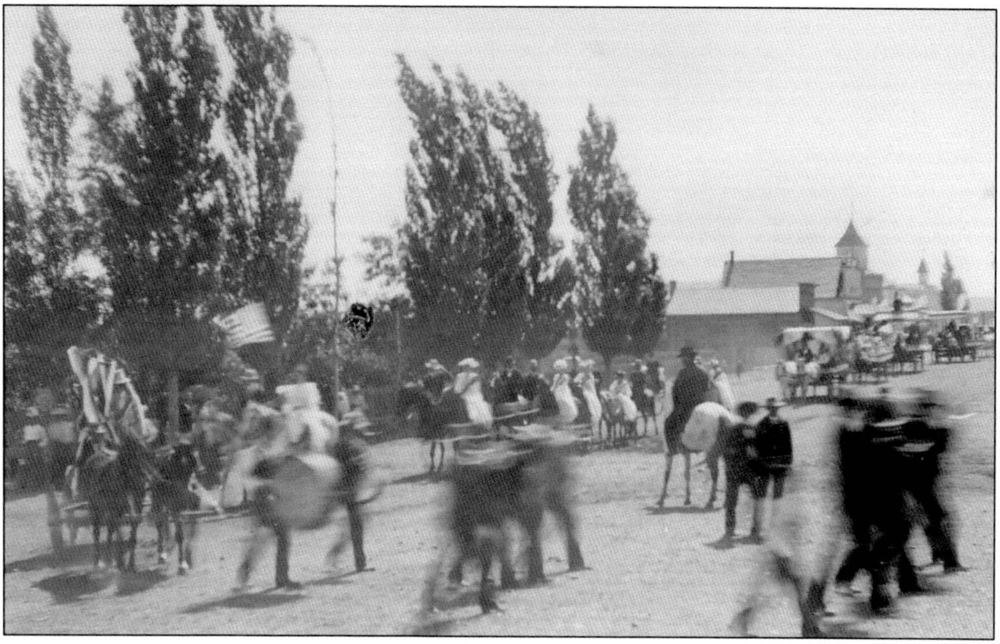

This picture shows the Fourth of July celebration parading down Commercial Street in 1895. (Courtesy St. Johns Historical Society and Museum.)

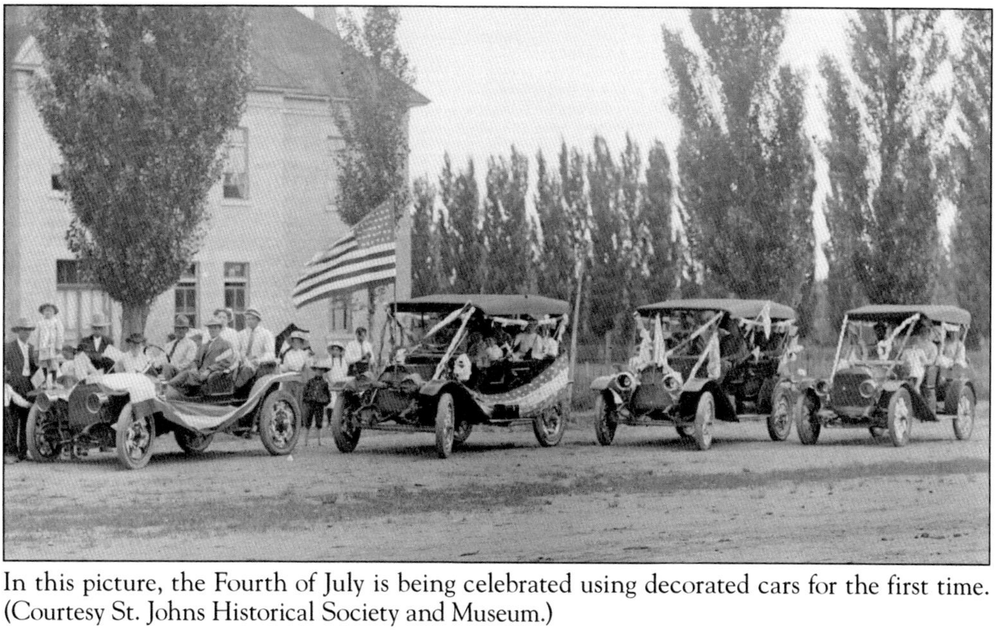

In this picture, the Fourth of July is being celebrated using decorated cars for the first time. (Courtesy St. Johns Historical Society and Museum.)

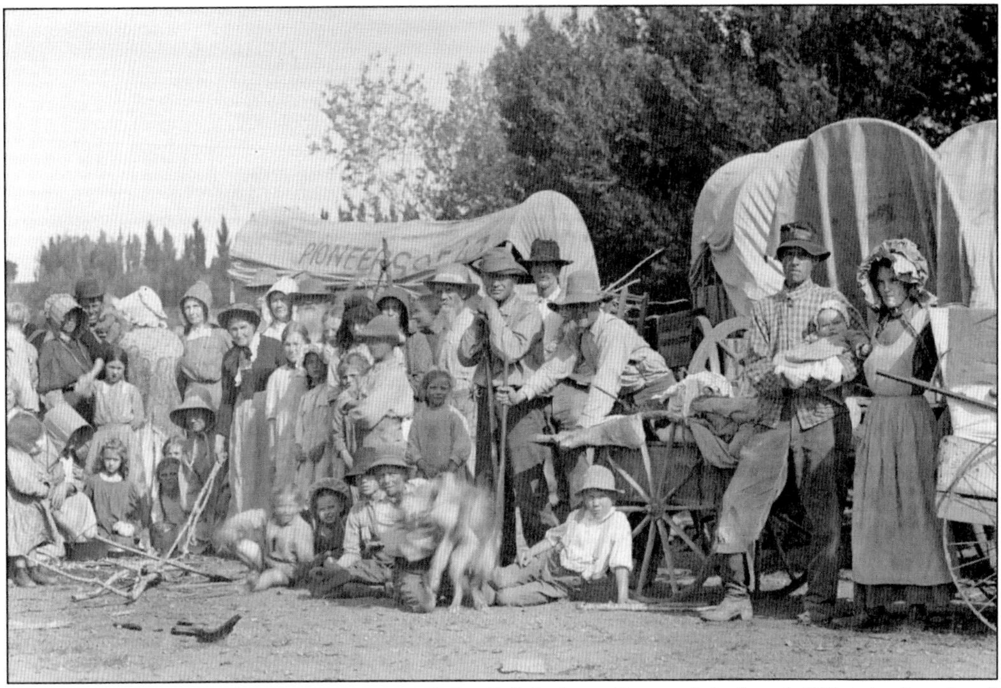

On July 24, 1849, Brigham Young entered the Salt Lake valley and declared, "This is the place" to a group of rather tired Mormons. Since then, Mormon communities have celebrated Pioneer Days every year on the weekend closest to July 24. Both these pictures show how the Mormons of St. Johns celebrated Pioneer Days in the early 1900s. (Both courtesy St. Johns Historical Society and Museum.)

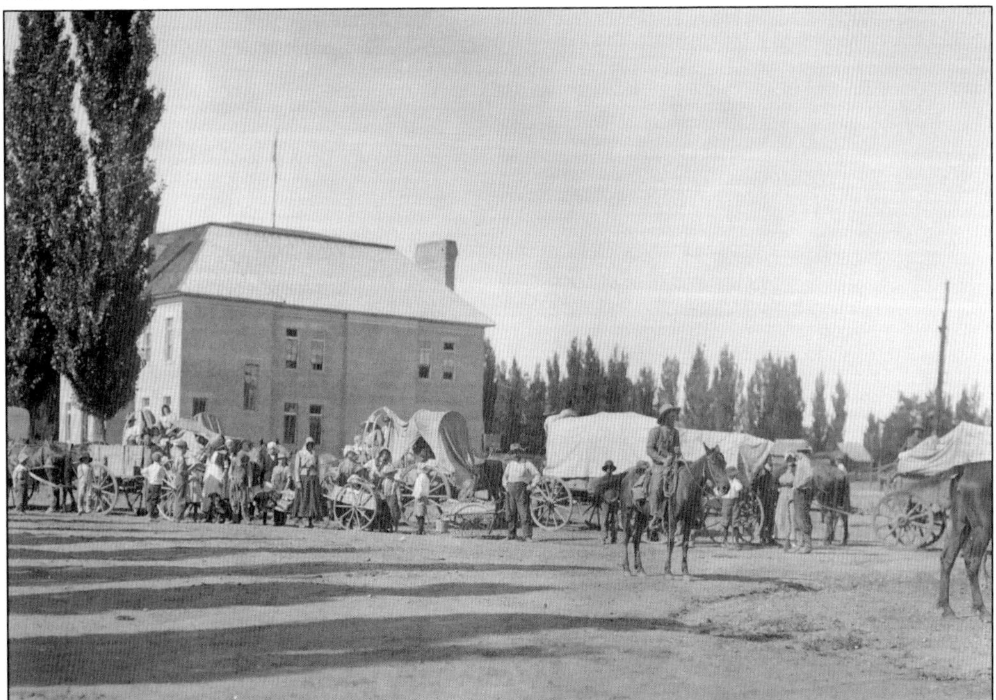

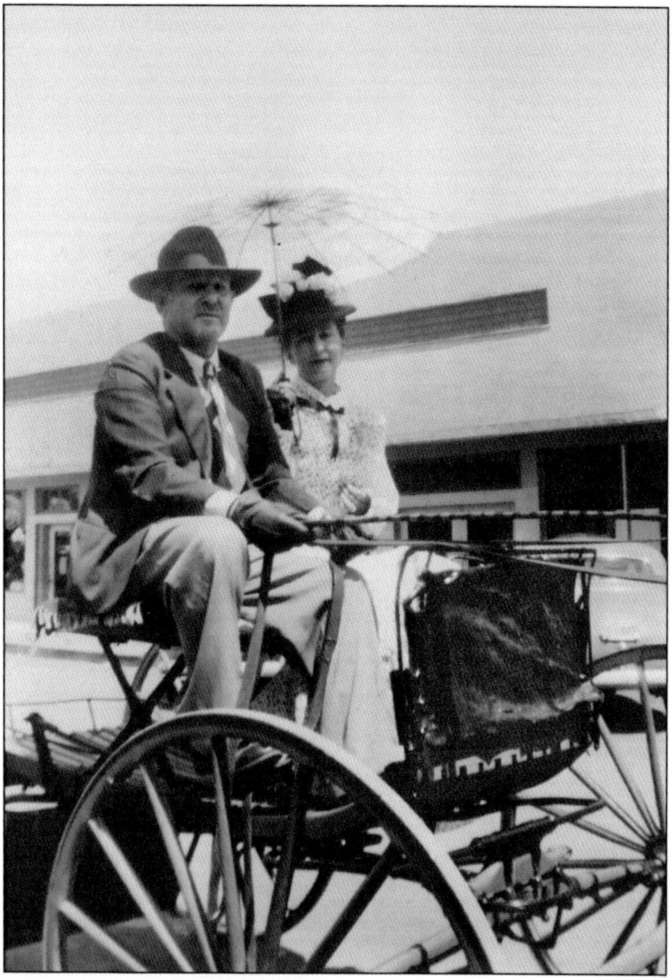

These pictures show the 1947 Pioneer Days celebration. At right are Jake and Allene Barth. (Both courtesy Barbara Jaramillo.)

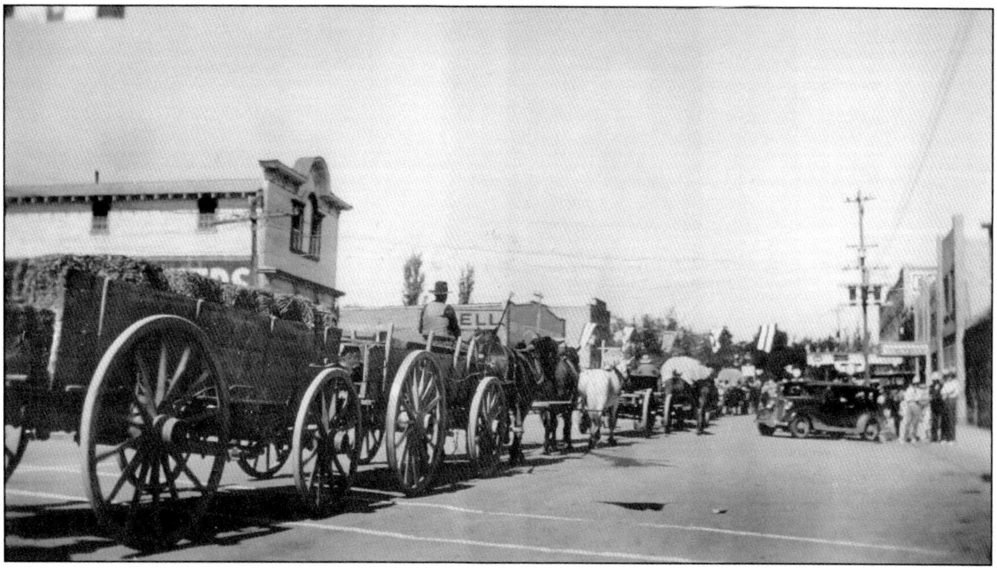

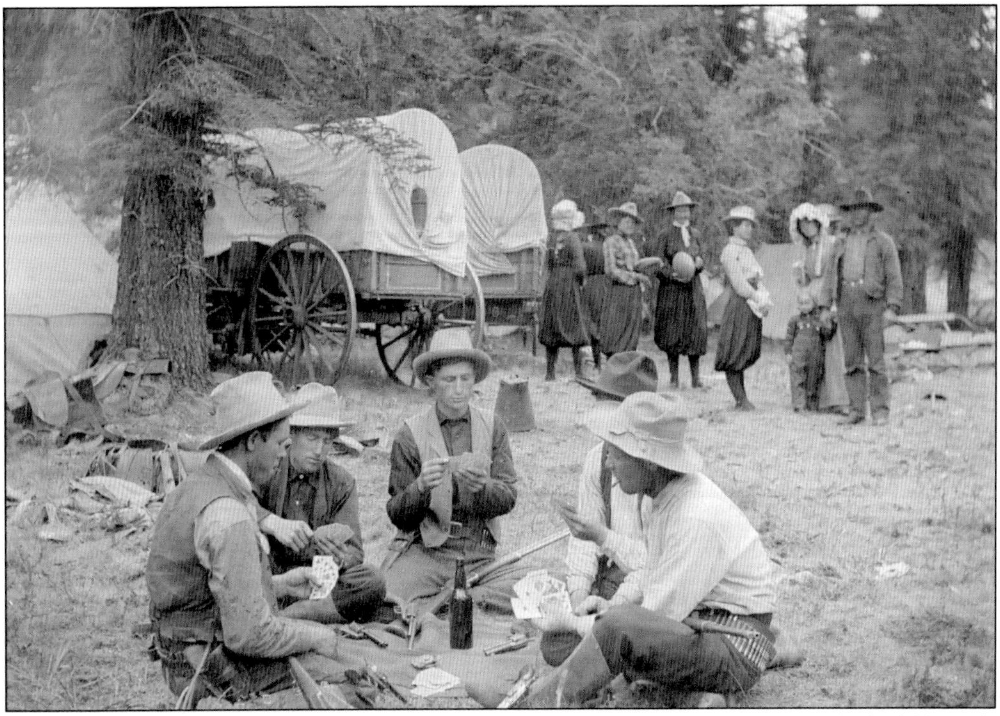

At the start of the 20th century, the Mormons decided to celebrate Pioneer Days a little differently by going to the White Mountains to camp, as shown in both of these pictures. (Both courtesy St. Johns Historical Society and Museum.)

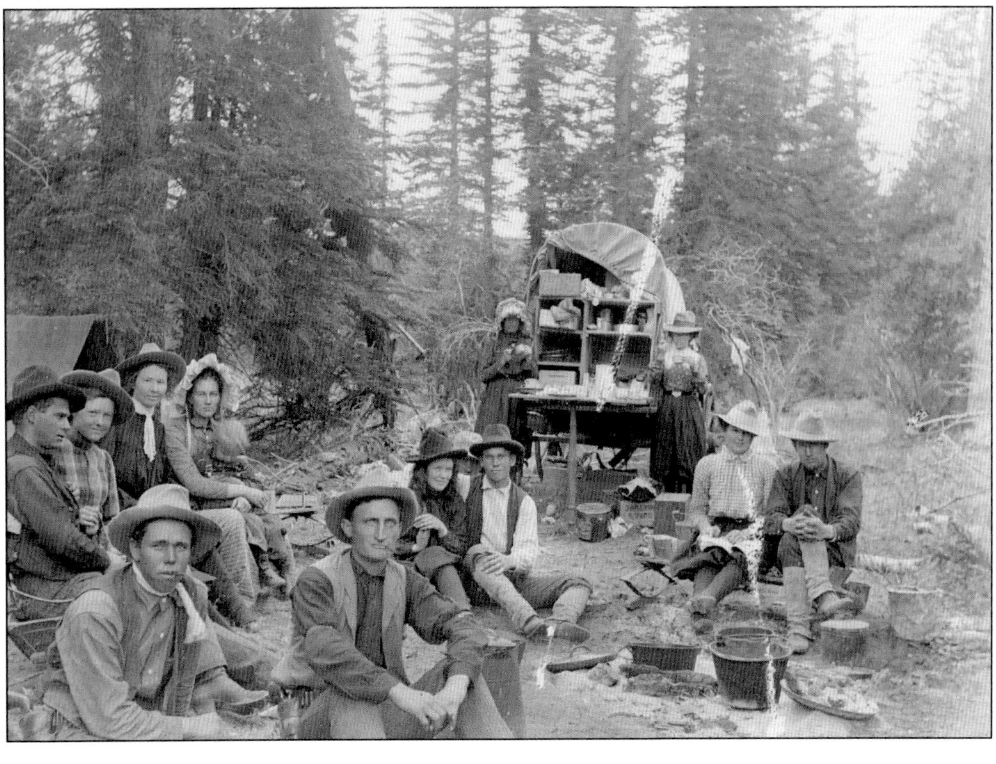

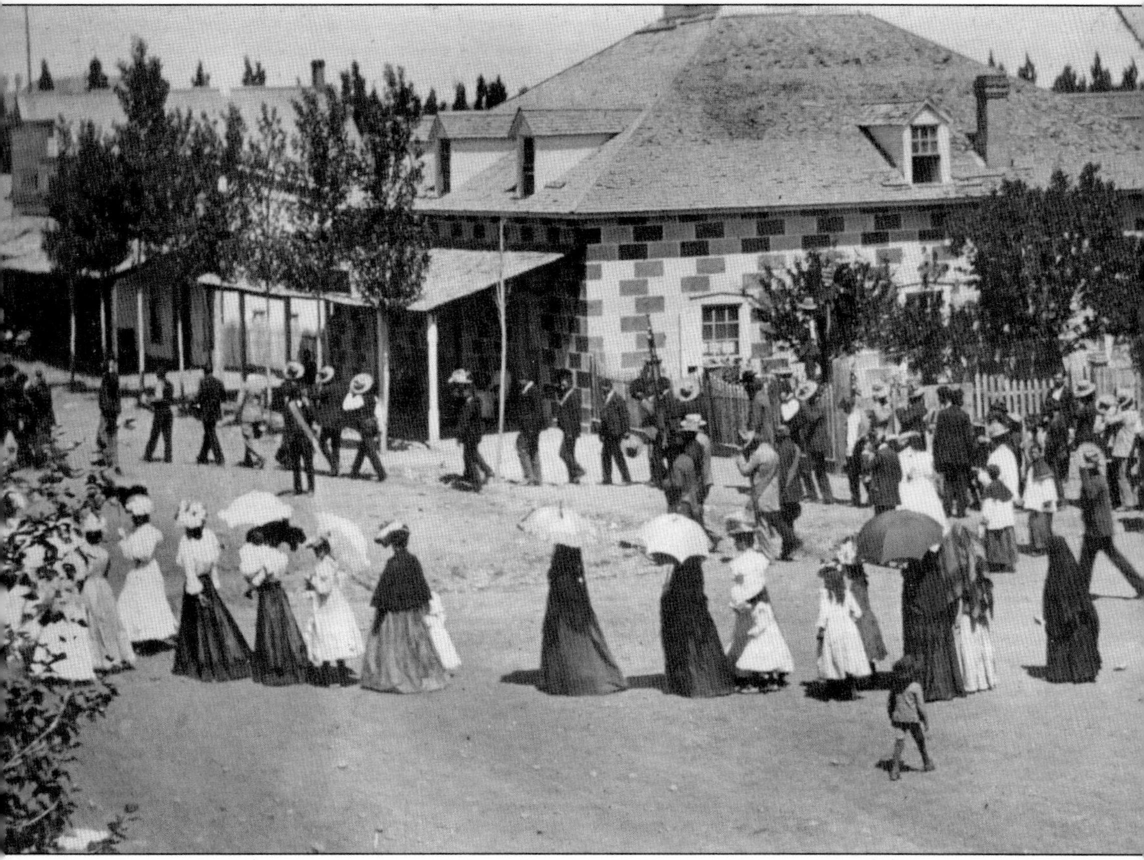

Every year on the weekend falling closest to June 24, the Catholic people celebrate the San Juan Fiesta in honor of St. John the Baptist, the patron saint for St. Johns. This picture shows the celebration in 1901. (Courtesy Barbara Jaramillo.)

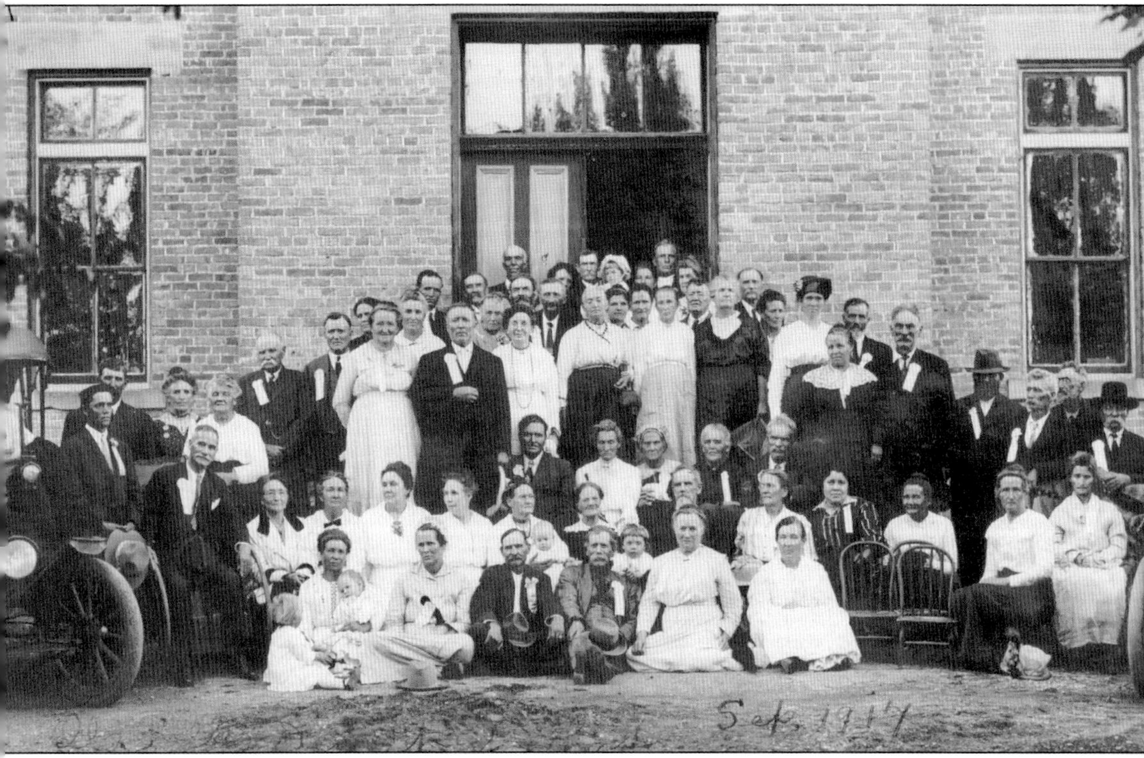

Shown here is the 1917 Early Settlers Day celebration, which used to be an annual event. This photograph has many of the original settlers. Pictured from left to right are (first row, seated) Mimie Richey holding an unidentified baby, Julia Greer, William Harris, Alex Shreeve, Amelia Peterson, and Annie Tenney; (second row) unidentified, Joseph B. Patterson (in wheelchair), Emily Patterson, Ruth Sherwood, Suzie Tenney, Charlotte Sherwood, Elizabeth Gibbons and unidentified baby, Catherine Waite and baby Katy, Solomon Waite, Refugio Barth, Josephine Schuster, Sadie Berry, Elsina Isaacson, Ada Plumb, and Henry Overson; (third row) Benjamin Richey (seated), Eliza Richey, Mrs. ? Wilson, Anna Maria Whiting, and Edwin M. Whiting; (fourth row) William W. Berry (face partially obscured), Rachel Berry, Frances Mineer with husband August behind her, John Brown (behind August), Thurza Brown, David K. Udall, Ella Udall, Claudina Jensen, Edna Shreeve, Amanda Thomas, Isaac Isaacson, Julia Johnson, Nettie McCray, Charles Whiting, Marion Jolley (in front of Charles), John Jolley (beside Charles), Thomas Berry, Andrew Gibbons, John Plumb, and Sol Barth; (fifth row, beginning behind John Brown) Nett Greenwood, Cynthia Brown, Margaret Jarvis, Moroni Richey, M. H. Peterson, Verona Whiting, Suzie Jarvis, and Heber Jarvis; (sixth row, beginning behind Cynthia Brown) Peter Peterson, Charles Jarvis, Willard Farr, Mary E. B. Farr, David Rencher holding an unidentified child, Bashebe Rencher, John T. Patterson, and Lizzie Patterson. (Courtesy St. Johns Family History Center.)

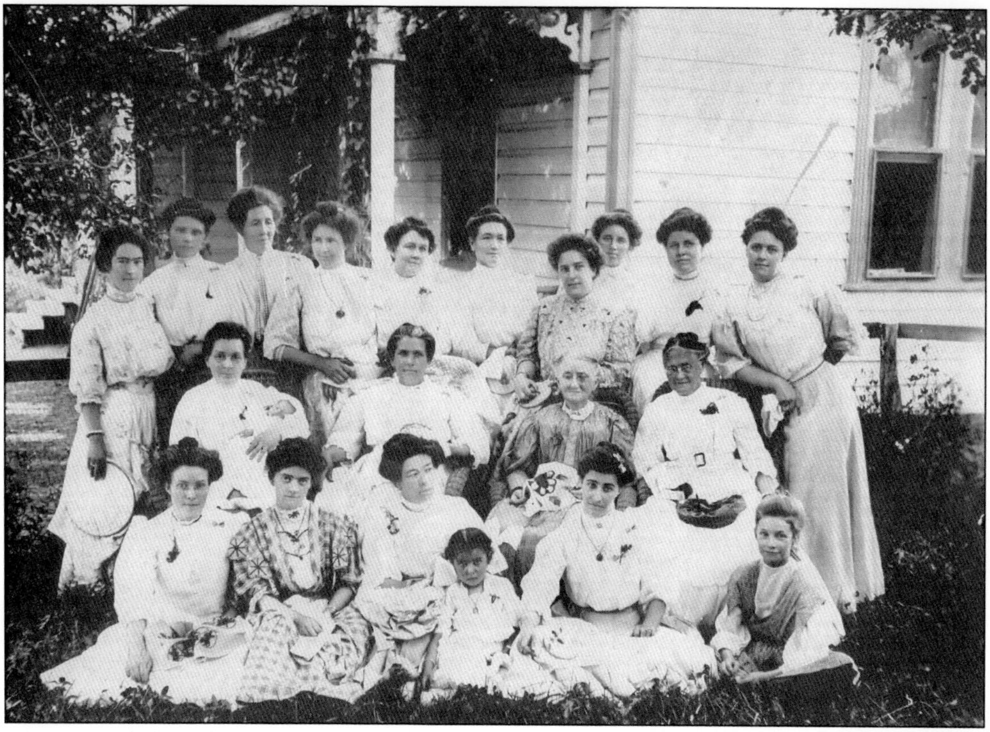

Women and their daughters got together for many reasons, like cross-stitching, shown here. Pictured from left to right are (first row) Charlotte Sherwood, Chessie Barth, Clara Barth, Ricka Backstein, Mrs. Paul Geary, and Mona Patterson; (second row) Ella Udall, Refugio Barth, Nellie Greer, and Mary Hogue; (third row) Cecilia Barth, Ida Rudd, Lou Knight, Charlotte "Lottie" Baker, Suzie Tenney, Emily Patterson, Adeliada Backstein, Alice Berry, Josephine Schuster, and Mrs. Roberts. (Courtesy Barbara Jaramillo.)

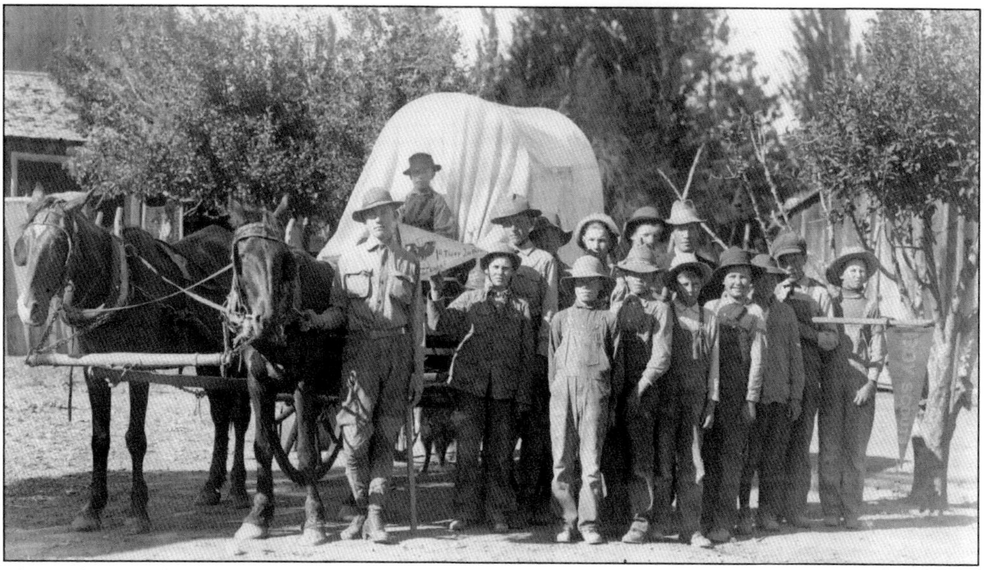

Shown here is the first Boy Scout troop in St. Johns, with George H. Crosby in charge. (Courtesy St. Johns Family History Center.)

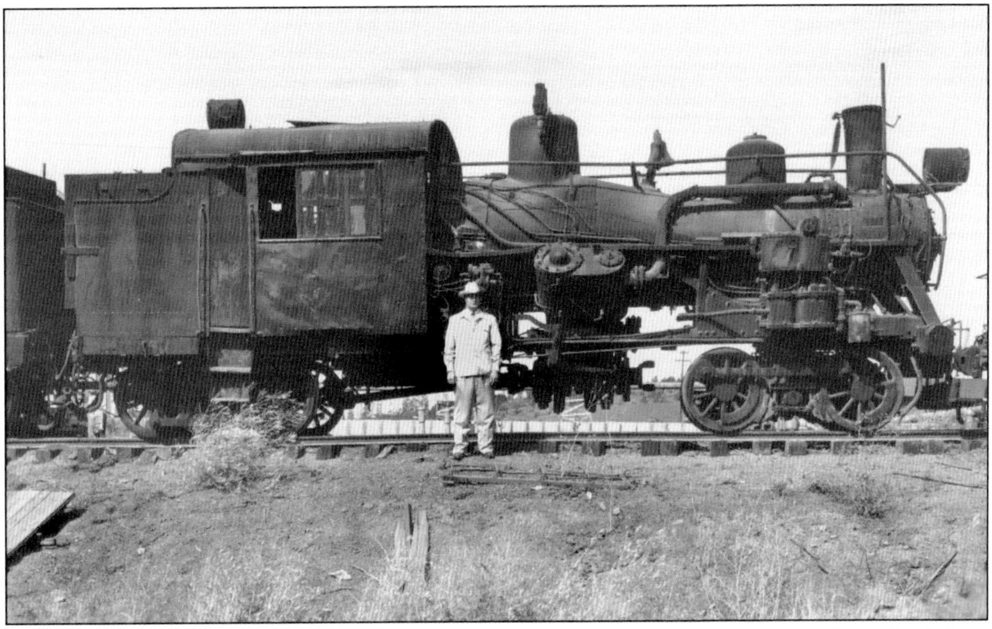

The Atlantic and Pacific Railroad was built through Holbrook, about 50 miles from St. Johns, in the early 1880s and served as the first connection St. Johns really had to the big world outside its borders. Here an unidentified man stands in front of a train. (Courtesy St. Johns Family History Center.)

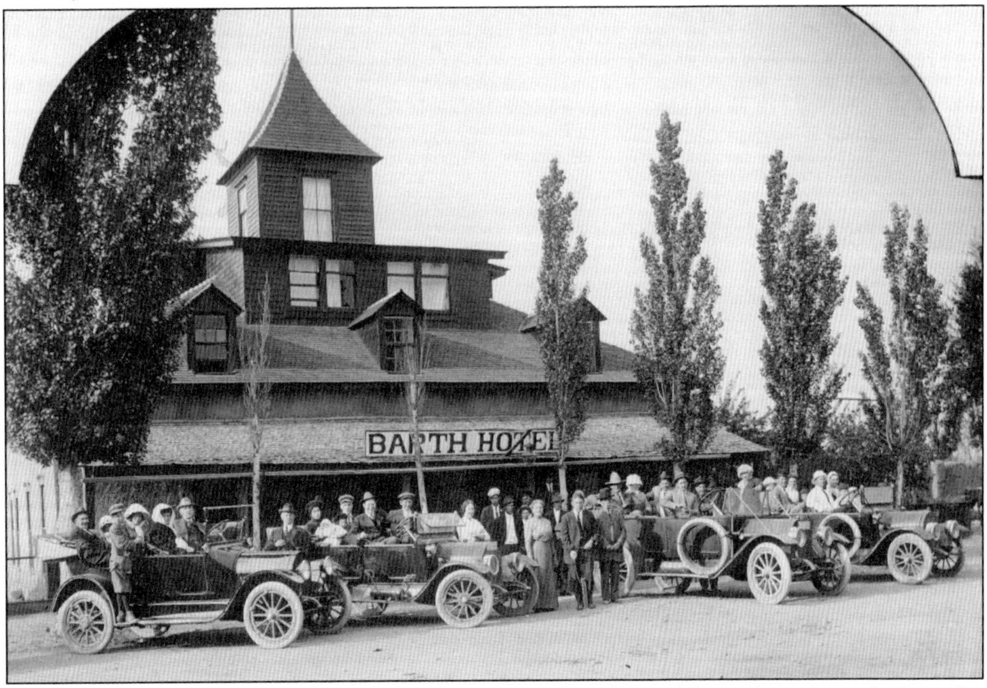

Although the railroad served as a connection to the rest of the world, cars brought with them the hope of faster travel to other places. In this picture, Gustav Becker, previously on the board of directors for the Arizona Good Roads Association, and his family park in front of the Barth Hotel to promote the newly released automobile. (Courtesy St. Johns Historical Society and Museum.)

Route 66 was what first really connected St. Johns to the rest of the world. In this picture, some Route 66 workers pose in front of the sign indicating the area of the legendary highway they helped build. (Author collection.)

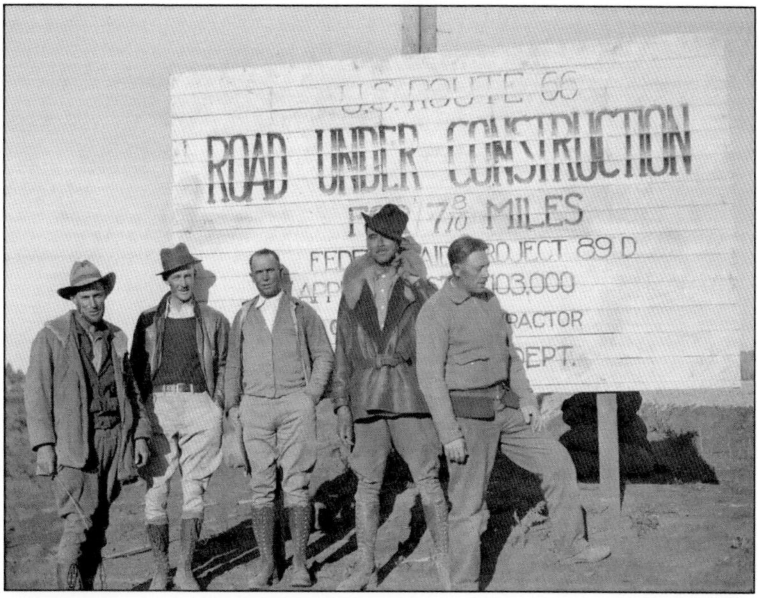

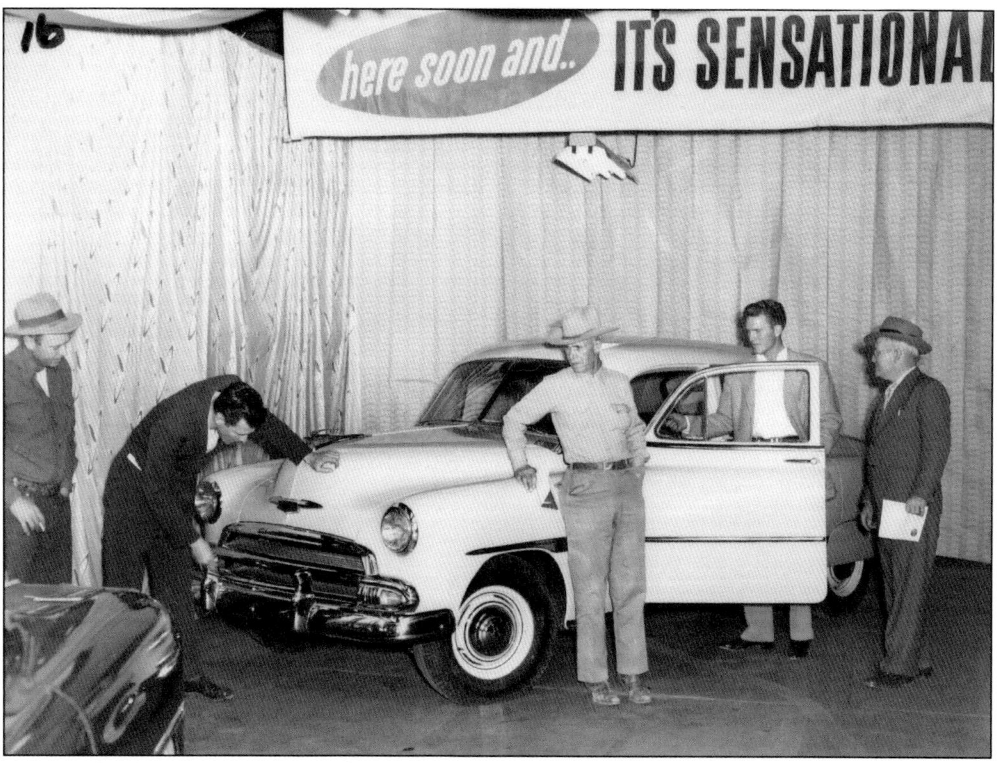

In 1922, Joy B. Patterson opened Patterson Motor Company, the first Chevrolet dealership in northern Arizona. In this picture, Joy's son-in-law John Bast checks out the grille of a new Chevy as an unidentified man and Tom Jones (leaning against the car) look on. Joy's son Jay Patterson is standing in the open door, and Marion Gibbons is beside him. (Courtesy St. Johns Family History Center.)

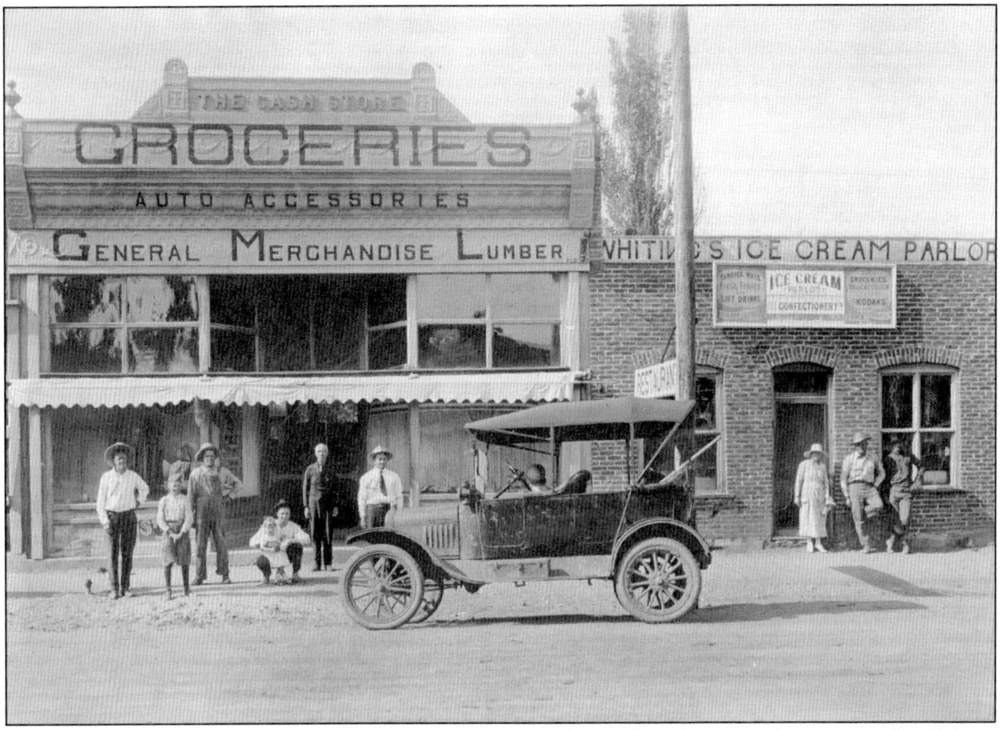

Whiting's Cash Store, which sold groceries and general merchandise, was first opened by Edwin Marion Whiting in 1901. Shown from left to right are Robert Overson, Ward Heap, three unidentified people, Willard Farr, Elmer Berry, and three unidentified people. (Courtesy St. Johns Historical Society and Museum.)

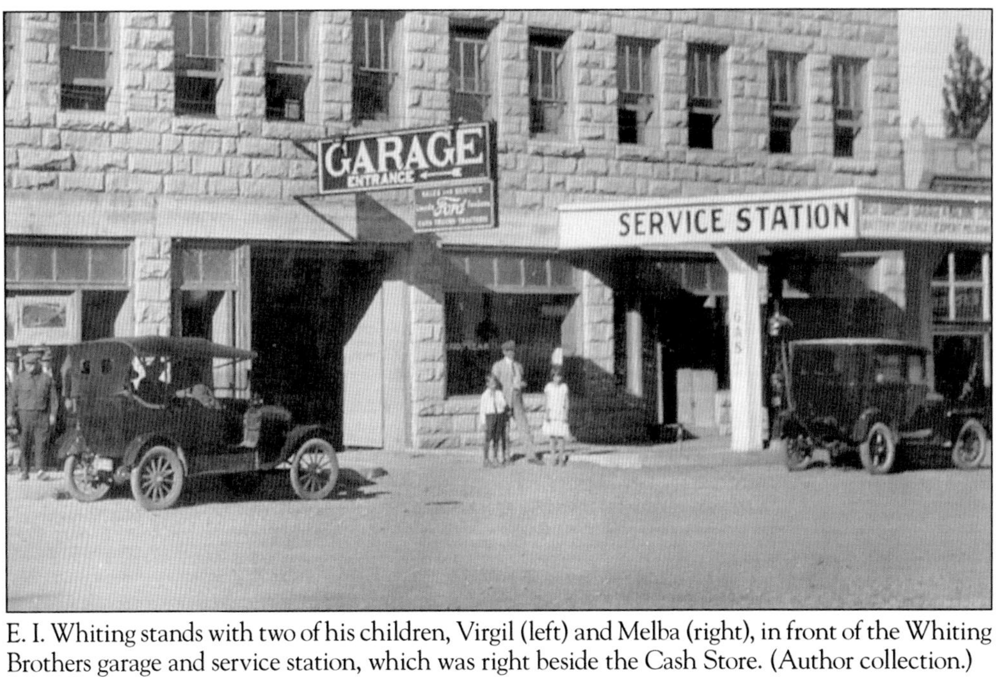

E. I. Whiting stands with two of his children, Virgil (left) and Melba (right), in front of the Whiting Brothers garage and service station, which was right beside the Cash Store. (Author collection.)

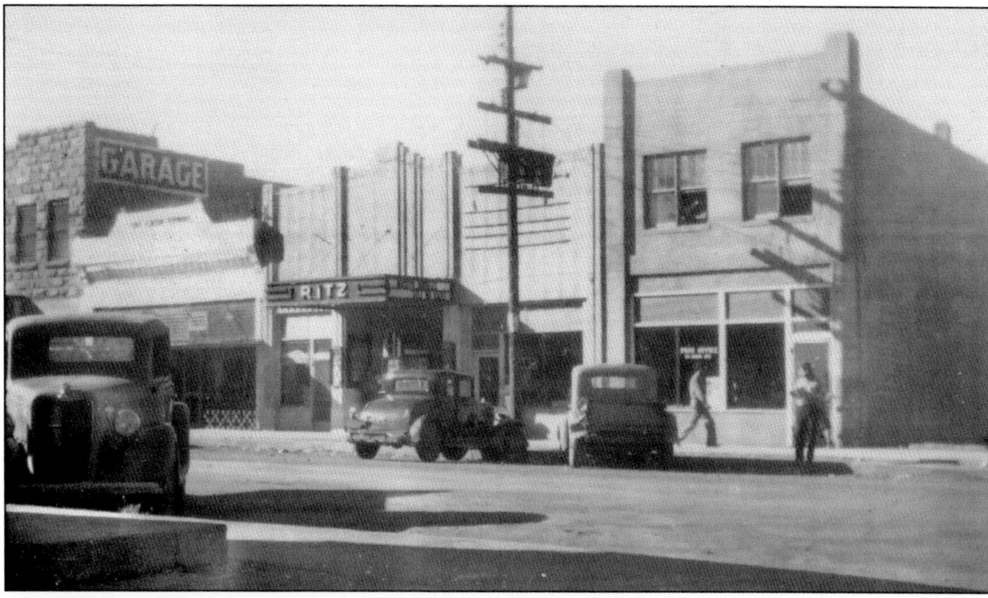

The Whiting Block contained the first Whiting Brothers service station, the Cash Store, a mercantile, and the Ritz Theater among other things. In March 1942, a butane tank connection broke inside the garage and caused an explosion. The heat from the burning garage caused a second butane tank on the back of a truck to explode. The force of the explosion not only broke windows in the homes within a five-block radius, but it shot through the Whiting garage at terrific speed, killing Marion Wilhelm and Sheriff John Nunn in the process. Members of the town assembled and tried to put out the blaze, but in the end it proved too much and all retreated to watch it burn down the entire block. When the flames had died down, E. I. Whiting and his wife, Ethel, went to assess the damage; a smoldering cash register lay in the snow rung up to "No Sale." E. I. turned to his wife and said, "Well, I guess we've lost everything Ethel, how do you feel?" To which Ethel responded, "I feel fine." (Both author collection.)

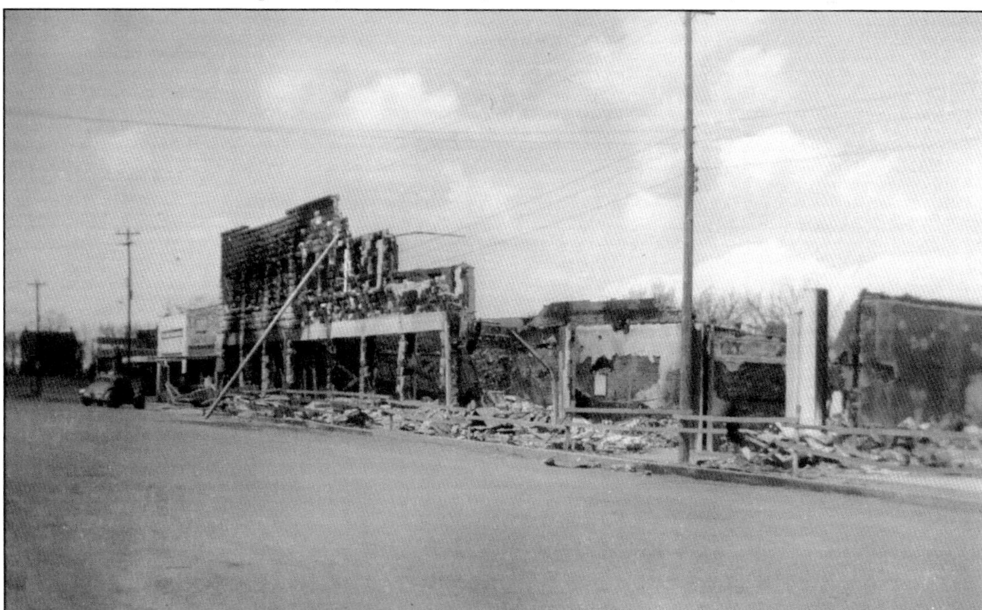

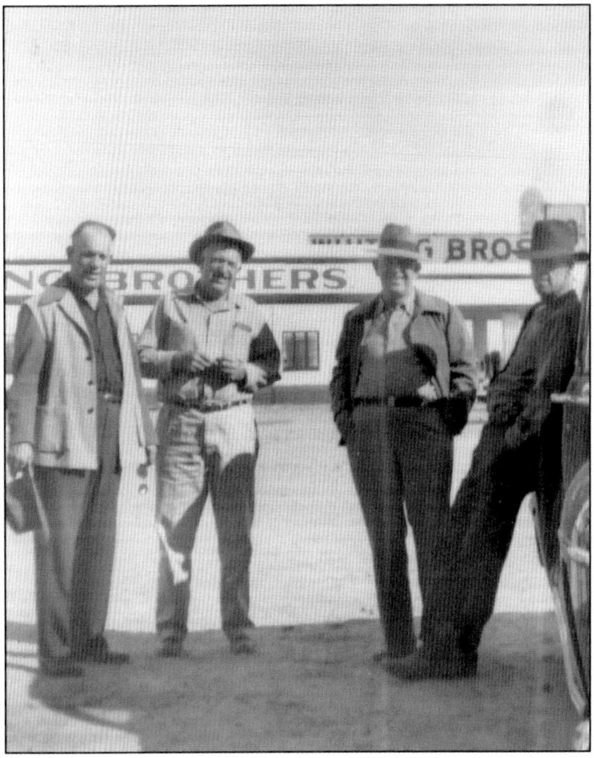

The Whiting brothers are pictured here outside one of their service stations. The yellow-and-maroon W/B sign advertising "quality gas for less" was a familiar sight for over 1,000 miles of Route 66. From left to right they are Arthur, Ernest, Eddie "E. I.," and Ralph. (Author collection.)

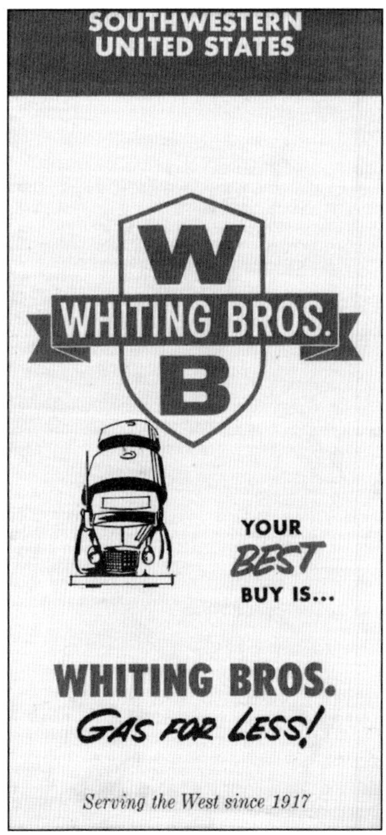

This Whiting Brothers map advertises "Whiting's Gas for Less." (Author collection.)

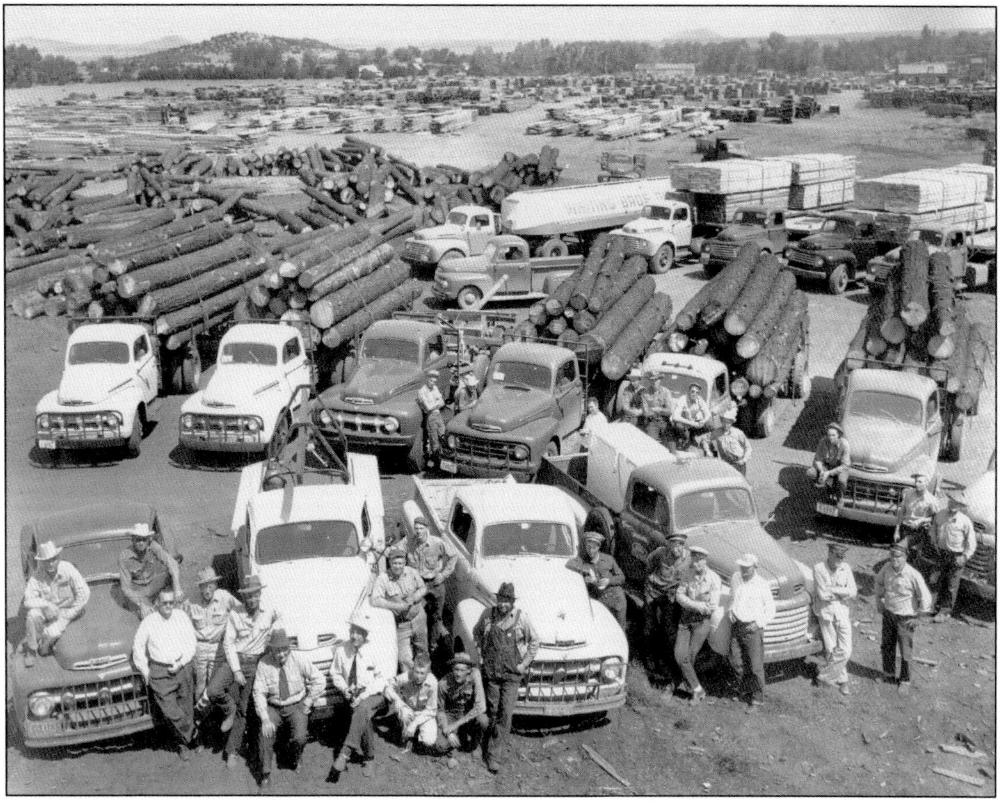

This photograph was a Ford advertisement taken at the Whiting Brothers sawmill in Eagar, Arizona. Pictured from left to right are Wilford Shumway, Sherwood Udall (both sitting on the hood of the truck at front left), two unidentified people, Virgil Whiting, unidentified, and E. I. Whiting. The rest are unidentified employees. (Author collection.)

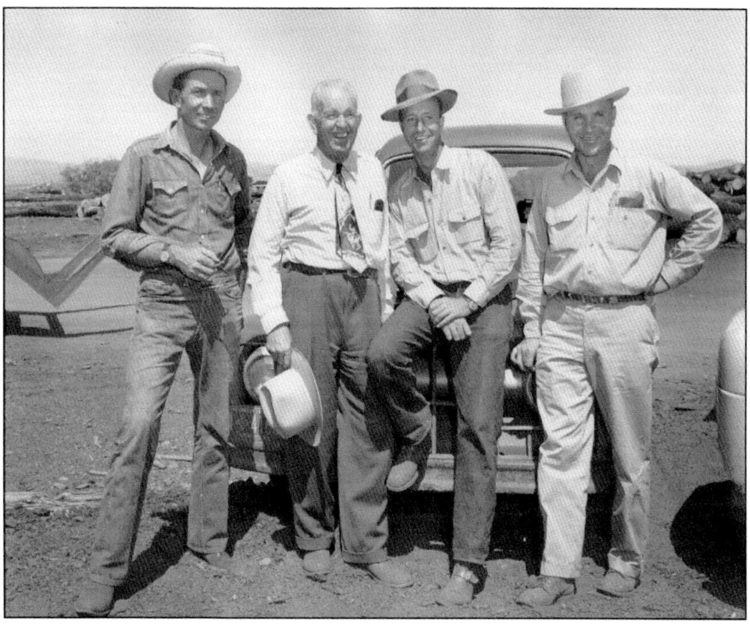

E. I. Whiting is pictured here with his sons-in-law Sherwood Udall (far left) and Wilford Shumway (far right) and son Virgil (beside E. I). (Author collection.)

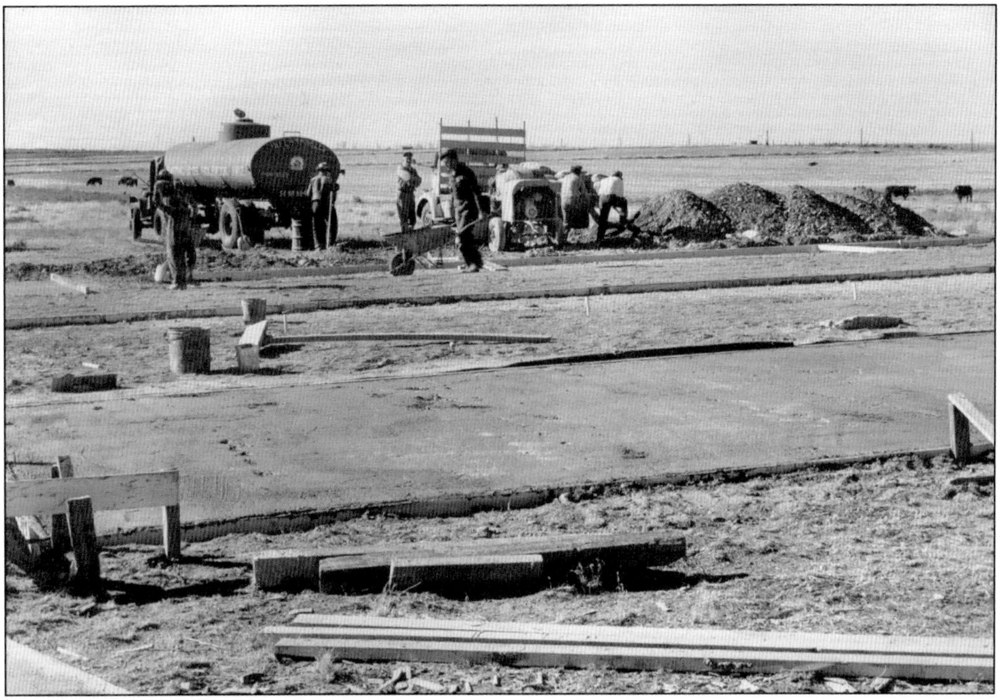

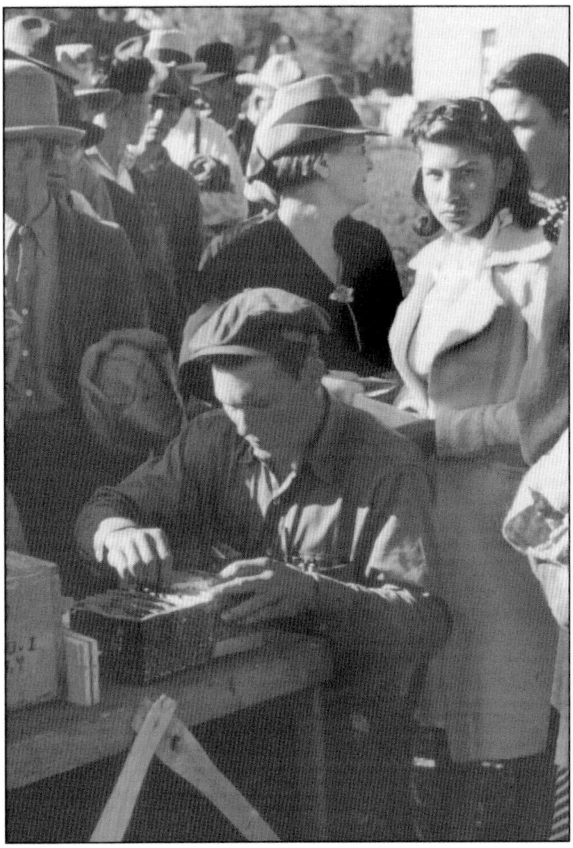

Whiting Brothers had a box factory, shown here being built, which was the first industrial undertaking in St. Johns. The factory employed 20 men and made government ammunition boxes. (Author collection.)

Giving back to their community in more ways than one, government relief workers distribute food in St. Johns. (Library of Congress.)

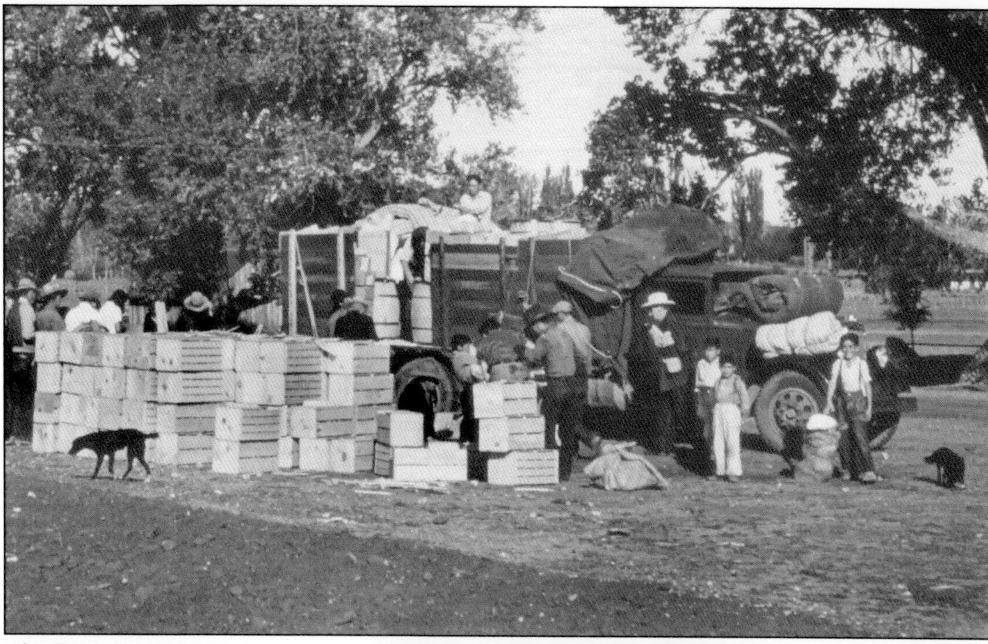

The Farm Security Administration was created in 1937 as a New Deal program designed to assist Americans. In order to better aid people, the government hired photographers to record and document rural living conditions throughout the United States. In October 1940, photographer Russell Lee arrived in St. Johns and photographed government relief workers distributing surplus commodities to grateful citizens (and dogs) in St. Johns. (Both courtesy Library of Congress.)

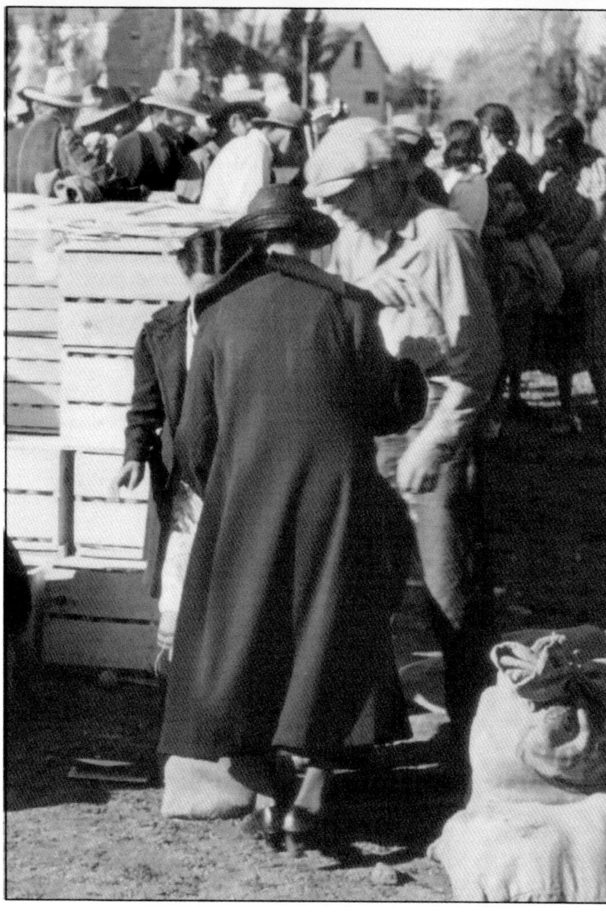

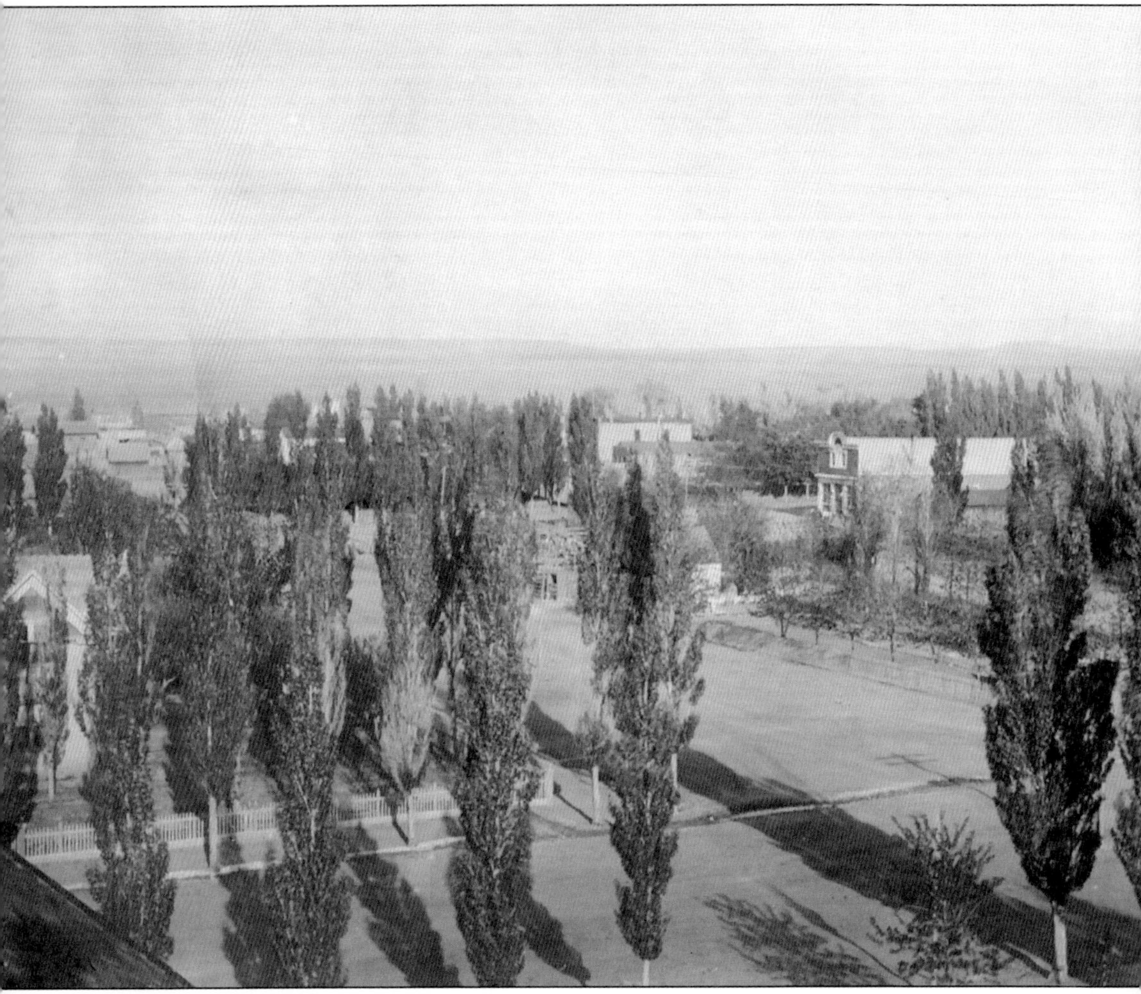

People would come from all over to see St. Johns, known as "Poplar Town" for the Lombardy poplars that lined every ditch. The wide streets and neat homes with white picket fences can be

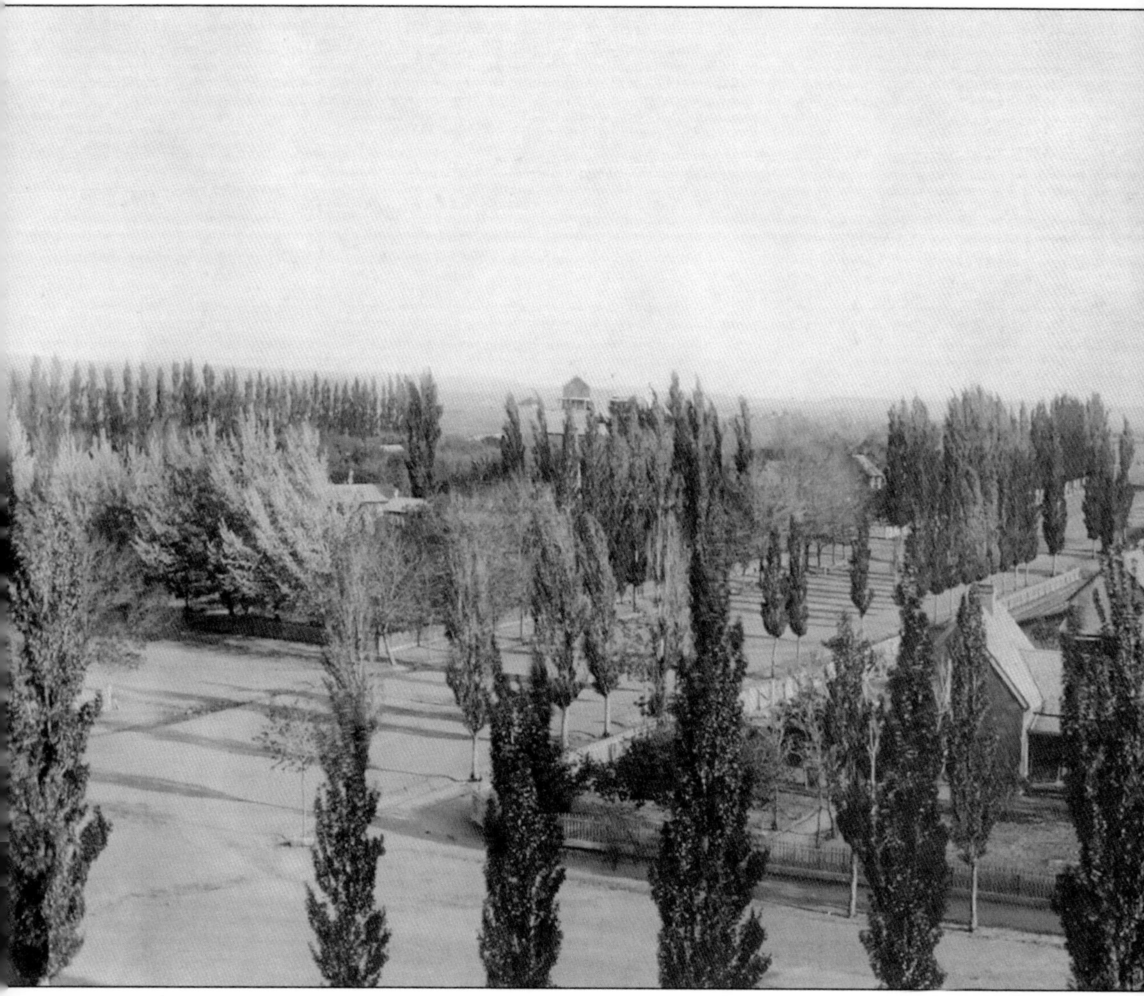

scene in this panoramic picture taken from the second floor of the academy. (Both courtesy St. Johns Historical Society and Museum.)

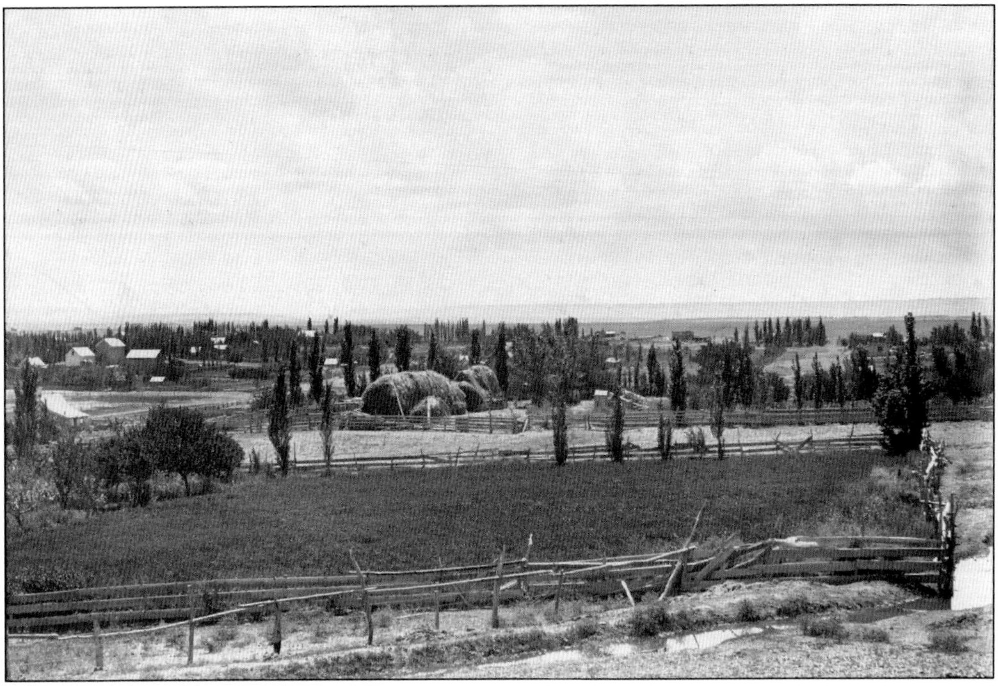

This panoramic picture showcases the surging agricultural goods consisting of wheat, barley, and hay produced in St. Johns. (Courtesy St. Johns Family History Center.)

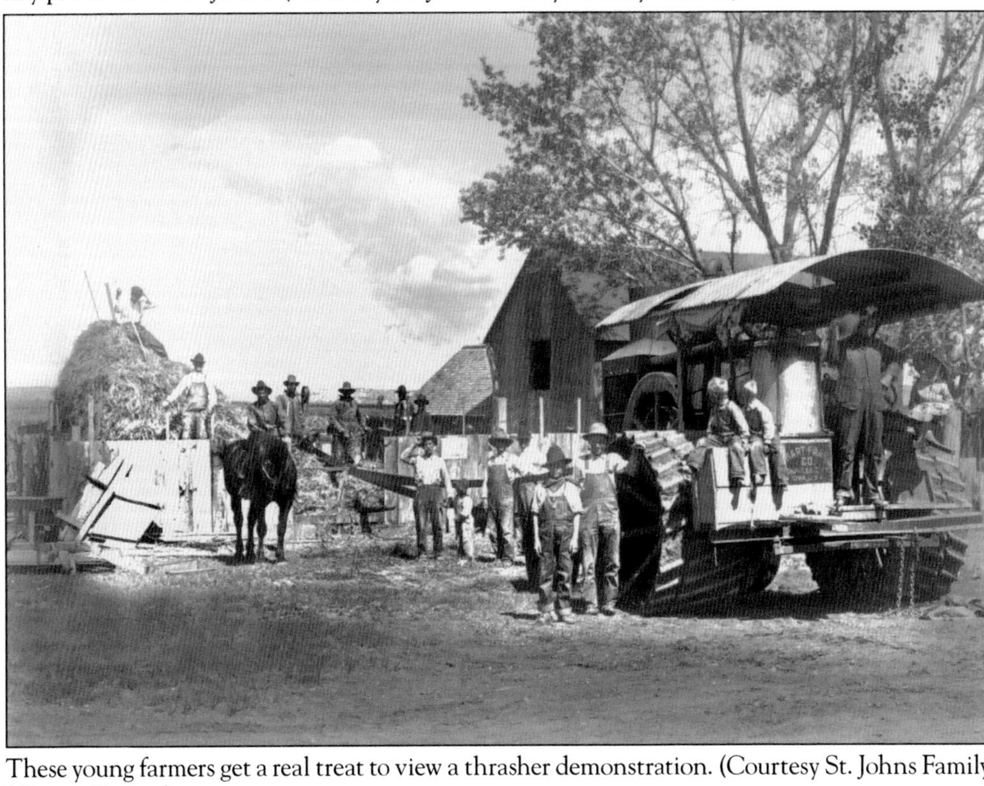

These young farmers get a real treat to view a thrasher demonstration. (Courtesy St. Johns Family History Center.)

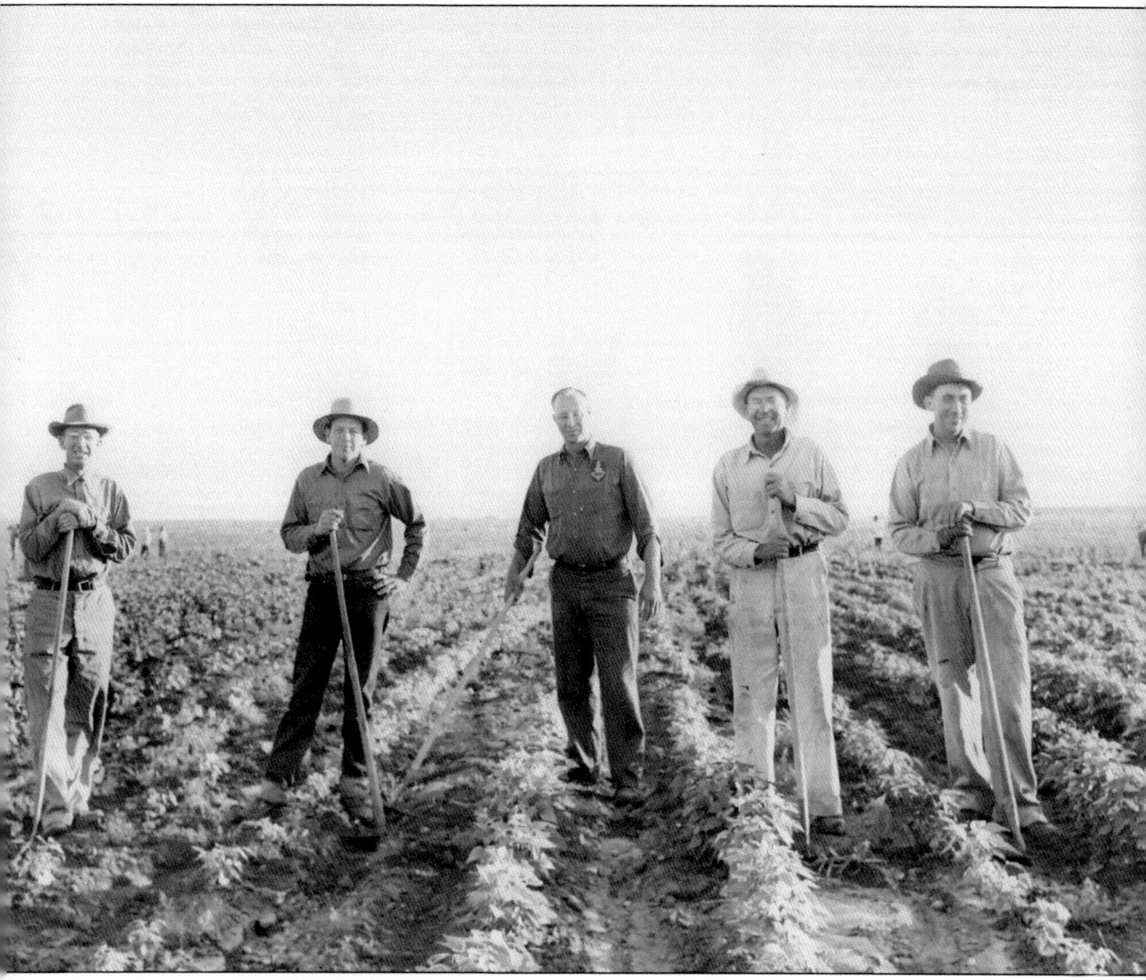

The ability to grow one's own food was pertinent to the survival of the people living on the Little Colorado River, and everybody farmed, including these local businessmen. Pictured from left to right are Nello Greer, Jay Waite, Carroll Shumway, Fred Whiting, and Albert F. Anderson. (Courtesy St. Johns Family History Center.)

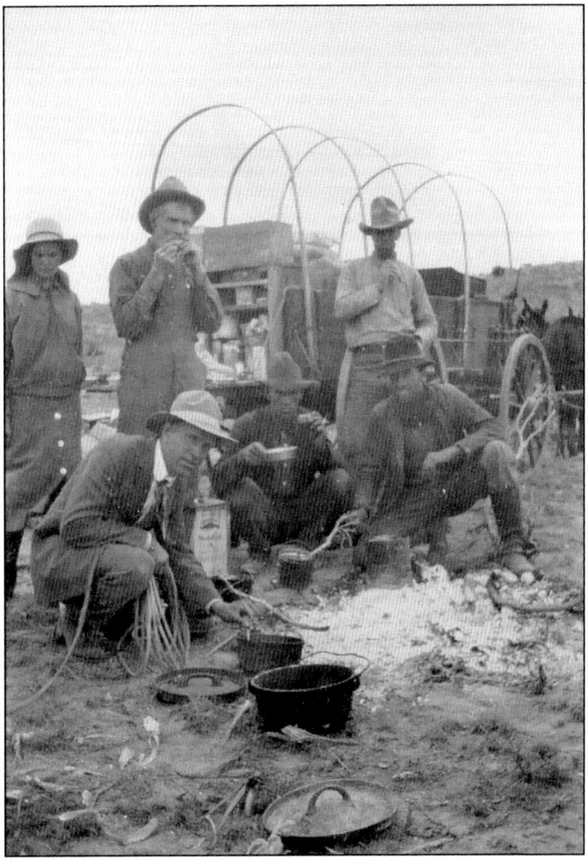

Camping out on the range and cooking with Dutch ovens, as shown in this picture, was how the cowboys lived. (Author collection.)

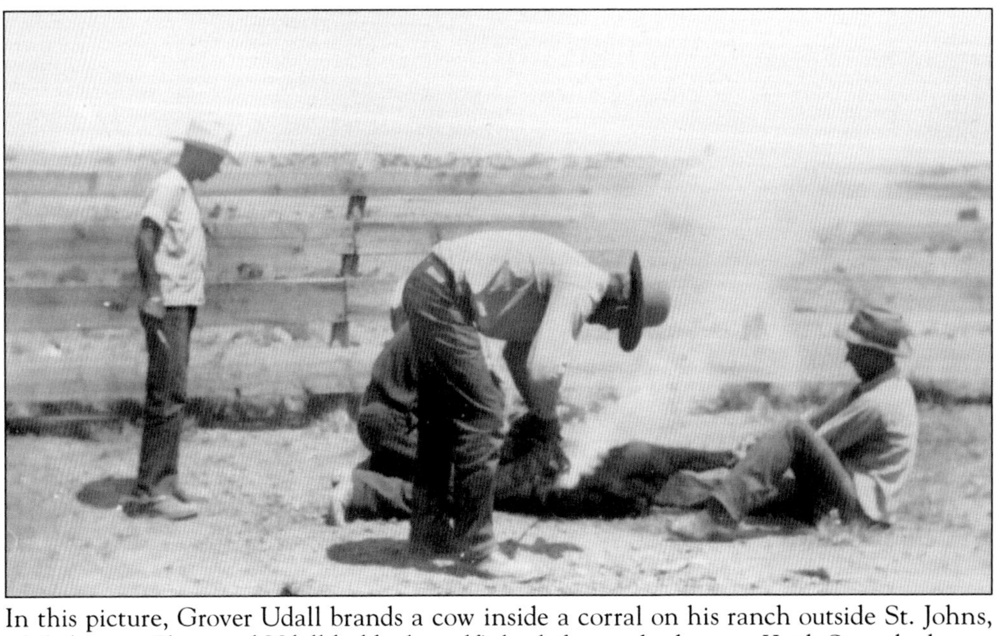

In this picture, Grover Udall brands a cow inside a corral on his ranch outside St. Johns, while his son Sherwood Udall holds the calf's back feet and other son Keith Steve looks on. (Author collection.)

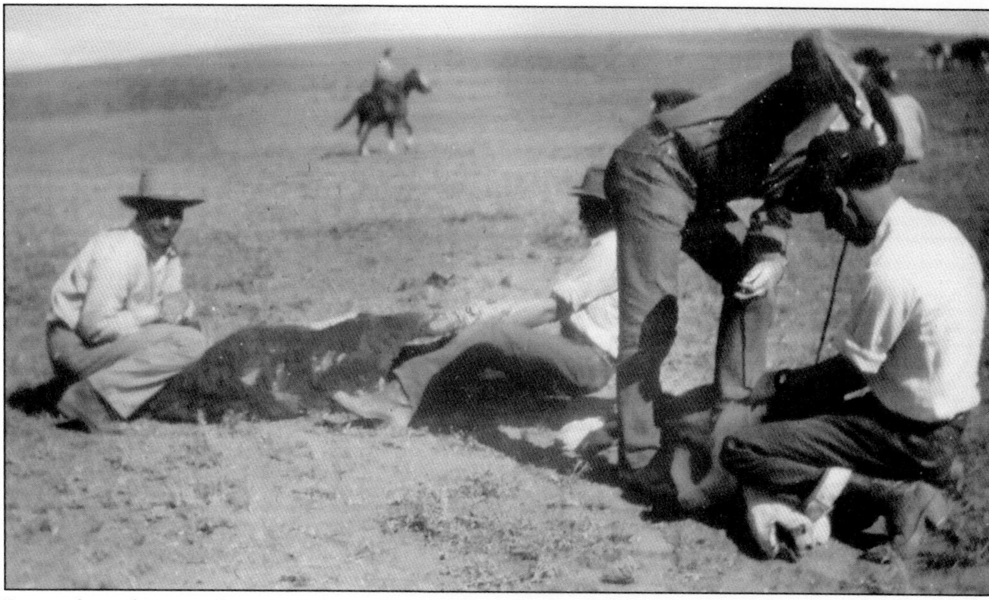

Range branding, as shown in this picture, was common back when ranches in the area were too large to try and gather cows to move them into a corral. (Author collection.)

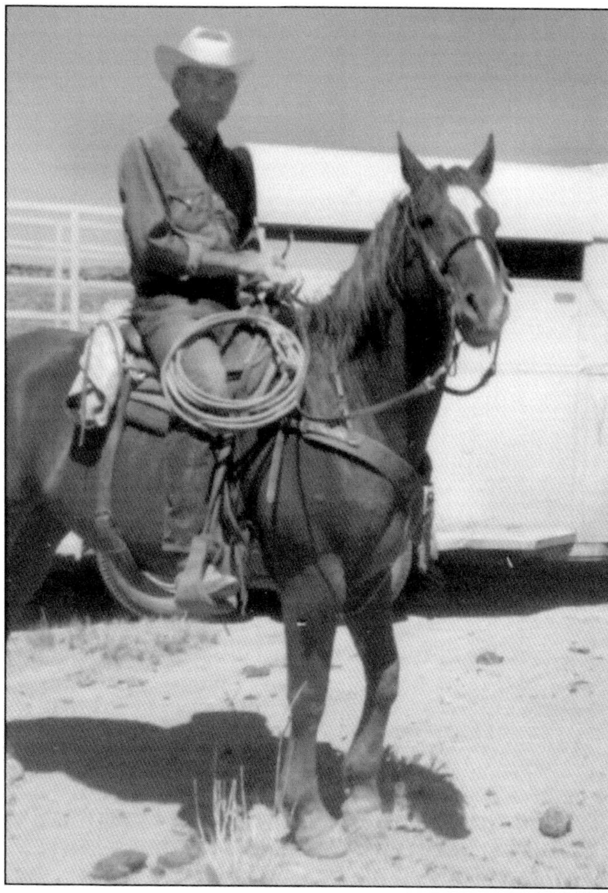

There is nothing like a day on the ranch for Sherwood Udall, who poses proudly on his trusty steed getting ready for long hours on the ranch. (Author collection.)

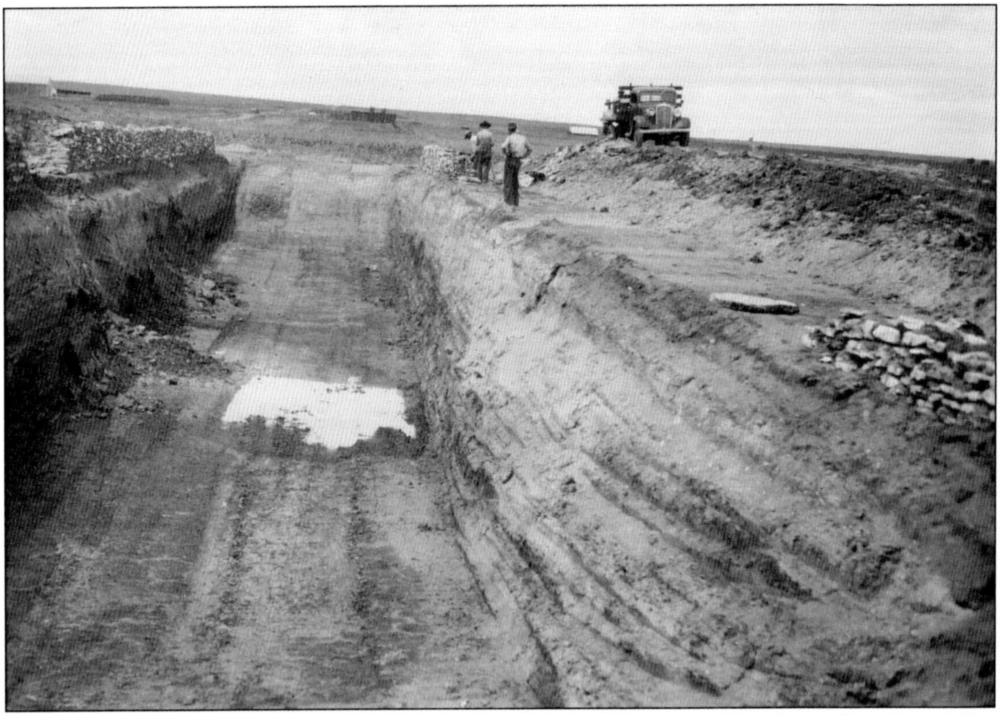

Before feedlots, ranchers and farmers grew corn for silage to feed their cattle before selling them. This picture shows a silo at a St. Johns farm. (Courtesy St. Johns Historical Society and Museum.)

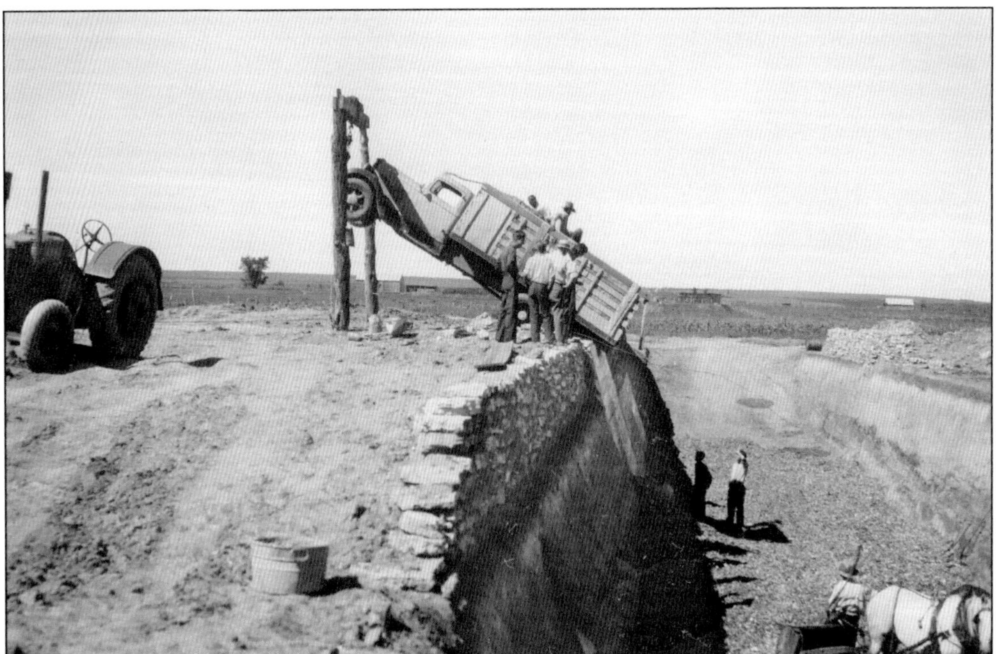

Here a group of ingenuous farmers demonstrates the St. Johns dump truck while some helpful and curious friends stand in the silo directly beneath the hoisted and ready-to-spill truck. It is unknown how this worked out for them. (Courtesy St. Johns Historical Society and Museum.)

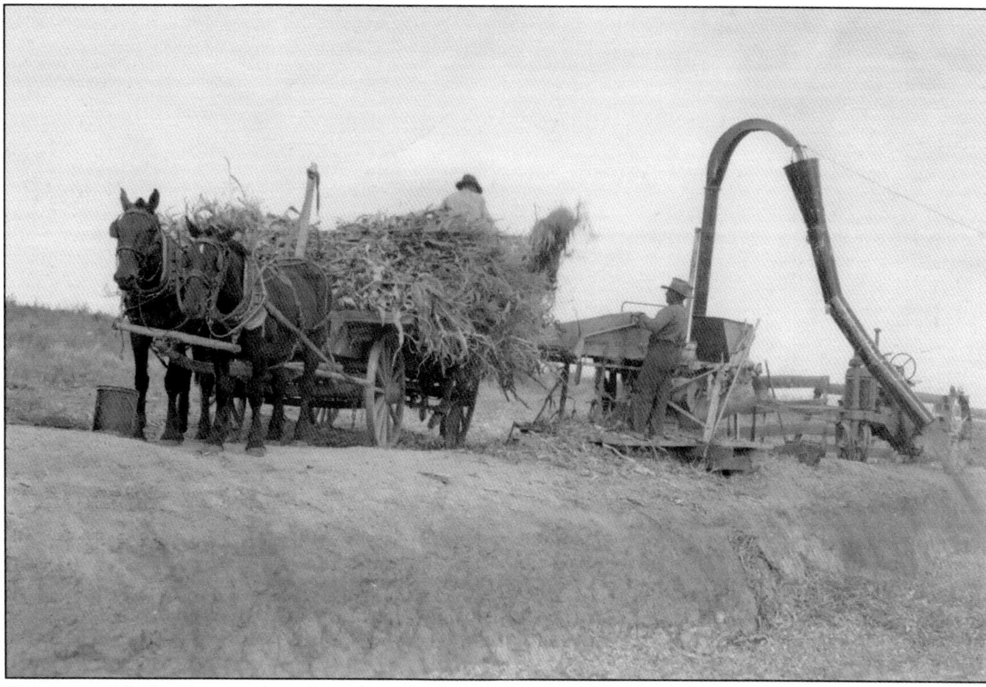

Silage could also be produced at the silo by feeding it into a machine that ground the corn. It was then spread in the silo as it was being made, shown here. (Courtesy St. Johns Historical Society and Museum.)

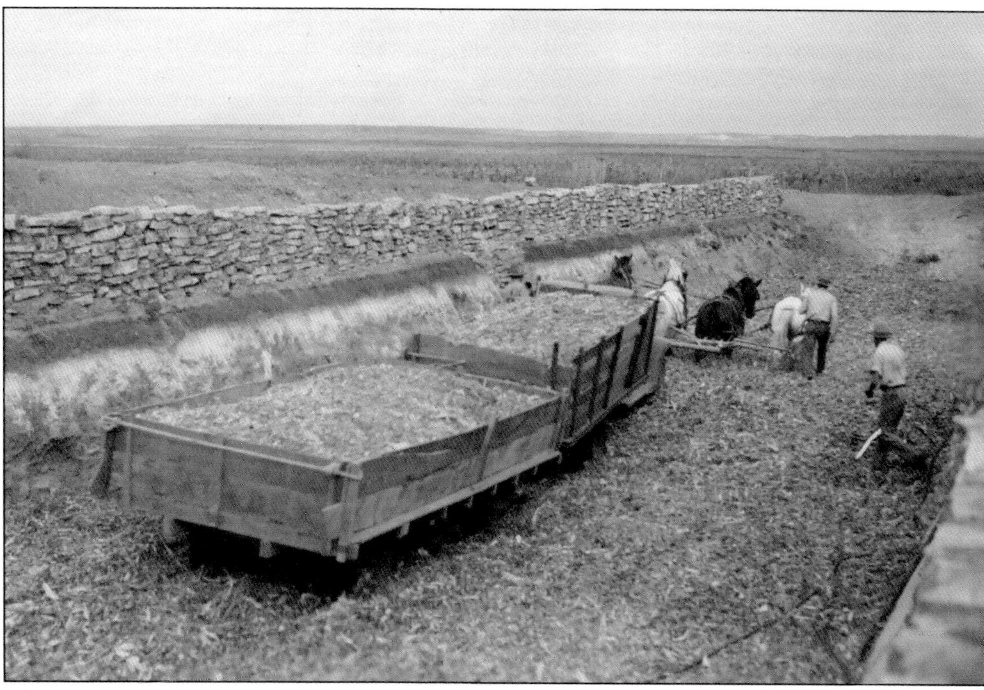

This picture shows a silo being filled and tamped down in the process. (Courtesy St. Johns Historical Society and Museum.)

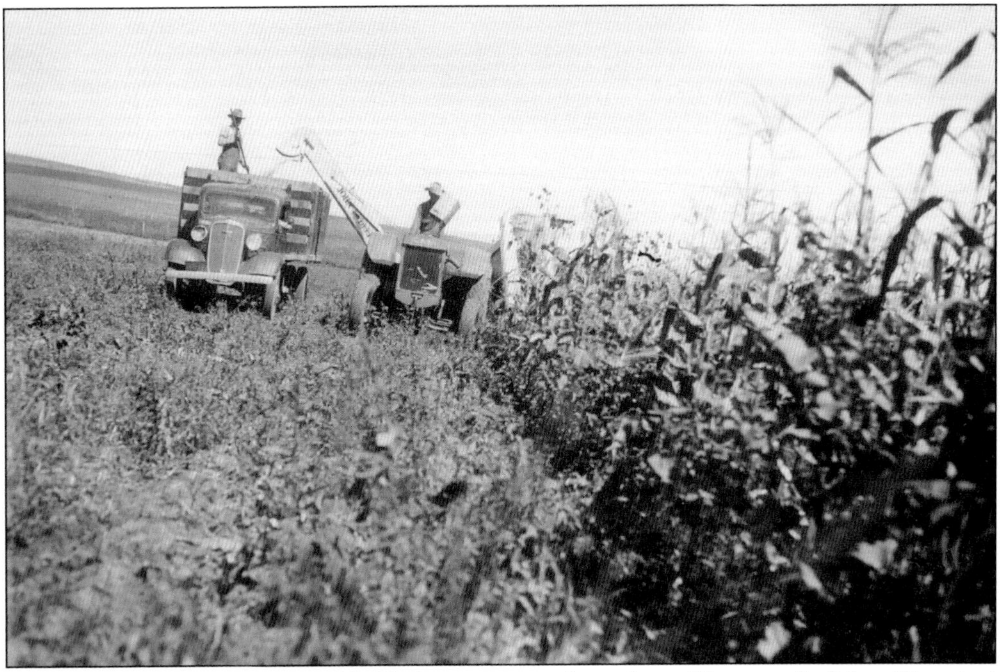

It was far easier to use a motorized field silage cutter, as shown here. (Courtesy St. Johns Historical Society and Museum.)

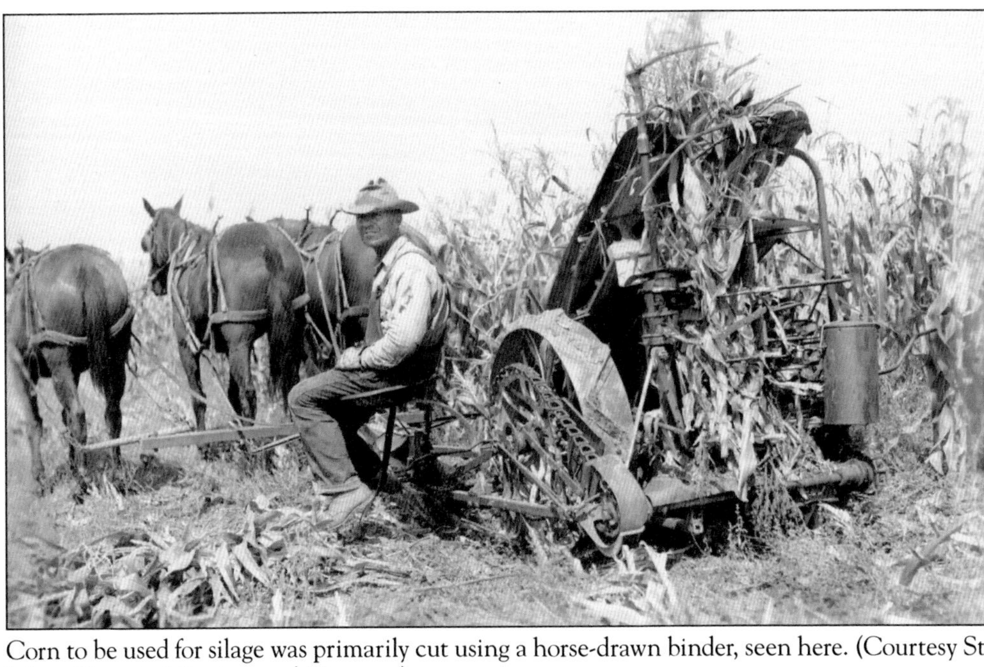

Corn to be used for silage was primarily cut using a horse-drawn binder, seen here. (Courtesy St. Johns Historical Society and Museum.)

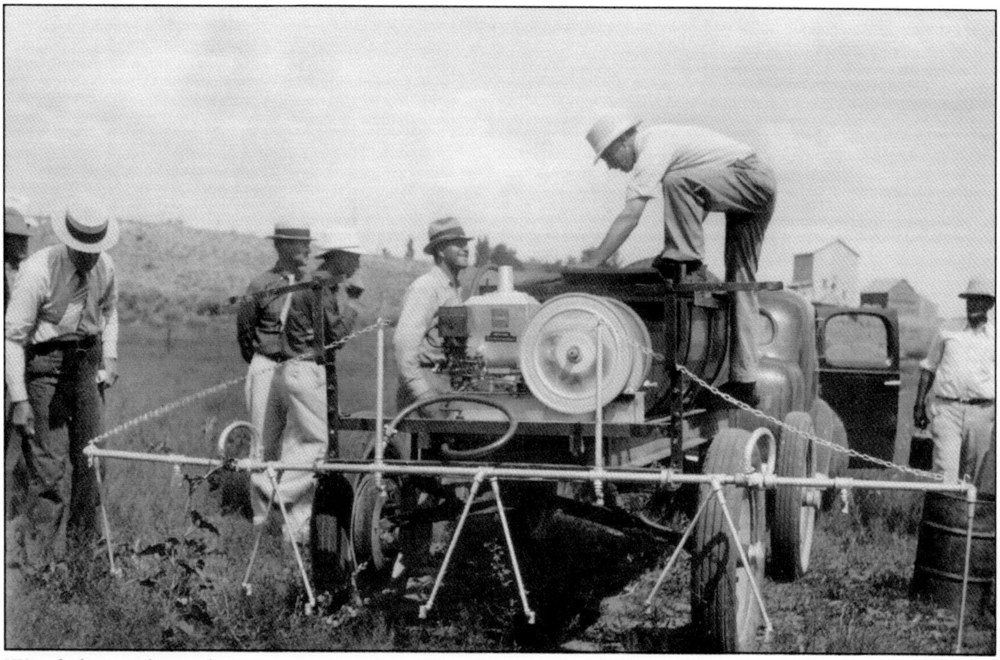

Weeds have always been a problem, and keeping them under control was a major priority. Preparations are being made for a weed-killing demonstration (above), and the weeds are being killed (right). (Both courtesy St. Johns Historical Society and Museum.)

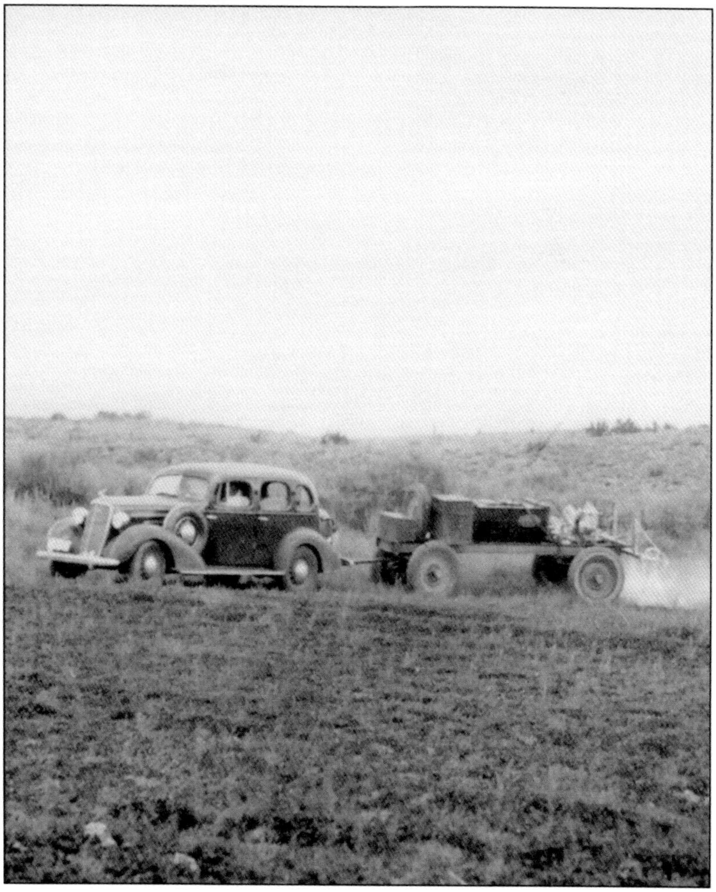

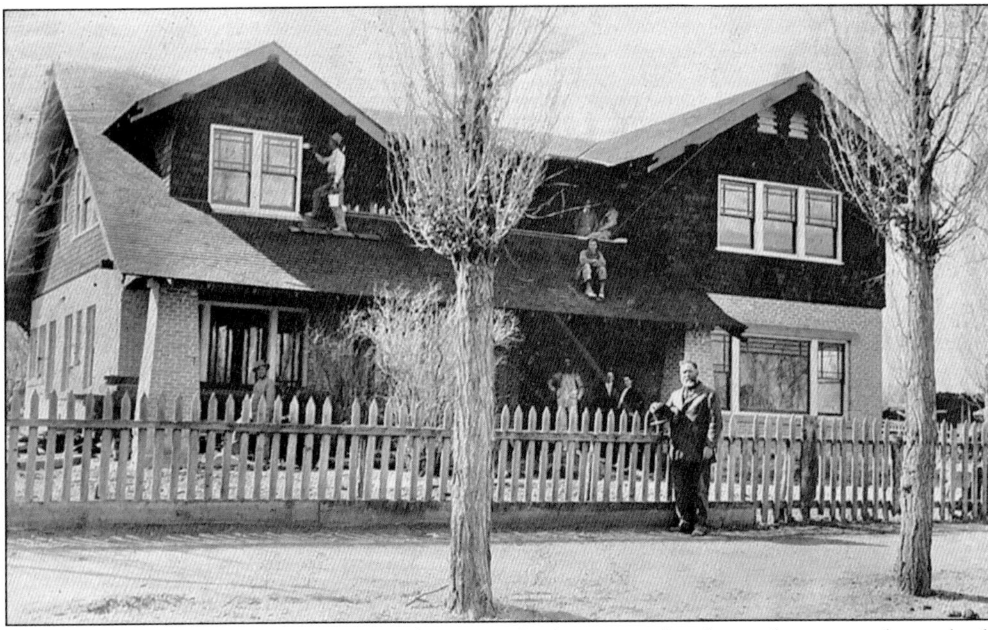

David King Udall is pictured here standing outside the gate as his dream home was being built in 1912. (Author collection.)

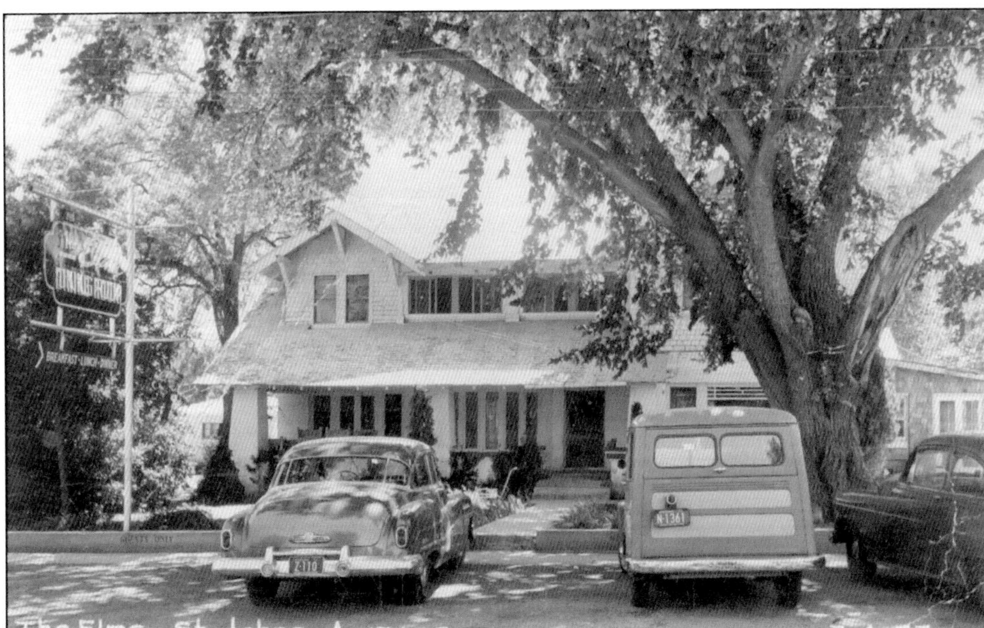

After David King Udall's death in 1938, his eldest son, Grover, and his family moved into the home. When Grover's untimely death made his wife, Dora, a young widow, she turned the home into a hotel, as shown here, called the Elm for the elm tree David King planted in the front yard in 1886 (shown at right, which was cut down in 2007). (Author collection.)

Before moving into his father's home, Grover Udall, shown here with his wife Dora, son Cal, and an unidentified friend, bought a farm and built a house (also shown here) on a hill, which at the time was way outside town. Because Grover was the only one who lived so far from town, the hill soon became known as Grover's Hill. This is the hill one travels over if entering St. Johns from the west. (Author collection.)

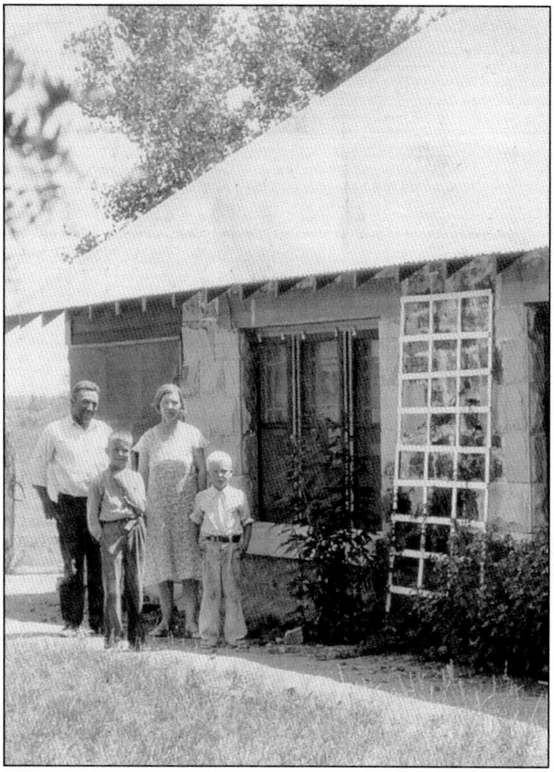

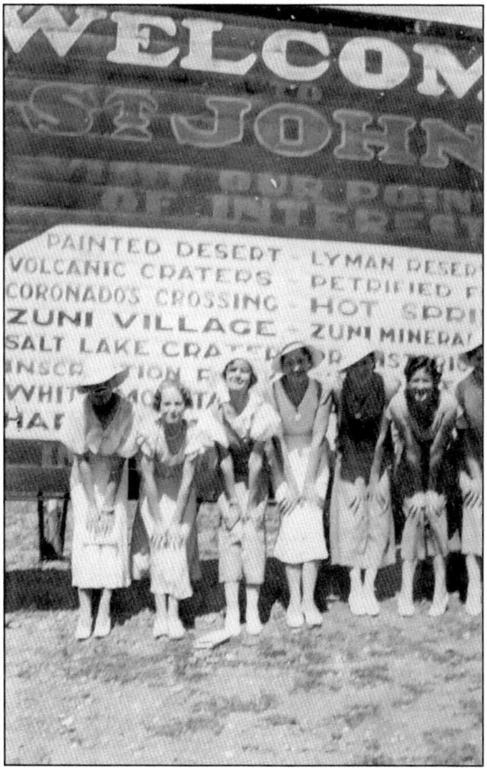

This welcome to St. Johns sign once appeared on the other side of Grover's Hill and was the first thing (minus the women in front) that people coming home saw before they topped Grover's Hill, yelled "I spy St. Johns!!" and knew they were home. (Author collection.)

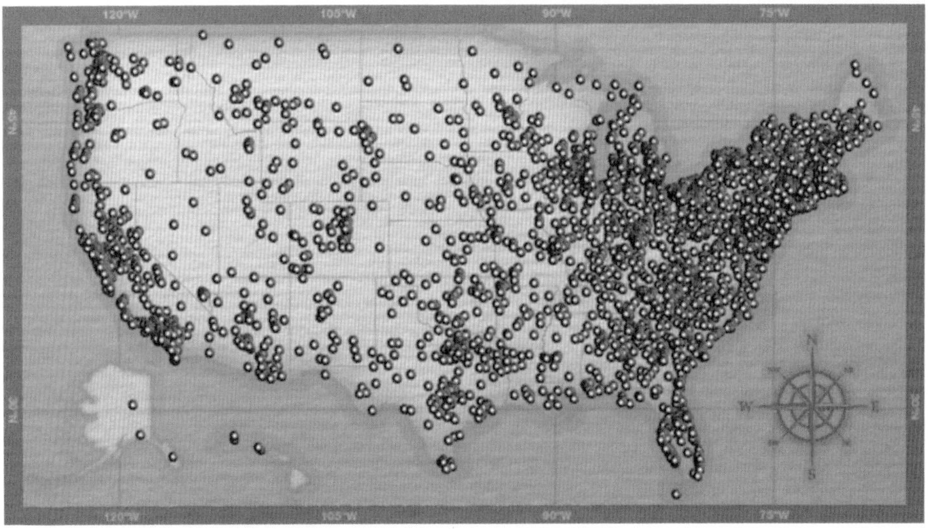